TEACHING ENGLISH GRAMMAR TO SPEAKERS OF OTHER LANGUAGES

This practical and research-based introduction to current and effective English grammar instruction gives pre-service and in-service teachers and teacher educators a strong foundation for teaching second language grammar and helps them develop their professional knowledge and skills. Written in a highly readable style for an international audience, it provides a thorough and rounded overview of the principles, strategies, techniques, and applications currently dominant in teaching L2 grammar in a range of instructional settings around the world. Chapter authors are world-class authorities in grammar and grammar teaching and learning. All chapters are based on theoretical frameworks and/or research foundations with a strong emphasis on practical applications and implications for classroom teaching, and highlight teaching methods, key concepts, and terminology associated with grammar instruction.

Part I examines the principles and foundations of grammar teaching that deal with the methodological options and instructional foci in grammar teaching. Part II is about strategies and techniques for the nitty-gritty of classroom grammar teaching. Part III focuses on grammar teaching for speaking and writing—the productive L2 skills in which the quality of learners' grammar matters most.

Illuminating the options and choices in grammar teaching from a contemporary perspective, *Teaching English Grammar to Speakers of Other Languages* is ideal as a key text for students in undergraduate and graduate MA-TESOL programs and as a resource for practicing ESL/EFL teachers, teacher educators, and teaching faculty.

Eli Hinkel is Professor, Linguistics and MA-TESL Programs, Seattle Pacific University, USA.

ESL & Applied Linguistics Professional Series
Eli Hinkel, Series Editor

Visit **www.routledge.com/education** for additional information on titles in the ESL & Applied Linguistics Professional Series.

TEACHING ENGLISH GRAMMAR TO SPEAKERS OF OTHER LANGUAGES

Edited by Eli Hinkel

Routledge
Taylor & Francis Group

NEW YORK AND LONDON

First published 2016
by Routledge
711 Third Avenue, New York, NY 10017

and by Routledge
2 Park Square, Milton Park, Abingdon, Oxon, OX14 4RN

Routledge is an imprint of the Taylor & Francis Group, an informa business

Library of Congress Cataloging-in-Publication Data
Hinkel, Eli.
Title: Teaching English grammar to speakers of other languages / Edited by
    Eli Hinkel.
Description: New York : Routledge, [2016] | Series: ESL & Applied
    Linguistics Professionals Series | Includes bibliographical references
    and index.
Identifiers: LCCN 2015035164 | ISBN 9781138906921 (hardback) |
    ISBN 9781138906938 (pbk.) | ISBN 9781315695273 (ebook)
Subjects: LCSH: English language—Grammar—Study and
    teaching—Foreign speakers.
Classification: LCC PE1128 .T3575 2016 | DDC 428.0071—dc23
LC record available at http://lccn.loc.gov/2015035164

ISBN: 978-1-138-90692-1 (hbk)
ISBN: 978-1-138-90693-8 (pbk)
ISBN: 978-1-315-69527-3 (ebk)

Typeset in Bembo
by Apex CoVantage, LLC

MIX
Paper from
responsible sources
FSC
www.fsc.org   FSC® C013056

Printed and bound in Great Britain by
TJ International Ltd, Padstow, Cornwall

CONTENTS

PREFACE

The goal of this textbook is to provide a practical and research-based foundation for teaching second language (L2) grammar for teachers and teacher educators who seek to develop their professional knowledge and skills. The book presents principles, strategies and techniques, and applications of current and effective English grammar instruction. The aims are to present a thorough and rounded overview of the principles and techniques currently dominant in teaching L2 grammar in a range of instructional settings around the world.

At present, despite an increased interest in the teaching of grammar at various levels of L2 teaching, it seems that no text presents an overview of grammar teaching principles and prevalent classroom methods. This book aspires to present a broader view of a range of approaches to grammar teaching. It goes without saying that in the end, classroom teachers anywhere are ultimately responsible for implementing grammar instruction in the best interests of their students. To this end, the book sets out to illuminate the options and choices in grammar teaching from a contemporary perspective.

The book is divided into three parts. Part I examines the principles and foundations of grammar teaching that deal with the methodological options and instructional foci in grammar teaching. Part II is about strategies and techniques for the nitty-gritty of classroom grammar teaching. That is, the chapters take a closer look at how grammar teaching can be implemented while keeping an eye on the advantages and disadvantages of each technique. Part III focuses on grammar teaching for speaking and writing, the productive L2 skills, in which the quality of learners' grammar matters most.

The Book Structure

Part I consists of five chapters. Chapter 1 (Marianne Celce-Murcia) presents grammar as a system used to create discourse in given contexts for given purposes. Chapter 2 (Sandra Lee McKay) examines what is meant by Standard English in the context of English as an international language (EIL). Chapter 3 (Susan Conrad) introduces findings from corpus analyses that have important consequences for the content of grammar instruction. Chapter 4 (Keith Folse) takes a look at how and why teachers would teach certain grammar points to address learners' goals in language production. Chapter 5 (Anne Burns) adopts a functional approach to teaching grammar in which language learning as primarily concerned with social interaction and meaning creation is discussed.

Part II includes four chapters. Chapter 6 (Penny Ur) provides an overview of different models of grammar teaching, focusing on the place of grammar practice within these models, as well as the learning theories that underlie their use. Chapter 7 (Rod Ellis) identifies three different senses of consciousness in language learning—consciousness-as-noticing, consciousness-as-understanding, and consciousness-as-control—and explains how these senses can be related to various teaching activities. Chapter 8 (Jack C. Richards and Randi Reppen) presents a view of grammar both as knowledge and as ability and proposes twelve principles as the basis for acquiring learning to use grammar in texts. Chapter 9 (Eli Hinkel) deals with applications of construction grammar to teaching L2 academic writing.

Part III addresses teaching grammar for productive skills. Chapter 10 (Michael McCarthy) considers the main findings of corpus investigations into spoken grammar and what it can contribute to grammar teaching. Chapter 11 (Dana Ferris) follows up with an overview of how language instruction (grammar/vocabulary development) can be integrated into a writing class syllabus in ways that are authentic, effective, and appropriately balanced with other writing concerns. Chapter 12 (Ken Hyland) briefly explores the most visible expressions of a writer's presence in a text, i.e., the use of hedges and first person pronouns, to show that there is actually considerable scope for the negotiation of identity in academic writing.

Acknowledgments

It is true of all books that the publisher's commissioning editor determines the destiny of each submission. The importance of the editors who work with the authors directly cannot be overstated. In the small and select group of such individuals, Naomi Silverman of Routledge is truly unlike any other publishing house editor that one is likely to encounter. Naomi is astute, brilliant, open-minded, thoughtful, supportive, kind, and patient—beyond compare. There is no telling how many books would never see the light of day if it weren't for Naomi's unique, perceptive, knowledgeable, and resourceful presence. Naomi, thank you.

For her creativity, originality, thoroughness, friendship, and insight, Sandra Fotos, a co-editor of an earlier grammar teaching book, deserves all the praise. Thank you more than I can say. There is no one like Sandy, and this is a fact.

PART I

Principles and Foundations of Grammar Teaching

1

THE IMPORTANCE OF THE DISCOURSE LEVEL IN UNDERSTANDING AND TEACHING ENGLISH GRAMMAR[1]

Marianne Celce-Murcia

Introduction

In the past, English grammar instruction focused primarily on the sentence level. Sentence-based drills were used to teach tenses, articles, negation, question formation, passive voice, and many other construction types. The problem with this narrow approach was that learning sentence-level grammar did not result in learners being able to use the English language for communication. There are in fact only a few local rules of English grammar that can be usefully taught and practiced as strictly context-free, sentence-level phenomena:

> Reflexive pronoun objects: Mary accidentally cut *herself.*
> Gerund verbals after prepositions: They were prevented from *leaving the party*.
> Determiner-noun agreement: *This book/These books* might interest you.

All other rules of grammar require some context in order for learners to understand when and why they are used.[2]

By artificially creating contexts through the use of adverbials, many verb tenses can be elicited and practiced at the sentence level:

> Present tense: She *rides* her bicycle for 30 minutes *every day.*
> Past tense: I *sent* my brother an email *yesterday.*
> Present progressive tense-aspect: We *are practicing* English *now.*

Such sentence-level examples and exercises can raise learners' awareness of grammatical resources that exist in English; however, they do not lead learners to being able to communicate their ideas effectively using these forms in speech and writing. This is because communication occurs at the discourse level, not at the sentence level. A sentence requires a subject and a verb. Discourse requires a communicative context and can consist of a word (e.g., *Stop!*), a phrase (e.g., *No smoking*), or any extended example of speech or writing that constitutes comprehensible communication (e.g., a conversation, an email message, a lecture, a news article, a research report, a short story or novel, etc.).

In communicative language teaching (CLT), the crucial linguistic level is discourse. CLT requires bottom-up resources (e.g., grammar, vocabulary, orthography/phonology) for the realization of discourse, but it also requires top-down context and information of various types (e.g., audience, purpose, content schemata, formal schemata,[3] politeness conventions, pragmatics, etc.) to ensure appropriate production and comprehension.

Getting Started

With beginning-level language learners, teachers often feel that it is not possible to use discourse-level strategies from the outset. Celce-Murcia and Olshtain (2000) make several suggestions indicating that this is not only possible but highly desirable. Early on, learners can be taught to express information about themselves at the discourse level based on models provided by the teacher. In one such exercise the teacher draws a basic, simple family tree on the board (Figure 1.1) and asks the students to do the same at their desks.

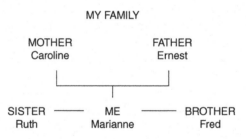

FIGURE 1.1 Illustration of a Family Tree

This requires the teaching and learning of some basic kinship vocabulary (*family, mother, father, sister(s), brother(s)*), three forms of the verb *be* (*am, is, are*), the conjunction *and*, the demonstrative pronoun *this*, and the possessive determiner *my*. Much of this vocabulary and grammar can be learned in context as a result of doing the activity. The teacher can provide a model of a simple discourse based on the family tree:

> This is my family. I am _____. My mother is _____, and my father is _____. My sister is _____, and my brother is_____.

This discourse should be practiced orally by each student in front of the class after the teacher models contractions in speech (*I'm, mother's, father's, sister's, brother's*) but uses full forms in the written model. One other sentence can be taught as an eliciting device so that students can practice telling the class about their families (*Tell me/us about your family*). This should allow the teacher to point out differences between singular and plural forms for siblings, depending on any given student's family tree: *my sister is/my sisters are; my brother is/my brothers are*. Once the model is well established, students can practice sharing information about their families in small groups while the teacher circulates to assist as needed. Finally, by writing up what they have first drawn and then reported orally, they carry out a useful reinforcement activity.

The follow-up activity provides practice with discussing the families just introduced in the third person. The students can use several classmates' family trees and practice describing them by referring to a model and making the appropriate choices. The elicitation utterance could be *Tell us about* _____*'s family*. The students will also learn the possessive *'s* inflection and *his* and *her* as possessive determiners.

> This is _____'s family. His/her mother is _____, and his/
> her father is_____. His/her sister(s) is/are _____,
> and his/her brother(s) is/are _____.

As written reinforcement, each student selects the family tree of a classmate and writes up the short discourse-based description.

Another discourse-based activity for beginners has each member of the class prepare a list of three or four things that s/he does every day with the help of the teacher as needed:

ANITA	HYUN
I go to school.	I go to school.
I ride my bicycle.	I play baseball/soccer.
I do the dishes.	I walk my dog.

This information can then be used to practice simple present tense narratives and to recycle and expand knowledge of personal pronouns. They should first each describe their personal everyday activities:

> I am Anita. Every day I go to school, (I) ride my bicycle, and (I) do the dishes.

The teacher points out that the *I* does not have to be repeated in the second and third activities. Then the same information can be used to practice third person simple present tense forms to describe the everyday activities of several different students, both male and female:

> Every day Hyun goes to school, he plays baseball and (he) walks his dog.

These constructions can then be used again at the discourse level to compare what Anita and Hyun do every day in an expansion of the preceding activity:

> Every day Anita and Hyun go to school. Anita rides her bicycle and does the dishes. Hyun plays baseball and walks his dog.

The same information can be used to learn and practice the past tense (and other tenses) at the discourse level with the teacher's help with irregular verb forms, etc.:

Question: What did you do yesterday?
ANITA: Yesterday I went to school, rode my bicycle, and did the dishes.

Once all students have practiced their personal narratives in the past tense, the class can move on to practicing the third person forms in this tense:

Question: What did Hyun do yesterday?
Response: Yesterday Hyun (he) went to school, played baseball, and walked his dog.

Again, it is a good idea to have students write out some of these informal narratives to reinforce the grammar and vocabulary. Such short, simple, and meaningful discourse segments, while not very long, are more authentic and complex than typical sentence-level drills taught to beginners in most ESL/EFL textbooks.

A bit later in the course, beginners can be given a short discourse frame to contrast past and current activities or states:

> I used to _____, but I don't anymore. Now I _____.

ANITA: I used to (usta) go to school in Mexico, but I don't anymore. Now I go to school in California.

They can also be given a short discourse frame to talk about their goals and plans for the future:

> I'm going to (gonna) _____, so I can _____.

HYUN: I'm gonna learn English, so I can study engineering.

Once again, after the class has practiced making first person descriptions, they can be asked to paraphrase these multi-clause statements with third person forms, followed by written reinforcement as part of the learning process. Starting to learn and produce language in discourse episodes longer than one-clause sentences from the outset, with content that focuses on their own lives, brings beginners closer to learning language as a system for communication rather than as an abstract system of decontextualized rules to be memorized. Grammar and vocabulary are acquired in the process of communicating at the discourse level.

Using Discourse Frames with Intermediate-level Learners

Discourse frames are often organized around verb tense, aspect, and modality, which Givón (1984: 269) has claimed are among "the major devices coding the connectedness/coherence of sentences in their wider discourse context." Likewise, Halliday and Matthiessen (2014) remind us that once we select one verb form, it greatly constrains what we can chose as a following verb form.

I have found that intermediate-level learners respond well to the fact that there are tendencies in English or any language[4] for describing events in a discourse episode such that one tense-aspect-modality form (usually a longer and more marked or salient form) initiates the discourse and another form elaborates or continues the episode. This is a notion that Suh (1992a, 1992b) put forward explicitly when she proposed her Frame-elaboration Hypothesis. For example, at the sentence level, past habitual actions or states can be described using either *used to* or *would*:

> My brother used to exercise every day.
> My brother would exercise every day.

There is no principled way to distinguish *used to* and *would* at the sentence level; however, in extended discourse episodes, Suh found that English speakers tended to begin (i.e., frame) their discourse with *used to* and to continue (i.e., elaborate) with *would ('d)* and also occasionally use the simple past. Here is one of the authentic examples she cites:

> The bad thing was they used to laugh at us, the Anglo kids.
> They would laugh because we'd bring tortillas and frijoles to lunch.
> They would have their nice little compact lunch boxes with cold milk in their thermos,
> And they'd laugh at us because all we had was dried tortillas.
> Not only would they laugh at us, but the kids would pick fights
> *(Terkel 1974: 32)*

This discourse pattern with *used to* framing and *would/'d* elaborating the habitual past narrative is supported by corpus research (see McCarthy 2015: 98).

Another useful frame, this one for future scenarios, involves the use of *be going to* and *will/'ll*. In this case, Suh (1992a) found that the tendency was for speakers to use *be going to* to frame the discourse episode and then to use *will/'ll* for elaboration with the occasional use of the simple present or the present progressive. The context for the following example episode is one where a medical doctor is informally describing the gastric restriction procedure for the morbidly obese:

> They're going to go in and, uh, have their gut slit open, their stomach exposed, and have it stapled off so that there'll be two pou . . ., an upper pouch in the stomach which will hold about two ounces of food; it's got a little hole right in. . . . in the middle of that pouch, where food, when it's finally ground up, will slowly go through.
>
> *(from Weinstein 1984[5])*

Here the initial *be going to* holds for the first long compound construction and *will/'ll* starts after *so that* in the second line. Then there is a descriptive digression for the next line and a half, which is in the simple present. After this, the final two lines continue the future narrative with *will* (e.g., *where food . . . will slowly go through*).

It has been my experience that intermediate learners can be presented with authentic examples like these two—ideally several authentic examples of each pattern. They should discuss the passages for comprehension and then can be asked questions that help them discover the discourse patterns, after which they are then able to apply these discourse-level patterns and create their own coherent narratives in response to prompts such as:

> Describe something you often did in the past or something that often happened then.
> What are your plans for the upcoming weekend?[6]

For further discussion of Suh's work, see Larsen-Freeman and Celce-Murcia (2016).

Since the ability to sequence tenses appropriately at the discourse level has never been taught in sentence-level grammars, this area has posed a pervasive learning problem for ESL/EFL learners. A discourse-based approach that all teachers should know about, because of its pedagogical usefulness, is Bull's (1960) Framework. Although Bull used his framework to describe and teach Spanish verb tenses, it was actually designed to describe the tense system of any language. It can be easily adapted to English, and Table 1.1 presents an abbreviated version for English of Bull's Framework.[7,8]

TABLE 1.1 The Bull (1960) Framework

Axis of Orientation	Time Before	Basic Axis Time	Time After
Present time	(present perfect)	(simple present)	(future of present)
Examples:	She has played soccer.	She plays soccer.	She is going to play soccer.
Past time	(past perfect)	(simple past)	(*would*/simple past)
Examples:	She had played soccer.	She played soccer.	She would play soccer.

Essentially what the Bull Framework tells us is that, once we establish an axis of orientation, e.g. present time, we need to stay in that axis moving left and right as needed to choose the proper tense unless the axis of orientation explicitly changes to another axis because an adverb signals a time change or because a brief generalization or aside intervenes in the discourse. This explains why, in the following discourse sequence, (a) is awkward and incoherent, whereas (b) flows smoothly and naturally:

(a) I have a splitting headache. I had it for two hours, so I will take some aspirin.
(b) I have a splitting headache. I've had it for two hours, so I'm going to take some aspirin.

Here is another pair of examples that illustrate the past axis rather than the present axis:

(c) Last night the girl had cried her heart out. She lost her doll and was convinced she will never find it.
(d) Last night the girl cried her heart out. She had lost her doll and was convinced she would never find it.

Native speakers of English are intuitively likely to produce sequences like (b) and (d), which follow from Bull's Framework and maintain axis time, whereas non-native speakers often produce sequences like (a) and (c), which are disjointed and awkward in their use of tense.

Familiarity with Bull's Framework, along with valid reasons for changing the axis of orientation, can help ESL/EFL learners produce more coherent tense sequences, which is especially important in their written discourse. They also need to understand that asides and intervening generalizations might occur in the present tense even when the discourse episode is in the past axis. These preferences for tense sequences can be demonstrated using well selected examples of authentic discourse and can be reinforced with appropriate feedback to learners when they produce awkward tense sequences in their written discourse.

Discourse Grammar for Intermediate and Advanced Learners

Cohesion

Intermediate- and advanced-level ESL/EFL learners need to understand how cohesion is achieved in English discourse and how cohesion contributes to coherence. The notion of cohesion, which is part of the grammar of discourse, was first described by Halliday and Hasan (1976), who propose four different types of grammatical cohesive devices: reference, substitution, ellipsis, and conjunction.[9]

Reference includes all types of pronouns and their related possessive and determiner forms. Reference also includes the demonstratives and certain uses of the definite article as well as some other items. Reference normally relates to preceding discourse (i.e., *anaphora*), but it can also refer to subsequent discourse (i.e., *cataphora*). For example:

Anaphora: John has a new car. He bought it last week. (*He* refers back to *John*; *it* refers back to *a new car.*)
Cataphora: Remember *this*: You have to file your taxes on or before April 15. (*This* refers forward to the entire following proposition.)

Substitution helps speakers and writers avoid repetition by referring to a common class of entities without implying coreference the way the preceding examples of reference do. For example:

Bill's old car kept breaking down, so he bought a new *one*. (*One* substitutes for *car*, not for *Bill's old car.*)

The nominal substitute *one* has the plural form *ones*:

I don't want the green apples. Give me the red *ones*. (*Ones* substitutes for *apples*, not *the green apples.*)

There are also verbal substitutes (*do, do it, do so*) and clausal substitutes (*not* and *so*).

Ellipsis occurs most often in oral discourse, specifically in conversation and other forms of informal speech. For example:

A: I'm really tired of this long, cold winter!
B: I am too! (*Really tired of this long, cold winter* undergoes ellipsis.)

In this case, the *too* in B's response is a conjunction that further serves to tie B's response to A's preceding complaint about the weather, which brings us to the final grammatical cohesive device introduced by Halliday and Hasan (1976).

Conjunction is a discourse-level signal to the listener or reader as to what the logical relation is between two propositions or two episodes in ongoing discourse. Simple and frequent conjunctions occur in conversation, like *and, but, then, so,* and *too.* However, the biggest problem for learners seems to be the accurate and appropriate use of more formal conjunctive elements at the discourse level. For example, otherwise advanced ESL/EFL writers often misuse *on the contrary* in contexts where *in contrast, on the other hand,* or *however* would be more appropriate, as in the following passage:

For example, a teacher might provide feedback for a student's error in an utterance elicited by the teacher in a question-answer sequence. *On the contrary*, if a student initiates a question with an error in the utterance, and whose approximate meaning is understood by the teacher, the teacher will answer the question instead of correcting the student's error.

(author data)

Many such examples could be cited to illustrate that using conjunctive adverbs correctly in academic writing is a problem even for advanced learners. In particular, learners do not seem to understand that the conditions for the use of *on the contrary* are highly constrained. One must first establish a general shared assumption. Then there is a specific instance where the assumption is negated or denied, after which *on the contrary* can then be used to explain what actually happened in the particular situation under discussion. The following example is a correct use of *on the contrary*:

> In Sime's view, gestures can be confusing since there is a lack of standardized patterns of gestures as opposed to the standardized meanings of words in a sentence. However, Sime's view does not explain how these students were able to understand their teacher. *On the contrary*, they proved adept at using their teacher's gestures in conjunction with her speech to decode her intended meaning.
>
> *(author data)*

I conclude this section of the chapter with part of an authentic text (excerpted from a letter written by a mother asking for advice on dealing with her preteen children) to illustrate how these cohesive devices all serve to help tie the text together grammatically across sentence boundaries, thereby contributing to a cohesive and coherent whole (the text has been divided into 4 parts):

1. I am a working mother with two preteens. After dropping them off at school,
2. I have to get right to work. But my children are disorganized and always late.
3. A few times, I have had to turn around and go back home because the older one
4. or the younger one forgot something.

> *(Clipping from personal data collection, cited in Celce-Murcia and Olshtain 2000: 7)*

The use of the pronoun *them* in part 1 is an anaphoric reference to *two preteens*. The conjunction *but* in part 2 signals the start of the unexpected complaint expressed in the following two parts. The phrase *always late* in part 2 is an elliptical form of the proposition *my children are always late*. The two instances of *one* in parts 3 and 4 substitute for *child*, linking back to *children* in part 2. Each part in the discourse thus has at least one grammatical cohesive device that contributes to the overall connectedness of the discourse.

Teachers should use authentic texts to help their learners understand and identify the cohesive ties so that they can learn to recognize and use such devices appropriately in their own discourse. The use of passages with blanks where cohesive devices are needed can provide a useful transition exercise between recognizing and identifying the cohesive devices in authentic text and using the devices in their own writing.

More Complex Frames in Spoken Discourse

Using Grammatical Forms as Pivots Within Discourse

Some constructions are pivotal in that they occur in the middle of a discourse segment with prior situational context or prior discourse, as well as follow-up discourse. The English present perfect progressive (PPP) is a good example of such a construction. Presented to learners out of context, a sentence with this verb form is impossible to interpret properly. For example:

> John has been walking.

Taken alone, this sentence does not make sense. The default context for this verb form is a general one that implies an adverb like *lately* or *recently*:

A: What has John been doing to lose so much weight?
B: He's been walking.

It's also possible for the PPP to occur in a specific context (e.g., this morning):

A: What has John been doing since he left the house at 7 a.m.?
B: He's been walking.

Celce-Murcia and Yoshida (2003) collected approximately 250 contextualized tokens of the PPP and found that it is typically part of a three-move structure:

1. The first move provides relevant background (simple present or present perfect tense).
2. The second move highlights an ongoing activity of concern (PPP).
3. The third move gives some evaluation or follow-up in the simple present tense.

What follows is an authentic example from a radio talk show (the proper names have been changed and the lines separate the discourse into its three moves):

Host: I'm Dr. Mary Smith and you're on talk radio. Hello?
Caller: Good afternoon, Dr. Smith. I'm Lucy and I'm 50.

I'd just like to share a positive thing that I have found in the last year or so.

I've been hiking,

---

and find that this is a wonderful way to keep your weight down and meet some people and just feel really good.

In this discourse segment, we get quite a bit of background because the interlocutors do not know each other, and the background must be established to ensure effective communication with the host and the radio listeners. Then the PPP comes up as the central focus of Lucy's discourse, and it is followed by an extended evaluation.

Another thing that Celce-Murcia and Yoshida (2003) found is that the PPP often occurs in complaints or laments and that sometimes the situational context can provide the necessary background such that a verbal first move to provide background is unnecessary (i.e., the situation itself is the first move):

Background: [You have waited in line for one hour to buy tickets for a newly released movie, and a young man cuts in line in front of you.]

Hey! I've been waiting in line a long time,

---

and I don't appreciate you butting in front of me!

In fact, Celce-Murcia and Yoshida even discovered one example where the first and last moves were implicit and unspoken but fully understood from the context:

Background: [Both A and B know that B has tried to stop smoking for some time now. As B enters the room, A sniffs and smells a strong odor of tobacco smoke on B's clothes.]

A: You've been smoking again!

[Unspoken evaluation: A negative assessment is implied, much like: *A:* That's too bad. / I'm disappointed in you.]

Another construction that tends to serve as a pivot in discourse but is rarely taught as such is the existential *there* construction. Typically, this construction is taught to ESL/EFL learners at the sentence level, often using objects as realia with focus on the subject-verb agreement rule:[10]

There is one book on the table.
There are two pencils.

In this chapter I want to focus on how the existential *there* construction is used in ongoing discourse. Lloyd-Jones (1987) found that using the existential *there* to locate objects in physical space, as in the two preceding constructed examples, accounted for only 10% of the tokens in her written and spoken data. How, then, is the existential *there* construction used at the discourse level?

Sasaki (1991) found that it functions as a pivot in oral discourse much as the PPP does. Here is one of her examples taken from data recorded and transcribed by Jan Frodesen, who interviewed a Great Lakes shipping captain:

1. Well, the things is, that when you see the boat at the dock
2. and you see that steel and that riveting, you think well,
3. there's nothing gonna harm this boat,
4. and when you're out on a big storm,
5. you're wondering what's keeping it all together.

In full form, line 3, the pivot of this discourse, would be:

There is nothing that is going to harm this boat.

The logical subject is *nothing*, and the relative clause that follows *nothing* makes an inference (i.e., nothing is going to harm this boat) based on the prior discourse in lines 1 and 2. The relative clause is thus anaphoric. However, the remaining discourse contrasts "seeing the boat at the dock" with "being out on a big storm," and it moves the discourse forward and offers an entirely different thought (i.e. *what's keeping it all together?*). Sasaki (1991) gives several other examples of how the existential *there* functions like a pivot—partly anaphoric and partly cataphoric—in oral discourse that is narrative in nature. I have emphasized the use of the existential *there* in oral discourse because its description has been grossly oversimplified in ESL/EFL grammar instruction. Whereas Sasaki has been the only one to publish research on oral discourse, there are many accounts of the use of the existential *there* in written exposition and academic discourse (see, among others, Huckin and Pesante, 1988; Ahlers 1991).

Using a Marked Tense to Signal an Important Conclusion

Earlier in this paper I discussed Suh's (1992a, 1992b) Frame-elaboration Hypothesis, whereby one tense-aspect-modality form frames a discourse episode and another shorter, simpler form then elaborates the discourse (e.g., *used to → would/'d; be going to → will/'ll*). I also discussed using a complex tense-aspect form (the present perfect progressive) as a pivot in the middle of a discourse episode. I now turn to examples from written discourse that illustrate the use of a marked tense (past perfect) to signal the end of a discourse episode in a manner that indicates an important fact, or what some analysts of literary stylistics might call a "coda" (see Celce-Murcia 2002, for a fuller discussion). Consider the following example:

1. In the 1980s researchers at Stanford University were trying
2. to teach American Sign Language to Koko, a female gorilla.
3. Koko was well cared for and was surrounded by interesting toys and objects.
4. Her caretakers continually exposed her to the signs for the foods
5. and toys in her environment. Koko particularly loved eating bananas.
6. One day she was hungry but couldn't find any bananas.
7. She went to the researcher and made a good approximation of the sign for *banana*.
8. Koko was rewarded with a banana, and the research team knew
9. that Koko had made the connection between a sign and the object it represented.

(author data)

The use of the past perfect in the last line of this discourse is not among the typical sentence-level uses of this tense-aspect form that get taught in ESL/EFL grammars. These uses tend to signal either (a) a prior event or (b) a past counterfactual condition:

a. Mary arrived after I had read the newspaper.
b. If you had studied harder, you would have passed the test.

In the preceding extended passage, the past perfect was explicitly used to make a point, i.e., to signal what the important point of the story was.

An interesting permutation of this discourse pattern occasionally occurs. We know from the work of Schiffrin (1981), Wolfson (1982), and others that in narrative discourse the present tense is sometimes used to refer to past time to make a narrative more informal and engaging for the listener or reader. We call this the historical present. In oral narrative, in fact, Schiffrin and Wolfson show that speakers often switch back and forth between past tense and present tense as they relate such narratives. In written discourse, other than fictional dialogue, there is less switching back and forth in narratives that describe a punctual action or an accomplishment (Vendler 1967). Thus we should not be surprised to see a sequence that is normally in the simple past with a past perfect climax become simple present tense with a present perfect climax when the historical present is used rather than simple past tense to make the discourse more immediate and engaging for the reader:

Life in an Icy Inferno

We're wearing harnesses and hard hats and descending on ropes and ladders into an ice cave known as Warren Cave, which has been hollowed out by steam from the volcano. We unclip the harnesses about 40 feet below the surface of the mountain . . . We're here to retrieve a temperature probe— one of the 23 the group left on the mountain a year ago in the hope of determining how much the soil temperatures change and thus whether these environments are relatively stable. As we move from the entrance, the light fades and we have to use our flashlights. Moore disappears down a corridor and after a few moments gives a shout. He's found the probe.

(Judson 2012: 115)

The full form of the final sentence is "He has found the probe." As in the previous discourse episode about Koko, the final sentence in the present perfect form signals a climax or coda of sorts. The only difference is that the discourse about Koko used past tense forms to narrate a past event whereas the preceding discourse used present tense forms (i.e., historical present) to narrate a past event in order to make the discourse more engaging for the reader. Otherwise, the structure of the two discourse patterns is parallel.

As suggested previously (Celce-Murcia 2002), I recommend teaching these patterns by presenting several authentic examples of any given pattern to learners and then engaging them in analysis of the verb forms, asking leading questions, as needed, until the pattern is identified. I then ask the learners to generate their own stories based on the patterns in the examples. These accounts can then be shared with classmates for feedback, which provides further reinforcement of the pattern.

Conclusion

The more complex discourse-based patterns in the preceding section are for high-intermediate and advanced learners. Knowledge of when and where to use them helps to make the writing of L2 learners more coherent and comprehensible. This is also true of the discourse patterns I discussed earlier that are intended for beginners or intermediate-level learners. The patterns discussed in this paper are not "rule based" in the way that sentence-level grammar constructions are viewed or described. They are, instead, tendencies, templates, or heuristics that learners can use to their advantage if they are aware of them; however, very few learners have ever been taught patterns like these. And while these patterns are never the only way to express a given message, they are very useful tools for achieving coherence and fluency at the discourse level.

All natural languages have such templates, but they do not normally transfer; they are different from language to language. Teaching English learners how to make their speech and writing cohere at the discourse level by making judicious grammatical choices is, I believe, what ESL/EFL teachers should be doing. Instructors need to move from teaching learners how to use grammar to form sentences to teaching them how to use grammar to create coherent and cohesive discourse.

Notes

1 My thanks to many colleagues and graduate students who have contributed to my views on discourse-based approaches to grammar analysis and instruction, especially my textbook co-authors Diane Larsen-Freeman, Elite Olshtain, and Sharon Hilles. Any errors or shortcomings in this chapter are mine alone.

2 Other rules that some have suggested are context free are subject-verb agreement and some-any suppletion. But these rules have been challenged rather convincingly by Lakoff (1969) and Reid (1991), respectively, who argue that these rules are dependent on meaning and context.

3 Content schemata are organized sets of information on a given topic typically shared by users of a language; formal schemata are templates for the form and organization of various discourse genres such as conversations, lectures, sermons, news articles, business letters, research papers, etc. as realized in a given language.

4 These tendencies, or templates, are different from language to language; the point is that all languages have such discourse templates, and they need to be researched and made explicit so that they can be used in language teaching materials.

5 This example comes from data collected and transcribed by Nina Weinstein (1984) for her MA thesis (only selected examples appear in the thesis). She was examining phonological features; we used her transcribed oral data to look at grammar in discourse. This segment can be edited for pedagogical purposes to make it clearer for learners:

> They're going to go in and have their stomach exposed and have it stapled off so that there'll be an upper pouch in the stomach which will hold about two ounces of food; it's got a little hole right in the middle of that pouch, where food, when it's finally ground up, will slowly go through.

6 Kyung-Hee Suh, in fact, collected some informal oral data to check against the transcripts she had found. She asked 10 native English speakers the question "What are your plans for the upcoming weekend?" and recorded their responses (with their consent). Out of the 10 consultants, nine followed the predicted template *I'm gonna . . . and then I'll . . . and I'll* with very minor variations.

7 For a more complete discussion of applying Bull's Framework to the English verb system, see Larsen-Freeman and Celce-Murcia (2016) and Larsen-Freeman, Kuehn, and Haccius (2002).

8 The progressive aspect (*be . . . -ing*) can combine with all the preceding tense forms:

> She has played soccer. → She has been playing soccer.
> She plays soccer. → She is playing soccer.
> She's going to play soccer. → She's going to be playing soccer.
> She had played soccer. → She had been playing soccer.
> She played soccer. → She was playing soccer.
> She would play soccer. → She would be playing soccer.

9 Halliday and Hasan (1976) discuss lexical cohesion as a separate topic in a separate chapter of their work.

10 For further discussion of the somewhat controversial nature of this subject-verb agreement rule, see Larsen-Freeman, and Celce-Murcia (2016).

References

Ahlers, E. (1991). A discourse analysis of nonreferential *there* in academic writing. Unpublished master's thesis. University of California, Los Angeles.

Bull, W. E. (1960). *Time, tense, and the verb: A study in theoretical and applied linguistics with particular application to Spanish*. Berkeley: University of California Press.

Celce-Murcia, M. (2002). Why it makes sense to teach grammar through discourse. In E. Hinkel & S. Fotos (Eds.), *New perspectives on grammar teaching in second language classrooms* (pp. 119–133). Mahwah, NJ: Erlbaum.

Celce-Murcia, M., & Olshtain, E. (2000). *Discourse and context in language teaching*. New York: Cambridge University Press.

Celce-Murcia, M., & Yoshida, N. (2003). Alternatives for teaching the present perfect progressive. *English Teaching Forum, 41*(1), 2–9, 21.

Givón, T. (1984). *Syntax*. Amsterdam: John Benjamins.

Halliday, M. A. K., & Hasan, R. (1976). *Cohesion in English*. London: Longman.

Halliday, M. A. K., & Matthiessen, C. M. I. M. (2014). *Introduction to functional grammar* (4th ed.). London: Routledge.

Huckin, T., & Pesante, L. (1988). Existential *there. Written Communication, 5*(3), 368–391.

Judson, O. (July, 2012). Life in an icy inferno. *National Geographic, 222*, 94–115.

Lakoff, R. (1969). Some reasons why there can't be any *some-any* rule. *Language, 45*, 608–615.

Larsen-Freeman, D., & Celce-Murcia, M. (2016). *The grammar book: Form, meaning and use for English language teachers* (3rd ed.). Boston: Heinle Cengage Learning.

Larsen-Freeman, D., Kuehn, T., & Haccius, M. (2002). Helping students make appropriate English verb tense-aspect choices. *TESOL Journal, 11*(4), 3–9.

Lloyd-Jones, M. (1987). A contextual analysis of nonreferential *there* in American English usage. Unpublished master's thesis. University of California, Los Angeles.

McCarthy, M. J. (2015). The role of corpus research in the design of advanced-level grammar instruction. In M. A. Christison, D. Christian, P. A. Duff, & N. Spada (Eds.), *Teaching and learning English grammar: Research findings and future directions* (pp. 87–102). New York: Routledge.

Reid, W. (1991). *Verb and noun number in English: A functional explanation*. London: Longman.

Sasaki, M. (1991). An analysis of sentences with nonreferential *there* in spoken American English. *Word, 42*(2), 157–178.

Schiffrin, D. (1981). Tense variation in narrative. *Language, 57*(1), 45–62.

Suh, K-H. (1992a). A discourse analysis of the English tense-aspect-modality system. Unpublished doctoral dissertation in applied linguistics. University of California, Los Angeles.

Suh, K-H. (1992b). Past habituality in English discourse: *Used to* and *would*. *Language Research, 28*(4), 857–882.

Terkel, S. (1974). *Working*. New York: Ballantine Books.

Vendler, Z. (1967). Verbs and times. In *Linguistics and philosophy* (pp. 97–121). Ithaca, NY: Cornell University Press.

Weinstein, N. (1984). The effects of levels of formality and tempo on reduced forms. Unpublished master's thesis. University of California, Los Angeles.

Wolfson, N. (1982). *The conversational historical present in American English narratives*. Dordrecht, Netherlands: Foris Publications.

2

TEACHING GRAMMAR

English as an International Language

Sandra Lee McKay

Introduction

Most of the chapters in this book deal with the teaching of Standard English. The purpose of this chapter is to examine what is meant by Standard English in the context of English as an international language (EIL). Specifically, we will focus on the variation that exists today in English usage and examine what this means for the concept of Standard English.

There are two main reasons for the many varieties of English that are spoken today. The first is due to the geographical spread of English, resulting in various Standard Englishes based on the country where English is being spoken (e.g., Australia, Singapore, the Philippines, etc.). Added to this diversity are differences in English due to the users of English, based on their educational and economic background, and the uses of English as, for example, the difference between spoken and written English. Given this diversity in English, in this chapter we explore what this means for teaching grammar. We begin the chapter by illustrating some of these variations in English.

The Current Status of English

Two significant facts about English that contribute to its being an international language are, first, it is widely spoken as a second language, and, second, it is spoken in many areas of the world. Many people do not realize that English is not the most widely spoken language in the world today in terms of the number of native speakers. Chinese and Spanish have more first language speakers than does English. (In millions, Chinese has 1,197 speakers, Spanish 406, and English 335.) However, English is by far the most widely geographically distributed language since it is spoken in 101 countries. The only language that comes close to this number is

Arabic, which is spoken in 59 countries (http://www.ethnologue.com/statistics/size, retrieved January 19, 2014).

One might ask why English is today considered an international language and not Mandarin or Spanish since they have far more native speakers. The answer to this puzzle rests in the current number of second language speakers of English. The British Council (http://www.britishcouncil.org/learning-faq-the-english-language.htm, retrieved January 12, 2014) summarizes the following estimates of the relative numbers of first and second language speakers of English.

- English is spoken as a first language by around 375 million people and as a second language by around 375 million speakers of the world.
- Around 750 million people are believed to speak English as a foreign language.
- Speakers of English as a second language outnumber those who speak it as a first language.
- One out of four of the world's population speaks English to some level of competence, and demand from the other three-quarters is increasing.

These numbers demonstrate two facts: first, there are far more L2 speakers of English than L1 speakers of English, and, second, if we consider the number of L2 speakers of English, the current number of speakers of English—both L1 and L2—far surpasses the number of people who speak either Mandarin and Spanish.

So what does all this mean for the teaching of English? First, it is important to note that even though English has official status in many countries of the world today, this does not mean that everyone in the country speaks English well. For example, in Singapore, Singlish (Colloquial Singaporean English) is a variety of English that developed from the influence of Chinese, Tamil, and Malay on the English that is used in Singapore. Most Singaporeans are familiar with Singlish and with standard Singaporean English, but there are some Singaporeans, generally older and less educated ones, who speak only Singlish.

Second, because today there are more L2 speakers of English than L1 speakers, learners of English have a far greater chance of using English with other L2 English speakers than with L1 speakers. The fact is that many learners of English will need to communicate with other L2 speakers who may have gaps in their knowledge of English, often in terms of grammatical accuracy. Hence, breakdowns in communication can occur. This has important implications for the teaching of English grammar.

Varieties of English: Common Features

Since most speakers of English today are bilingual, they have another language that they use on a daily basis. In many instances, these other languages affect their use of English; generally, the most obvious influence is on pronunciation. However, differences in grammar are also common, though few impede comprehension. By way of illustration, let us examine some of these differences.

In a seminal work on the varieties of English, Kachru (1983) argued that the different roles that English serves in countries around the world are best conceived of in terms of three concentric circles: (1) the *Inner Circle*, where English is the primary language of the country, such as in Australia, Canada, the United States, and the United Kingdom; (2) the *Outer Circle*, where English serves as a second language in a multilingual country, such as in Singapore, India, and the Philippines; and (3) the *Expanding Circle*, where English is widely studied as a foreign language, such as in China, Japan, and Korea. Recent scholars have convincingly maintained that such a categorization is an oversimplification of a complex situation of language use. For example, in some Outer Circle countries such as India or South Africa, segments of the population have little or no knowledge of English and hence make no use of English on a daily basis. Nevertheless, in those contexts in which a large bilingual population makes use of English along with one or more languages on a daily basis, there are bound to be changes in all of the languages used due to phonological and grammatical transfer and the borrowing of words. These varieties of English are called *World Englishes.*

Researchers who subscribe to this framework seek not only to document the uniqueness of various varieties of English but also to argue that such varieties should be seen as legitimate and standard in the local context. They contend that rather than have a monocentric basis of standardization based on Inner Circle native speakers, there should be a recognition of the pluricentric nature of current English use with standards based on the language used and accepted in the local context. There is then an emphasis in discussions of World Englishes on the uniqueness of each variety of English. Nevertheless, many of these varieties share common features. The following list provides examples of some of these shared features in reference to grammar.

Drawing on the work of Platt and colleagues (1984), McKay and Bokhorst-Heng (2008) note the following grammatical innovations in World Englishes:

Nouns (65)

1. A tendency not to mark nouns for plural.

   Up to twelve year of schooling. (India)
   A province will be divided into district. (Philippines)

2. A tendency to use a specific/nonspecific system for nouns rather than a definite/indefinite system, or to use the two systems side by side.

   • Nonspecific:

     I really want to spend some time in village, definitely if I get chance. (India)

- Specific:

  Got one boy, morning also eat instant noodles, afternoon also eat instant noodles, night also eat instant noodles. Suddenly he died. The doctor found a lot of wax in his stomach. (Malaysia)

3. A tendency to change the form of quantifiers.

   Don't eat so much sweets. (Singapore)
   You are expected to say some few words. (Sri Lanka)

4. A tendency to convert certain uncountable nouns to countable (examples cited by Shim 1999: 252, taken from a high school English textbook).

   Although it is a hard work, I enjoy it. (Korea)
   An old man showed a great patience. (Korea)

5. A tendency not to make a distinction between the third person pronouns *he* and *she*.

   My mother, he live in kampong. (In Malaysia, a kampong is a small village.)
   My husband who was in England, she was then my fiancé. (East Africa)

6. A tendency to change the word order within the noun phrase.

   Ninety over cheques. (Singapore/Malaysia)
   That your brother will he come? (Nigeria)

Verbs (85–86)

1. A tendency not to mark the verb for third person singular in its present tense form.

   Instead of "She drinks milk," a speaker of Philippine English might say, "She *drink* milk."

2. A limited marking of verbs for the past tense.

   I move to hostel. (India)
   Last year I stay three months in Germany. (Singapore)
   Some of them are crying because teacher ask them to read stories in Filipino. (Philippines)

3. A tendency to use an *aspect* system (completed or ongoing action) rather than a *tense* system (past or future) or to use both systems side by side.

   It was during that time these people make some arrangement with law enforcement agencies. (West Africa)
   I still eat. (instead of *I am/was eating*; Malaysia)

4. A tendency to extend the use of *be* + *verb* + *-ing* constructions to stative verbs.

She is knowing her science very well. (East Africa)
The squad we are having here is good enough to beat Namibia. (South Africa, from Kamwangamalu 2001: 58)

5. The formation of different phrasal and prepositional verb constructions.

Her name cropped in the conversation. (East Africa)
You can voice out what you are not satisfied with at the meeting. (Singapore)
Each and every day one was well informed to cope up with any eventuality. (written English, West Africa)
The older generation finds it difficult to do with young people. (Korea, from Shim 1999: 251)
Gardens come on life again. (Korea, from Shim 1999: 251)

It is important to note that an individual's use of English can vary greatly depending on the formality of the context, the class and educational background of the speaker, whether the speaker is writing or speaking, and the purpose for which English is being used (e.g., an email versus a formal letter). Many speakers of English today can shift their use of English depending on the context, using a standard variety in formal situations and an informal variety, with many of the features just listed, in informal contexts. Often this ability to shift is a factor of education since individuals who have a high level of proficiency in English are generally familiar with several varieties of a World English from the most standard to the most informal. For example, in Singapore, highly educated Singaporeans are able to use Standard Singapore English, which is almost identical to Standard American English, in formal contexts. However, with friends or family and in informal situations, they can switch to Colloquial Singaporean English, or Singlish. However, there are cases in which individuals who have a full command of Standard Singapore English are not fluent in Singapore Colloquial English, and there are cases where less educated Singaporeans are not fluent in Standard Singapore English. In this way, diversity in English grammar is affected by educational level and social class.

In most cases the grammatical features of World Englishes just listed are far more prevalent in spoken, informal English than in written English. Formal written English tends to display far fewer of these features and in many ways comes closest to what might be thought of as a universal standard. By and large, there is great consistency in most academic, professional, and diplomatic writing. It is this more or less universal written Standard English that is the target for a good deal of high-stakes assessment of English proficiency. Given the diversity in English use previously noted, let us now examine what this means for teaching grammatical standards in classrooms where a variety of non-Standard English is spoken.

Standard English and EIL

Standard English is the variety regarded as the target for many educational contexts and is typically used as a yardstick by which to measure other varieties. Several scholars have attempted to define the term more precisely, leading to the following definitions:

- A particular dialect of English, being the only nonlocalized dialect, of global currency without significant variation, universally accepted as the appropriate educational target in teaching English; which may be spoken with an unrestricted choice of accent. (Strevens 1983: 88)
- The variety of the English language which is normally employed in writing and normally spoken by "educated" speakers of the language. It is also, of course, the variety of the language that students of English as a Foreign or Second Language (EFL/ESL) are taught when receiving formal instruction. The term *Standard English* refers to grammar and vocabulary (dialect) but not to pronunciation (accent). (Trudgill and Hannah 2002: 1)
- We may define the Standard English of an English-speaking country as a minority variety (identified chiefly by its vocabulary, grammar and orthography) which carries most prestige and is most widely understood. (Crystal 1995: 110)

The assumption in this chapter, based on these definitions, is that Standard English is the variety of English normally employed in formal writing, that it is a minority variety that carries great prestige, and that it is typically the educational target in the teaching of grammar.

In their article on selecting an instructional variety for an EIL curriculum, Matsuda and Friedrich (2012) contend that there are three prevalent alternatives in selecting a target for EIL instruction: an international variety of English, the speaker's own variety of English, and an established variety of English. The first, an international variety, is the variety that would be "intelligible and effective in all international communication" (17). This variety is fairly homogeneous and is used primarily in the formal texts of academic and professional writing. One advantage of using such a target in an EIL classroom is that it is far easier to teach and assess. However, as Matsuda and Friedrich (2012) point out, there are disadvantages to using this variety as a pedagogical target.

> [S]uggesting one or a limited set of specialized varieties of English for international use does not reflect the reality of international communication and the use of EIL. In most communicative exchanges that involve language users from different linguistic and cultural backgrounds, which variety of English . . . is used depends on the speakers involved and is thus unpredictable.

(18)

A second possibility for a pedagogical target is to teach the speaker's own variety of English, such as Singapore English or Indian English. The advantage of this alternative is that it legitimizes the student's own use of English. The disadvantage, of course, is that it limits the student's familiarity with variation in English to the student's own variety. As such, students are not given access to the varieties of English that have greater international currency.

The final possibility that Matsuda and Friedrich (2012) suggest is "to select one of the established varieties as the dominant instructional variety while introducing other varieties as part of common classroom practice" (21). Established varieties are ones that "are codified, are used for a wide variety of communicative functions (so that students can learn to do what they need/want to do in English) and are relatively well accepted in different kinds of international contexts as well as different realms of use (e.g., business, academic and entertainment)" (22). Such varieties need not be only British or American English but could also be Indian or Singaporean English. They argue that this approach will increase students' ability to use several varieties of English and more importantly to know when to use each one. Ultimately, however, it is the needs of the students, the resources available, and the local context that should determine which of these alternatives to select.

No matter which alternative is selected, it is essential that all EIL students are aware of the fact that there are many varieties of English and that they differ in range and power. This awareness, as Matsuda and Friedrich (2012) point out, can be developed in several ways. One is to familiarize students with different varieties of English through the teaching materials themselves, using, for example, listening tapes that include different varieties of English. A second possibility is to provide opportunities for students to interact with English speakers who speak a variety different from their own. This can be done by hiring teachers not only from Inner Circle countries but also from Outer and Expanding Circle countries. A final strategy is to provide students with knowledge about English variation through readings on the dialects of English.

In her discussion of grammar teaching and standards, Gupta (2012) maintains, as we have done here, that formal written English is fairly universal in its consistency. She points out, however, that written texts do display grammatical differences depending on their level of formality so that the grammatical features of newspaper headlines, short message service (SMS) messages, postcards, and advertisements tend to be quite different from the features of a formal text written for academic or professional purposes. She also argues, rightfully so, that differences that exist in formal prose based on regional variation tend to be less categorical than a matter of frequency. So, for example, while the use of the present perfect in relation to the use of the past tense is more common in British and Australian English than in American English, the feature still exists in American English. For Gupta, the differences that exist in formal writing based on region have been given far too much emphasis in language classrooms. She contends that "all teachers of

English need to pay the greatest attention to areas of grammar where the rules are clear and the same across the world" (254).

Grammar Teaching in EIL Classrooms

Larsen-Freeman (2014) argues persuasively for the acceptance of a three-dimensional grammar framework. She contends that the goal of grammar teaching should be to enable learners to use English accurately, meaningfully, and appropriately. As such, grammar instruction should give attention to form/structure, meaning/semantics, and use/pragmatics. Hence, all language instruction needs to examine three questions:

1. How is the structure formed?
2. What does it mean?
3. When/why is it used?

The fact that English is an international language with a broad geographical spread, resulting in many varieties of English, adds to the complexity of answering these questions and teaching grammar. Let us first consider the issue of form.

Grammar Teaching and Form

As noted, particular varieties of English have different standards in regard to count and noncount nouns in English. In the Philippines, for example, the use of *luggages* is considered correct in that it is used in formal academic writing. The same is true for *furnitures* in Nigeria. How then should count and noncount nouns be dealt with in EIL grammar classes? Here the importance of making localized grammatical decisions is critical. English teachers in the Philippines should teach that *luggage* is one of the countable nouns in English while teachers in the United States should teach that *luggage* is noncountable. These decisions would be based on which form is acceptable to the majority of local users of English, particularly in written discourse, and is codified in local grammar books and style guide sheets. However, it would also be important with more advanced English learners to make students aware of the fact that which nouns are countable will differ among the varieties of English. This will prepare students to be competent users of English in the local context and alert them to the fact that some grammatical standards will vary depending on the context.

In determining whether a particular structure is standard, grammar teachers need to keep two facts in mind. First, some uses of questionable grammatical forms may be due to gaps in the learners' English proficiency and the influence of those they interact with (e.g., the use of "She drink coffee every morning."). On the other hand, some questionable grammatical forms may be innovations, which in time will be accepted as standard (e.g., the use of "We discussed about that at the last meeting." and "I am enjoying the party."). EIL grammar teachers need to keep both of these facts in mind when making decisions about grammatical correctness and to localize their decisions so that the standards they teach reflect local norms. At the same time, they need to prepare students for the differences in standards they will encounter in other contexts.

Grammar Teaching and Semantics

To be competent users of English, students need to acquire not just the forms of English but also the meaning of particular forms. For example, it is not enough for users of English to learn that some phrasal verbs are separable (e.g., *look up* and *keep up*) while others are not (e.g., *come across* and *go with*). Users also need to know the meaning of the form. For example, to use the phrasal verb *come across* in a meaningful way, it is useful to know that *come across* has two meanings: "to discover by chance" (e.g., "I came across the old photo when looking at my grandmother's album.") and "to make an impression" (e.g., "He came across as arrogant."). The teaching of semantics in EIL classrooms, however, is complicated by the fact that a good deal of lexical innovation is occurring in the development of World Englishes.

Brown (1999), for example, points out various features of Singapore Standard English (SSE) that differ from Standard American English (SAE). For example, while *upkeep* can be used only as a noun in SAE (e.g., "He paid for the upkeep of his mother's house."), it can also be used as a verb in SSE (e.g., "An old car is expensive to upkeep."). Also, although in SAE *since* is used either as a preposition followed by a noun (e.g., "since my childhood") or a conjunction followed by a clause (e.g., "since I was young"), *since young* is a common phrase in SSE (e.g., "I tend to prefer Mandarin since young."). The coining of compound nouns also adds to the differences that exist between SAE and SSE. For example, the phrase *coffee money* does not mean money used to buy coffee as it would in SAE; rather it means a bribe (e.g., "He gave the policeman coffee money."). And *black face* does not mean a face with a black skin color as it does in SAE, but rather it means an individual is in a grumpy, surly, or bad mood, a translation from a Cantonese expression.

Some terms used in several varieties of English can have different meanings in different countries. For example, Matsuda and Duran (2012) note the following example:

> Tea: India—a milky hot and sweetened beverage served anytime; Australia—evening meal or dinner; Singapore—late lunch; UK—afternoon light meal; U.S.—formal afternoon occasion.
>
> *(217)*

Such examples highlight the richness of World Englishes but pose particular challenges for language learners.

What do such examples suggest for the teaching of semantics? Such examples can provide teachers with an opportunity to make students aware of the innovations that are occurring in the use of English. While it is clearly not necessary for English learners outside of Singapore to learn phrases such as *coffee money*, it is a fascinating aspect of English to study by means of readings on the development of World Englishes. In addition, studying such examples provides a context for students to investigate the lexical innovations that are occurring in their first language.

Grammar Teaching and Pragmatics

Perhaps the most complicated aspect of EIL grammar teaching has to do with the pragmatic aspect of our three-dimensional grammar framework. When speakers have pragmatic ability, they understand the intended meaning of what is said. This ability is important because people can say things indirectly. For example, the same sentence (e.g., "When are you leaving?") can have different intended meanings (e.g., "May I have a ride with you?" or "Don't you think it is time for you to go?"). In intercultural encounters, these indirect meanings may not be understood by the listener and hence can cause misunderstandings.

Pragmatic ability includes both sociopragmatic and pragmalinguistic competence. When speakers have *sociopragmatic* competence, they know, for example, when it is appropriate to apologize. If the speaker and listener have different expectations about when an apology is warranted, this can lead to cross-cultural misunderstandings and stereotyping. When speakers have *pragmalinguistic* competence, they know the correct linguistic form to use to express an apology, depending on the seriousness of the offense, the formality of the situation, and the role relationship of the speakers. For example, speakers with pragmalinguistic competence know when it would be appropriate to say a simple "I'm sorry" and when they should say, "I apologize." Hence, the teaching of pragmatics needs to give attention both to when particular speech acts are expected and to how the speech act should be expressed.

It is difficult to overemphasize the importance of pragmatic competence in EIL exchanges. In the majority of EIL exchanges, speakers have different levels of competence in the grammar of English, as well as differences in their sense of pragmatic appropriateness. In order for communication to proceed smoothly, speakers have to work to negotiate understanding and adjust the form of their language so that the listener is able to comprehend the intent of the message. Canagarajah (2007) goes so far as to argue that in EIL exchanges, form can in some ways be less important than meaning and use, pointing out that in EIL exchanges,

> form receives reduced significance, or, rather, form gets shaped according to the contexts and participants in an interaction. More important are the range of other skills, abilities, and awareness that enable multilingual speakers to

negotiate grammar. In addition to grammatical competence, we have to give equal importance to language awareness that enables speakers to make instantaneous inferences about the norms and conventions of their multilingual interlocutors; strategic competence to negotiate interpersonal relationships effectively; and pragmatic competence to adopt communicative conventions that are appropriate for the interlocutor, purpose and situation.

(928)

If the present-day community of EIL speakers is composed of individuals speaking different varieties of English, at different levels of proficiencies for different purposes, a truly competent speaker of EIL must be able to shift among these contexts. Proficiency in EIL then means "the ability to shuttle between different varieties of English and different speech communities. In this sense, the argument becomes irrelevant whether local standards or inner-circle standards matter. We need both and more—that is the ability to negotiate the varieties in other outer- and expanding-circle communities as well" (Canagarajah 2006: 233). Developing such proficiency and assessing it is challenging. However, it is important to point out, that in order to accomplish this task, learners do not need to be proficient in every variety of English that exists. Rather, as Canagarajah (2006) points out, we need to shift our focus both in pedagogy and assessment to developing negotiating skills.

Such realizations suggest the need for an important shift in assessment practices. From focusing overly on proficiency in grammar or in abstract linguistic features, we have to focus more on proficiency in pragmatics. Sociolinguistic skills of dialect differentiation, code switching, style shifting, interpersonal communication, conversation management, and discourse strategies are important for shuttling between English varieties.

(McKay 2005: 233)

Ultimately, we need to shift our emphasis "from language as a system to language as social practice, from grammar to pragmatics, from competence to performance" (Cangarajah 2006: 234).

Given the importance of strategic and pragmatic competence in EIL exchanges, an essential aspect of EIL classes should be to develop these competencies. McKay (2011) argues that all EIL curricula should focus on the following components of language use:

1. Explicit attention should be given to introducing and practicing repair strategies, such as asking for clarification and repetition, rephrasing, and allowing wait time.
2. A variety of conversational gambits or routines should be introduced and practiced, including such items as expressing disagreement and disagreement, managing turn-taking, and taking leave.

3. The curricula should seek to promote students' understanding of how pragmatic norms can differ cross-culturally.

4. Students should be free to express their own pragmatic norms but also to recognize that, to the extent these differ from the norms expected by their listener, there may be cross-cultural misunderstandings.

(133)

What does this three-dimensional grammatical framework of form/structure, meaning/semantics, and use/pragmatics suggest for classroom activities? This is the topic we turn to now.

Classroom Activities

Before discussing specific grammatical activities that might be used in grammar classes in EIL contexts, it is important to point out the major goals of these activities. All of the suggested activities are based on the following assumptions:

- All learners of English should be aware of variation in English use based on geographical area, the level of formality, and the speaker's economic and educational background.
- All learners of English should be taught a standard variety of English.
- All varieties of English should be equally respected with a realization that different varieties of English are the most suitable for specific contexts.
- Since grammatical competency depends on an understanding of form/structure, meaning/semantics, and use/pragmatics, attention to the development of strategic intercultural competence should exist in all EIL classrooms.

Activities for Beginning-level Students

One might argue that because beginning-level students are struggling to learn basic structures and simple vocabulary, they should not be faced with any of the preceding goals. Yet in teaching contexts in which students share a mother tongue, several activities could be undertaken to help students understand the variation in present-day English use. Two such activities are presented next.

Activity One: Awareness Activity

Ask students to gather examples of differences in the use of their mother tongue that exist based on geographical regions. These could be pronunciation differences, lexical differences, or grammatical differences. Use these examples to make the point that any language will differ based on geographical differences. Then point out how English also differs by geographical region. Here you might give two or three examples of how English varies based on geographical region, using some of the examples included in the chapter.

Activity Two: Awareness Activity

Ask students to bring in examples of different written texts in their own language—emails, blogs, SMSs, newspaper articles, textbooks, novels, and so on. Using these examples, select two or three sentences from each text without identifying where they came from. Then ask students to guess where the sentence came from. Ask then to identify specific items in the text that helped them to decide on the source of the text. Use this activity to make the point that the language used in any text will vary depending on the purpose of the text and its level of formality.

Activities for Intermediate Students

Intermediate-level students have much more English to use in discussing the manner in which English varies. The following are some activities that might be used with this level of student.

Activity One: Attention to Meaning/Semantics

Put students in groups of three or four, and ask them to search the web for sites that list differences in the words used in British and in American English. They should then make a list of equivalencies in the two dialects similar to the following list. Tell them that whichever group has more words wins the game.

American English	British English
Gasoline	Petrol
Cookie	Biscuit
Round trip	Return
Elevator	Lift
Crosswalk	Zebra crossing
Subway	Underground
Apartment	Flat

Activity Two: Attention to Use/Pragmatics

In order to begin to familiarize students with the manner in which language appropriateness can differ cross-culturally, you might give them the following example upon receiving a compliment.

When someone compliments the watch you are wearing, how would you respond?

1. Say, "Oh this cheap thing?"
2. Give it to him.

3. Say, "Thanks" and smile.
4. Say, "Would you like to have it?"

Ask them which response they would most likely make if they answered in English. Then ask them which response they would most likely make if the answers were translated into their mother tongue. Many students from Asian countries will select something like the first response, which is technically called a downplay, or a way of sounding humble when accepting a compliment. Use this example to illustrate the manner in which what is acceptable can differ cross-culturally.

The point of this activity is twofold. First, it helps students understand that how a compliment is received depends on such things as how well the speakers know each other, what is being complimented, and what message the speaker hopes to make. In this way, form very much depends on the context. The second goal of the activity is to make students aware of the fact that different cultures may tend to have specific ways of receiving a compliment. For example, in America the most common response to a compliment is the third one, a simple thank you. However, in many cultures, it is common to use a downplay.

Activity Three: Attention to Form/Structure

Put students in groups, and ask them to search for websites that include errors in the use of English, such as the *New York Times* article "Strange Signs from Abroad" (http://www.nytimes.com/interactive/2010/05/11/travel/funny-signs.html#/all/). Use this example to make the point that many users of English today make errors in the way they use English. Hence, in using English with people who speak English as a second language they may find that speakers make errors and that sometimes these errors may cause problems in understanding. You could then follow this activity with Activity Four on how to repair breakdowns in communication. You could also follow this activity with a homework assignment on having them gather examples from their local context of signs or written documents where they see errors in the use of English.

Activity Four: Attention to Use/Pragmatics

Using the examples gathered in Activity Three, make the point that speakers of English who are not fluent in the language will make errors in their use of English. These errors can often cause problems in understanding. When these occur, tell them they can use a variety of expressions to try to clarify meaning. These include the following:

- *I'm sorry. Could you say that in another way?*
- *I'm sorry. I don't know what you mean by X.*

- *Do you mean* X*?*
- *Could you say that again?*

In order to give them practice in using these forms, give them sentences in which there are either errors in form that need clarification (e.g., "Yesterday I go to the store," where the tense is not clear) or errors in meaning that need clarification (e.g., "The cheese will blow off," in which it is not clear what the speaker means by "blow off").

Activities for Advanced Students

At this level of proficiency students can undertake activities that make them fully aware of variation in present-day English. Some possible activities follow.

Activity One: Attention to Form

Search the web for current newspapers published in English in an Outer Circle country such as India, the Philippines, or Nigeria. Select a simple article from the newspaper that displays particular semantic and grammatical features that differ from the standard variety of English being taught in the class. Give the article to the students, and ask them to identify words and grammatical forms that differ from what they have learned. Ask them to identify which ones get in the way of understanding. Use this activity to make the point that different varieties of English will have minor differences in semantics and grammatical structures but that such differences typically do not impede comprehension.

Activity Two: Attention to Form and Meaning

Put students in pairs, and have each pair select a particular variety of English that they would like to know more about (e.g., Australian English, Indian English, Singapore English, etc.). Then have them research on the web the grammatical and semantic features of this particular variety. Have them share their findings. Then ask them to identify which grammatical features, if any, they believe would lead to misunderstandings and why. In addition, have them list lexical items that might lead to misunderstandings. Ask them to list expressions they might use to make the meaning of these words clear.

Activity Three: Attention to Semantics

Bring in an example of an advertisement that makes use of a newly created blended word or a play on an English word. For example, in Bangkok there is a pet store called Dogburi, which is a blend of the English word *dog* and the Thai word *buri* for city. There is also a Thai restaurant called Thai Tanic, a play on the name of the American ship called the *Titanic*. Tell students such words are frequently created to give prestige to a product or store because some English is used. Have them find examples in their own environment of such examples.

Activity Four: Attention to Form

Have students use the Google search engine to find where particular grammatical features or semantic features are used. Gupta (2006), for example, found interesting differences between American and British English in the use of "I was stood" and "I was standing in a. . . ." The former grammatical structure is found primarily in British English in sentences such as, "A few weeks ago I was stood in a balloon basket for the first time." The latter expression is used in American English in sentences such as, "I was standing in a bar in Sydney when I saw a good friend." Gupta suggests students search items such as the following to see where each form is predominantly used.

- *I wrote (to) my mother and . . .*
- *The bacteria/bacterium are/is . . .*
- *There is/are several . . .*
- *I am/have been here since . . .*
  (2006: 107)

Conclusion

This chapter has focused on the teaching of grammar in EIL classrooms. We began the chapter by highlighting the diversity in form that exists in present-day English use. We pointed out that the use of specific varieties of English is often a factor of geographical region, proficiency in English, and the level of formality of the exchange. The use of more widely accepted standard forms of English appears to be related to greater proficiency in English and a higher level of formality. We maintained that what is termed Standard English is generally the type of English used in academic writing.

We next examined the teaching of standards in reference to EIL classrooms. We pointed out three prevalent possibilities in the selection of a target standard for the curriculum: to teach the local variety of English, to teach the English norms present in academic writing, or to teach a widely accepted standard of English while introducing other varieties of English as well. Which standard to teach in the classroom depends on a variety of local conditions, including the proficiency level of the teacher, the goals of the students, curriculum guidelines, and available resources.

We then turned to the teaching of grammar in EIL classrooms. We argued for the adoption of a three-dimensional framework for grammar teaching that includes attention to form/structure, meaning/semantics, and use/pragmatics. Only by focusing on all three aspects will an individual be able to use English effectively and appropriately in intercultural exchanges. We noted that the teaching of form is complicated by the fact that there are many varieties of English that are constantly undergoing innovation both in form and in lexicon.

We devoted attention to the teaching of pragmatics and use since, in most EIL exchanges, form gets shaped by the context and participants of the exchange. Because many speakers of English have gaps in their proficiency, they often need to adjust their language to suit the listener's level of proficiency and to clarify meaning. In order to be able to do this, we advocated that EIL classrooms devote attention to strategies for clarifying meaning and repairing breakdowns in communication.

Finally, we presented a variety of activities that can be used with students at various levels of English proficiency in order to make them aware of the diversity that exists in present-day English use. We believe that such awareness can begin even with less proficient students by drawing on parallel phenomena in their first language.

The issues raised in the chapter lead to several principles in EIL grammar teaching:

Principle 1: The concept of grammar needs to be broadened in the teaching of EIL. Attention to form must be linked to contexts of use so that a determination of what is correct and what is appropriate is made in reference to a specific context.

Principle 2: All EIL students need to understand the manner in which grammatical standards vary in English depending on the geographical region, the level of formality, and whether it is spoken or written English.

Principle 3: Attention to the development of strategic intercultural competence should exist in all EIL classrooms.

The goal of this chapter has been to make the rationale for these principles transparent and to suggest ways of implementing them in EIL classrooms.

Discussion Questions

1. What do you see as the advantages and disadvantages of making students aware of the many varieties of English that are spoken today? In answering this question, consider situations in which you believe such knowledge is critical and situations in which you believe such knowledge can impede the goal of attaining proficiency in Standard English.

2. The success of many of the activities described in the chapter depend on the teacher supplying the students with clear examples that will help students undertake the task at hand. In order to have some of these examples to use in the future, complete the following tasks. You may need to use the web or your local environment to complete the task.

   • For the beginning-level Activity One described in the chapter, gather examples of the unique vocabulary of one variety of English as, for example, Australian English or Singapore English.

   • For the beginning-level Activity Two, find a simple email text in English, as well as an excerpt from a beginning-level textbook. Use these examples to demonstrate how even written English differs depending on the level of formality.

- For the intermediate-level Activity Three, find examples of signs in English in the local environment that display errors in the use of English. Use this as a basis for having students find additional examples.
- For the intermediate-level Activity Four, find examples of when learners make errors in their use of grammar or vocabulary choice that impede comprehension. Use these examples as a basis for an activity in which the listener tries to clarify the meaning of the statement. You might gather these examples by listening to your own students' use of English with you and with other students.
- For the advanced-level Activity One, find a current newspaper published in an Outer Circle country such as Nigeria, the Philippines, or India. Use this article as the basis for the activity described in the chapter.
- For the advanced-level Activity Three, find examples in your own local environment where English has been used in creative ways in the names of stores, products, advertisements, or pop lyrics. Use these as a basis for having students gather further examples.
- For the advanced-level Activity Four, do a google search of the four grammatical structures suggested by Gupta to find out what your students may encounter in doing this activity.

3. Watch the YouTube video entitled "World Englishes: An Investigation of International Students' Goals and Experiences," and discuss the questions posed in the video:
   - In your opinion, are some varieties of English more "correct," coherent, or logical? If so, in what way? If not, why do you think some varieties are labeled as such?
   - In your opinion, how does communicating with a non-native speaker of English differ from communicating with a native speaker? What are the pedagogical implications of such differences?

Suggestions for Further Reading

Alsagoff, L., McKay, S., Hu, G., and Renanyda, W. (Eds.). *Principles and practices for teaching English as an international language*. New York: Taylor & Francis.
This book provides a clear introduction to the concept of English as an international language and what this means for the teaching of grammar. The articles by A. Gupta and S. L. McKay are especially helpful in reference to the teaching of grammar.

Matsuda, A. (Ed.). *Principles and practices of teaching English as an international language*. Toronto: Multilingual Matters.
Two chapters in this book are particularly relevant to the teaching of grammar from an EIL perspective. The first is by Matsuda and Friedrich on selecting an instructional variety of English to use in classes where there is a focus on EIL. The second, by Matsuda and Duran, provides EIL activities and tasks, many of which are relevant to the points made in this chapter.

References

British Council. (n.d.). Frequently asked questions. Britishcouncil.org. Available online at http://www.britishcouncil.org/learning-faq-the-english-language.htm

Brown, A. (1999). *Singapore English in a nutshell.* Singapore: Federal Publications.

Canagarajah, S. (2006). Changing communicative needs, revised assessment objectives: Testing English as an international language. *Language assessment quarterly, 3*(3), 229–242.

Canagarajah, S. (2007). Lingua franca English, multilingual communities, and language acquisition. *The Modern Language Journal, 91,* 923–939.

Crystal, D. (1995). *The Cambridge encyclopedia of the English language.* Cambridge: Cambridge University Press.

Ethnologue. Summary by language size. Ethnologue.com. Available online at http://www.ethnologue.com/statistics/size

Gupta. A. (2006). Standard English in the world. In R. Rubdy & M. Saraceni (Eds.), *English in the world: Global rules, global roles* (pp. 95–109). London: Continuum.

Gupta, A. (2012). Grammar teaching and standards. In L. Alsagoff, S. L. McKay, G. Hu, & W. Renandya (Eds.), *Principles and practices for teaching English as an international language* (pp. 244–260). New York: Routledge.

Kachru, B. (1983). *The Indianization of English: The English language in India.* New York: Oxford University Press.

Larsen-Freeman, D. (2014). Teaching grammar. In M. Celce-Murcia, D. Brinton, & M. A. Snow (Eds.), *Teaching English as a second or foreign language* (pp. 256–270). Boston: Cengage Learning.

Matsuda, A., & Duran, C. S. (2012). EIL activities and tasks for traditional English classrooms. In A. Matsuda (Ed.), *Principles and practices of teaching English as an international language* (pp. 201–237). Toronto: Multilingual Matters.

Matsuda, A., & Friedrich, P. (2012). Selecting an instructional variety for an EIL curriculum. In A. Matsuda (Ed.), *Principles and practices of teaching English as an international language* (pp. 17–27). Toronto: Multilingual Matters.

McKay, S. L. (2005). Teaching the pragmatics of English as an international language. *Guidelines, 27*(1), 3–9.

McKay, S. L. (2011). English as an international lingua franca pedagogy. In E. Hinkel (Ed.), *Handbook of research in second language teaching and learning* (Vol. 2, pp. 122–139). New York: Routledge.

McKay, S. L., & Bokhorst-Heng, W. D. (2008). *International English in its sociolinguistic contexts.* New York: Routledge.

Platt, J., Weber, H., & Ho, M. L. (1984). *The new Englishes.* London: Routledge and Kegan Paul.

Shim, R. J. (1999). Codified Korean English: Processes, Characteristics and Consequences. *World Englishes, 18*(2), 247–258.

Strevens, P. (1983). What is 'standard English'? In L. Smith (Ed.), *Readings in English as an international language* (pp. 87–93). Oxford: Pergamon Press.

Trudgill, P., & Hannah, J. (2002). *International English* (4th ed.). London: Arnold.

3

USING CORPUS LINGUISTICS TO IMPROVE THE TEACHING OF GRAMMAR

Susan Conrad

Introduction

When I began teaching ESL grammar many decades ago, it didn't take me long to question what a textbook was teaching. I remember looking at constructions the textbook told my students to use and thinking, "Wait a minute. I don't think I'd write that" and "Well, that's not wrong exactly, but I'd never use it." As these thoughts accumulated, they brought a host of other questions: Was it just me— were my grammar choices different from everyone else's? Were there British-American differences I didn't know about? Did I actually use English differently than I thought I did? Were these textbook writers envisioning a certain setting that I wasn't familiar with?

I didn't want to teach just accurate grammar; I wanted to give my students practice with appropriate and effective grammar. To do that, I wanted to get beyond using my own intuition or a couple of examples I could easily find. I wanted evidence of what a large number of proficient English users say and write in different settings. In sum, I wanted *corpus linguistics*—an area of applied linguistics that didn't exist then but that, in recent decades, has developed into an area with substantial impacts on grammar teaching.

This chapter is not about the *how* of grammar teaching so much as the *what*. Traditionally, this was considered obvious: grammar teachers teach the rules of structure in English. However, as I realized with the first textbook I used, accurate structures are only one part of proficient grammar use. It is true that students need to learn the rules for the structure of English. For instance, English uses prepositions to signal certain physical relationships (e.g. *I placed the book on the table*) rather than postpositions (**I placed the book the table on*) or no preposition (**I placed the book the table*). But it is also grammatical to use a pronoun in the prepositional phrase (*I placed the book on it*), to use the passive voice (*The book was placed on the* *table*), or even to front the prepositional phase (**On the table** *I placed the book*). The meaning of each is similar, but the choices are not equally effective for all contexts. Grammar teachers need to determine how important it is for their students to know certain alternatives when there are so many to choose from. They need to explain to students when different alternatives are appropriate. They need to provide practice with language that is effective for students' needs and goals. They even need to help students learn to figure out patterns of grammar variation for themselves. Corpus linguistics helps with all these challenges.

Some teachers think everything students need will be in a course textbook. Certainly a good textbook is invaluable for most teaching situations, but textbooks are not always selected by thoroughly analyzing their grammar content. Furthermore, even the best textbook cannot cover everything that is important for all contexts and all students. Several times in this chapter I compare findings from corpus research to coverage in grammar textbooks. My point is not to attack these textbooks. In fact, they have many excellent characteristics. But the comparisons illustrate how teachers can make content and practice more consistent with realistic language use and more targeted to their students' needs if they integrate corpus linguistics into their teaching.

Of the next three sections of the chapter, the first ("What Is Corpus Linguistics?") provides a basic overview of what corpus linguistics is and how corpus analyses are conducted. The second section ("Findings from Corpus Analyses that Improve the Teaching of Grammar") then illustrates corpus linguistics' contributions to grammar teaching in four areas: (1) revealing frequency information that can be incorporated into content and sequencing decisions, (2) clarifying the importance and the nature of context-dependent grammar choices, (3) differentiating the grammar of academic writing from the grammar of conversation, and (4) connecting grammar and vocabulary. The final section ("Applying Corpus Linguistics in Your Own Teaching") then moves on to suggestions for what you as a teacher can do to take advantage of the benefits of corpus linguistics.

Throughout the chapter I primarily refer to corpus-based research on American and British English. If this is not a target for your students, you can consult analyses of corpora of World Englishes or English as a Lingua Franca (see the final section) for more appropriate information. The principles for using corpus linguistics to improve grammar teaching remain the same even if the variety of English is different.

What Is Corpus Linguistics?

Corpus linguistics is an approach to studying people's use of language that employs computer-assisted analyses. Speakers and writers adapt their grammar to different contexts—according to factors such as different modes (written, spoken, electronic, etc.), different audiences, different purposes, different settings, and many others. Some grammar choices are conscious, such as if a writer is told to use the passive voice for the methods section of a lab report, but most are not, so intuition or anecdotal evidence can be misleading. A corpus study covers many users, so it is possible to see what is typical and what is unusual for a large number of people in certain circumstances.

Many different specific techniques are used within corpus linguistics, but all corpus studies share certain characteristics, three of which are especially important for grammar teachers to understand. First, they use a corpus—a large, principled collection of texts (writing or transcribed speech) that were produced in real communication situations. Corpora can contain any kind of text. Academic books and articles, casual conversations, dialog from TV sitcoms, recipes, newspaper articles, email, tweets, lectures, or any other type of text could be included. Since we are trying to generalize about people's language use from corpus studies, corpora need to be carefully designed to represent a category of language use. For example, a corpus that is meant to represent published academic prose could not include only research articles from one psychology journal and one chemistry journal. It would have to include many kinds of academic texts (textbooks, review articles, etc.), many disciplines, and many publishers and authors. Important details for corpus design can be found in numerous articles and corpus linguistics handbooks (see e.g. O'Keeffe and McCarthy 2010: chapters 3–8), but the overall principle concerns representing a large number of speakers or writers so that results are more generalizable than the study of just a few individuals. (An exception to this is for studies of individual speaker or author style, but even then the individual is often compared to a large group.)

Many corpora are now freely available to download or to search on the Internet. In this chapter I include many examples from the Corpus of Contemporary American English, (COCA) (Davies 2008–). This corpus contains 450 million words in five categories (unscripted TV and radio speech, fiction, popular magazines, newspapers, and academic prose) and is available for searches on the Internet. A large, general corpus like the COCA is useful for many grammar classes. It allows teachers to compare grammar in speech and several types of writing. The British National Corpus is 100 million words of British English, and other readily accessible corpora cover English as a Lingua Franca, World Englishes, spoken academic English, and certain English for Specific Purpose categories. The final section directs you to several corpora. It is also possible to create your own corpus for a specific purpose; for instance, you could compile a corpus of travel blogs and create grammar activities with it before asking your students to write their own travel blogs. You can download free software for analyzing the corpus, as explained in the final section. Other corpora, such as the Longman Spoken and Written English Corpus and the Cambridge English Corpus (two large corpora with several categories of writing and conversations), are available only to authors working on projects for the owners of the corpora, but results of their analyses are often published.

The second and third characteristics of corpus analyses—frequency counts and interpretation of those counts—highlight the interplay of computers and humans that is typical in corpus linguistics. Typical corpus analyses include frequency counts conducted with a computer. Frequency counts allow us to judge whether a grammar feature is typical or rare in a certain context. Traditionally, textbooks included descriptions such as *often, typical, common,* or *rare* without quantitative analysis, but corpus studies can now provide that evidence. Using a computer for the counts allows analysis of much more text than by hand; even when a human user must interact with the computer to make counts more accurate, the computer conducts faster, more reliable quantitative analysis. However, frequency information tells us nothing about the function or impact of grammar features, so the third characteristic of corpus analyses is that they include human interpretations of functions.

The following example illustrates these characteristics of corpus work. Imagine that I am teaching a unit about passive voice to my class in an English for Academic Purposes (EAP) program. Besides the practice in the textbook, I wonder if any passives are especially common in classes at universities because I know my students need to be prepared to comprehend lectures. I have a concordancer, the easiest and most common type of software used in corpus linguistics, and I have the Spoken and Written Academic Language corpus, a corpus of university language from four U.S. universities that colleagues and I compiled for Educational Testing Service (see Biber, Conrad, Reppen, Byrd, and Helt 2002). The corpus is grammatically tagged, making it possible to search via grammatical categories, so I run a search for all passives in the class sessions. (You will learn how to do this and try it with COCA in the last section.)

Table 3.1 displays the frequency information for the 10 most common passives in the class sessions. Immediately I see three interesting bits of information. First,

TABLE 3.1 Passive Verbs in Class Sessions of the Spoken and Written Academic Language Corpus

Raw Count	Count per 1,000,000 Words	Percentage of Passive Occurrences in the Class Sessions	Verb
413	331	5.6%	called
256	205	3.5%	done
207	166	2.8%	used
112	90	1.5%	given
111	89	1.5%	made
99	79	1.3%	involved
84	67	1.1%	based
83	66	1.1%	written
78	62	1.0%	considered
77	62	1.0%	divided

Hit	KWIC
223	e plane of the ecliptic and beyond Neptune and the other region **is called** the Oort. O.O.R.T. um cloud, which is a more of a spherical re
224	al (maristems). and the lateral (maristems) are of two types, one **is called** (cort camping) or the super tough name (felgic) the other is c
225	called (cort camping) or the super tough name (felgic) the other **is called** vascular (cambium). and finally there is a third exceedingly r
226	de out of I'm not sure I did. the type of wax that makes this stuff, **is called** S.U.B.E.R.I.N. Suberin S.U.B.E.R.I.N.. the cuticle is made out
227	ells divide, this the swelling is produced. [679] the big swelling, **is called** a nodule N.O.D.U.L.E., a root nodule. in this particular instance
228	most, but not all, most leaves have two basic parts. this part here **is called** the (blathe) and the little stalk like thing, that most leaves hav
229	d the (blathe) and the little stalk like thing, that most leaves have **is called** a petiole, P.E.T.I.O.L.E.. so a (blathe) and a petiole ... leaves ha
230	gs. the basic leaf type shown on the left is the primitive one. this **is called** a microphyll. a microphyll ... the one on the right is the more
231	c ones. that I've drawn for you on that page. this leaf on the left **is called** a microphyll because of two very special characteristics num
232	fermented, carbonated, and put in bottles, sometimes in, to what **is called** here, real (fuel). [223] But then you decline that when I say, r
233	cally comb out or rake the fibers into long linear strips. And that **is called** (hackelling). Not what you do to a performer on stage, when
234	hing), and (hackelling). OK? And then the third and last process **is called** decorticating. And this is typically done for things like sisal [I
235	are called bolls. When they ripen the cotton is found the, which **is called** lint. That's the actual (uniseriate) called single-celled wide h

FIGURE 3.1 Part of the Concordance Listing [KWIC (key word in context)] Display for *Called* in University Class Sessions, Using the AntConc Concordancer

there is great diversity in the verbs used in passive voice; the 9th and 10th most common verbs account for only 1% of occurrences, so there are many verbs occurring infrequently. Second, no single verb is very common. The most common occurs 331 times per million words; a million words is about 140 hours of speaking, so this is an average of slightly over twice each hour. Third, I am interested in the most common passive, which accounts for over 5% of the occurrences: *called*. I wonder how it is used, so using the concordancer, I run a concordance listing [also called a Key Word in Context (KWIC) display, Figure 3.1]. Looking at the lines, I see that *called* is used in definitions, giving the technical term for an item that has been explained. In our course textbook, *Grammar Connection* (Carlisi 2008), the chapter about passive voice does a good job of describing passive structure, and it exposes students to passive voice with almost 50 different verbs. However, when *call* appears, it is in the sense of a phone call. Nowhere is the more common academic meaning used—even though the book's back cover advertises, "Connect learners to academic success." I thus know that when I provide extra practice with passives for my students, I want to include receptive work with *call* used to introduce technical terms. A little expansion into the textbook component of the Spoken and Written Academic Language (SWAL) corpus will give me even more to work with. (In case you wonder, *call* is used in the same way, but two other verbs are more common as passives in the textbooks: *be used for/by* and *given*.)

This short exploration of passives took longer to describe than to conduct. Thus, even with fast searches on their own, teachers can gain useful information from corpora. With more advanced techniques, more patterns can be analyzed. For example, Conrad (1999) illustrates how multiple characteristics and their interactions can be taken into consideration with interactive computer techniques. Six features are examined in a study of linking adverbials (transition words such as *however* and *therefore*): frequency, semantic category, grammatical structure, placement within the clause, the specific item used, and the type of text (academic prose, newspaper reporting, fiction, and conversation). All of these features are important for understanding linking adverbial use. Even if you start to work with corpora on your own, it is useful to keep reading results of other studies, especially studies that use techniques beyond a concordancer.

Through the study of frequency, interpretation of functions, and analysis of patterns of use, corpus linguistics can do much to transform teachers' understanding of grammar and to improve on the coverage of a traditional grammar course. The next section introduces four specific ways.

Findings from Corpus Analyses That Improve the Teaching of Grammar

A. Incorporating Frequency Information into the Content and Sequencing of Teaching

One way that corpus studies contribute to grammar teaching is by adding frequency information into teachers' and textbook writers' decisions about what to cover and in what order to cover it. Frequency information does not override other pedagogical concerns such as students' needs and backgrounds, learnability and teachability, etc., but it provides an additional type of information that teachers could only guess at before corpus studies became common. Frequency alone cannot tell you if a feature should be taught to your students, but it can make you consider forms and functions that you would otherwise neglect. As Biber, Conrad, and Cortes (2004) put it:

> [W]e do not regard frequency data as explanatory. In fact we would argue for the opposite: frequency data identifies patterns that must be explained. The usefulness of frequency data (and corpus analysis generally) is that it identifies patterns of use that otherwise often go unnoticed.
>
> *(376)*

For teachers, the knowledge that a particular grammar feature is very common should lead to questions such as the following:

- Why is this feature so useful? For example, does it serve multiple functions? Does it fulfill a single purpose that is very common when people speak or write?
- Under what circumstances or in what contexts is this structure so useful?
- In what ways is this feature important for my students? Do they need to be able to understand its use or also produce it—or neither, given their current levels and their goals?
- What is challenging about this feature's use? Is it teachable/learnable at the level of my students? What do they need to know beforehand to understand this feature's use?

Answering these questions can help lead to sensible content and sequencing decisions. For instance, Biber and Reppen (2002) question the decision by many popular grammar textbooks to teach present progressive verbs (e.g. *am eating, are sleeping*) before or in the same chapter as simple present (e.g. *eat, sleeps*) and to use model conversations that have an unusually high frequency of progressives. They note that corpus analyses have found that simple aspect verbs are 20 times more common than progressive verbs in conversation. In addition, simple present verbs have many uses—including talking about present states and habitual actions. Present is also a simpler structure than progressive since it does not require a form of *be*. Many teachers also notice students overusing progressives. For all these reasons, you might decide, like Biber and Reppen, that introducing simple present before present progressive is a better sequence. Alternatively, you may decide for other reasons to cover progressive first, but a modern, well-trained grammar teacher needs to make a deliberate, informed decision, not just follow tradition.

Corpus studies can also give grammar teachers useful information for rare features. If a feature is rare, it is worth asking why it is used at all. Usually, special discourse or social contexts are associated with the feature. Explaining those contexts to your students is important. For example, *that*-complement clauses are grammatical in the extraposed position or subject position. Consider this example from a sentence in the introduction of this chapter (and see more details of this analysis in Biber et al. 1999: chapter 9):

> Extraposed: It is true *that students need to learn the rules for the structure of English.*
> Subject position alternative: *That students need to learn the rules for the structure of English* is true.

Readers generally find the subject-position clause harder to process, and subject position is rare. However, subject position occurs occasionally. When it does, it is virtually always in writing, and two discourse factors are associated with it. Almost always, the information in the *that*-clause has already been presented or is generally accepted as true, and, in many cases, the main clause predicate has a complicated structure with additional clauses (such as another *that*-clause). For example:

> [T]he sample size may not have been large enough to detect significant differences across sites, nor to detect tinidazole resistance or high-level metronidazole resistance. *That we did not detect isolates with such resistance* suggests that its prevalence in this population is low.
>
> *(COCA academic)*

In the past, textbook writers who wanted to address the use of the subject-position clauses made only vague statements; for example, Danielson and Porter (1990) noted that "[t]he *it*-pattern usually seems more natural with *that*-clauses" (278; see further Conrad 2000). This is a clear illustration of how further information from corpus analysis is helpful. Other useful illustrations with relatively rare structures often covered in advanced grammar, including subjunctives, are in McCarthy (2015).

Another use of frequency information involves the analysis of learner corpora—that is, corpora of speech or writing by learners of English. Such corpora can be analyzed to see what errors persist over time from learners of many different first languages. This error information could then be used to inform many teaching materials (see Nesselhauf 2004). Currently, however, learner corpora are most commonly used to include explicit warnings against specific errors in corpus-informed textbooks (described in the last section) or the teacher's own work with students (e.g. see Gilquin and Granger 2010).

Although this section focuses on frequency of use, it has been difficult to address it without mentioning the conditions that correspond to patterns of use, such as registers and discourse factors. The next section considers just how important such patterns of use are for describing grammar, expanding on the notion in the introduction that grammar cannot be considered just an accurate/inaccurate dichotomy.

B. Addressing Grammar as Appropriate Choices for Contexts

In 1998, speaking at the international TESOL convention, Larsen-Freeman sought to "challenge the common misperception that grammar has to do solely with formal accuracy," arguing instead for a "grammar of choice" (2002: 103). Similarly, O'Keeffe, McCarthy, and Carter (2007) have argued that we need to think of probabilistic grammar—features that are more or less likely in particular social or discourse circumstances. Other writers call these "patterns of use" (e.g. Biber, Conrad, and Reppen 1998). All these grammarians are concerned with describing grammar as appropriate choices for different contexts, and these descriptions are precisely what corpus analyses facilitate.

If you are a novice grammarian or used to thinking of grammar as structural accuracy, you may wonder if there are truly so many influences on grammar choices that it is worth your attention. As a sampling of grammar patterns of use, Table 3.2 presents a list of characteristics and one example corpus analysis to illustrate each. As you can see, patterns of use correspond to many different types of factors: register (type of text), language features in the co-text (words and grammar in adjacent text), meanings (semantic categories of words, meaning in surrounding discourse, and positive/negative contexts), social factors (such as politeness), principles related to cognitive processing (such as end weight and information flow), and regional variation. They affect not just choices between grammatical alternatives but also the placement of features within clauses (e.g. linking adverbials) and specific words within structures (e.g. verb or adjective choices). To make matters more complicated, many of these factors interact. For example, the deletion or retention of *that* in *that*-complement clauses is associated not just with register but

TABLE 3.2 Factors Found to Correspond to Grammar Choices in Corpus Analyses

Grammar Choices Correspond to	*Example*
1. Register (also called genre, category of text, or type of text)	*That*-complement clauses of verbs (sometimes called noun clauses) are grammatical with or without the *that* complementizer. In academic writing, nearly all *that*-clauses include *that*. In conversation, the great majority of *that* clauses omit *that*. Newspaper writing is similar to academic writing in retaining *that*, but the proportion is not as extreme, and fiction is similar to conversation in omitting *that*, but the proportion is not as extreme (see Biber et al. 1999: 681–682 and Conrad and Biber 2009: 94–94). *She said he'd landed a top secret government job . . .* (COCA spoken) *Newton never claimed that he could explain the source of gravity . . .* (COCA academic) See subsection C of this chapter for more on register differences.
2. Words associated with the grammar feature	Linking verbs + adjectives are used to describe the subjects of sentences (e.g. *I am happy*). There are myriad combinations possible, but most linking verbs are common with a specific set of adjectives to express a certain type of meaning. Two examples are *get* and *become*, which have similar verb meanings (concerning change) but different typical uses: get + negative changes: *get* + *angry, bored, cold, lost, mad, sick, tired*, etc. become + changes in understanding or importance: *become* + *apparent, clear, difficult, evidence, familiar, important* (Conrad and Biber 2009: 22). This is a type of lexico-grammatical relationship, covered further in subsection D of this chapter.
3. Other grammar features in the clause	Hypothetical or counterfactual *would*-clauses are usually taught with an adjacent *if*-clause (*If I were you, I would . . .*). In fact, the majority of such *would*-clauses are *not* adjacent to an *if* clause (Frazier 2003). Instead, a common pattern is for the *would*-clause to occur with implied, covert conditionals and to have infinitives or gerunds also in the sentence, as in this example from Frazier (2003: 457): *Letting the administration take details off their hands **would** give them more time to inform themselves about education as a whole. . .*

Grammar Choices Correspond to	Example
4. Semantic categories	Although verbs are grammatical in many tense-aspect combinations, certain semantic categories exhibit a preference for certain combinations. In academic writing, verbs expressing discovery (especially *discover, find, show, reveal, uncover*) are often used in the present perfect, emphasizing that results continue to be important or relevant (e.g. *Research has shown that . . .*), while verbs having to do with existence (e.g. *consist of, comprise, contain, correspond, illustrate, include, represent,* etc.) usually do not occur in the present perfect. Instead they are used in simple present to describe a state or logical relationship. For example: *Our alphabet writing system represents the sounds of speech.* (Conrad and Biber 2009: 7)
5. Meaning in the surrounding discourse context	Linking adverbials (transition words like *therefore* and *however*) are grammatical in more than one location in a sentence. They are most common as the initial element of a sentence, but they can be placed after the subject. When initial placement is not used, the subject of the sentence often provides a contrast with the previous sentence. For example: <u>*At first sight*</u>*, it would seem that there are two possible results from the reaction.* <u>*Closer consideration*</u>*,* **however***, reveals that this cannot be the case.* (Conrad and Biber 2009: 88)
6. Semantic prosody (neutral grammatical features become associated with positive or negative meanings)	The passive voice is usually formed with *be* + the past participle (e.g. *was eaten*). However, it can be formed with *get* (e.g. *get eaten*). These "*get*-passives" are used more widely in negative contexts—e.g. *get* + *arrested, caught, stolen, mocked, hit, killed. Get married,* a common structure, might be an exception to this pattern—but it is important to check if the larger context has negative associations. For example: *Soon after that he got married, and soon after that he left his wife.* (COCA) See further discussion in O'Keeffe, McCarthy, and Carter (2007: 106–114).

(*Continued*)

TABLE 3.2 (Continued)

Grammar Choices Correspond to	Example
7. Other principles of language structuring—end weight and information flow (related to cognitive processing)	Most passive voice sentences do not state the agent in a *by*-prepositional phrase, but some do. The use of passives with *by*-phrases corresponds to two principles of language structuring: (1) the principle of end weight—i.e. longer ("heavier") structures tend to be placed at the end of clauses—and (2) information flow—i.e. already established or generally accepted information is placed before new information in clauses. In a section entitled "The Use of the Long Passive Across Registers," Biber, Conrad, and Leech (2002: 169) use their own sentence as an example: *In principle, the long passive can be replaced by an active clause with the same meaning.* Here, *the long passive* is already established information because it has been the focus of the section. The longest (weightiest) constituent is *by an active clause with the same meaning*. Thus, use of the *by*-passive in this sentence conforms to end weight and information flow principles.
8. Politeness	The past tense most often refers to past events or states. However, it is sometimes used to make a polite offer in face-to-face situations, especially with the verbs *want* and *need*. For example: *Did you want more coffee?* (Conrad and Biber 2009: 1) The meaning is present time, and answers use the present, present progressive, or modals.
9. Geographic regions	British and American English speakers in conversation differ in their preference for modals to express obligation. *Must* and *have to* are possible in both, but British more often use *must*, while Americans favors *have to* (Carter and McCarthy 2006: 881–882). *I have to get home.* (COCA spoken) Differences also exist for less widely known World Englishes. For example, progressive aspect has greater use with stative verbs in some varieties, including Xhosa English in South Africa (de Klerk 2006). For example: *I'm having two points* (p. 141) rather than *I have two points.* (When such use is systematic, even if it differs from traditional norms, it constitutes a regional variant, not an error.)

also with specific verbs and grammatical features in the co-text (see summary in Conrad and Biber 2009: 94–95). In sum, for a proficient speaker or writer, choices are a big part of grammar competence.

Two teaching implications are clear from Table 3.2 and its associated corpus studies. First, variation in the use of grammar is so much a part of grammar that it should not be ignored in teaching. To take just one example, it is not fair to ask students to practice linking verbs and adjectives in a completely random way when proficient speakers tend to use certain verb + adjective combinations for specific types of meaning. We have a great deal of information about grammar use now, so teachers can move beyond the accurate/inaccurate dichotomous view of grammar and give students practice with typical patterns of use.

A second implication is that, given so many facets to grammar choices, it would be easy to overwhelm students. As always, teachers need to make thoughtful pedagogical decisions. At low proficiency levels, the introduction of patterns of use might remain implicit, for example, simply using typical linking verb + adjective combinations in practice activities. Covering patterns of use could also mean recycling items in a syllabus, adding a new function to a feature, such as adding the politeness function for past tense after students are familiar with using it for past time. In an ESL setting, teachers might address some variation by asking students to listen for how people outside the classroom use grammar differently than what they learned and then answer questions about what they notice. Other students, such as advanced EAP students, are likely to want explicit information about grammar in academic settings. There is no single right way to address patterns of use; what's important is not to ignore them.

C. Differentiating Between Academic Writing and Conversation

Grammar choices associated with registers—the first category in Table 3.2—deserve particular emphasis. Registers are categories of texts defined by their situational characteristics—purpose, audience, amount of time for planning and editing, mode of transmission, and many others (see further discussion in Biber and Conrad 2009). Many corpus studies have compared the use of features between registers, and they consistently find substantial differences. Most notably, *The Longman Grammar of Spoken and Written English* (Biber, Johansson, Leech, Conrad, and Finegan 1999) has about 300 investigations of linguistic features, with most of them compared across approximately 20 million words representing conversation, fiction, newspapers, and academic prose. Teachers of English for Specific Purposes might need information about more specific registers, but all ESOL teachers need to appreciate the differences between grammar in academic writing and conversation. The purposes, need for specificity, time for planning and editing, concern for threats to a person's face, and many other factors are fundamentally different between academic writing and conversation—and are reflected in grammar use.

As an example, consider the definite article (*the*). The definite article is grammatical with singular and plural count nouns and noncount nouns (e.g. *the table*, *the tables, the furniture*), but choosing among it, the indefinite article (*a/an*), and no article is difficult for many learners, especially if their language has a different system for specifying nouns. Textbooks tend to give very basic guidance, such as the following: "Use *the* when you know or assume that your listener is familiar with and thinking about the same specific thing or person you are talking about" and "Use *the* for the second mention of an indefinite noun" (Azar and Hagen 2009: 118). This information is true as far as it goes, but corpus research shows a far more detailed picture that can help teachers provide explanations and design helpful practice for their students.

Table 3.3 displays reasons for using the definite article (summarized from Biber et al. 1999: 266 and Conrad and Biber 2009: 64–65). Previous mention in the text accounts for 25–30% of the uses of the definite article in conversation and academic writing. Great differences exist, however, for shared situational context and modifiers of the noun. Shared situational context accounts for 55% of the uses in

TABLE 3.3 Reasons for the Definite Article Use in Conversation and Academic Writing (summarized from Biber et al. 1999: 266 and Conrad and Biber 2009: 64–65)

Reason for Use of the Definite Article	Examples (from COCA)	Conversation	Academic Writing
Previously introduced in the text	The police had *a robot* that they sent up the driveway. And that enraged him. And he started screaming at them on the phone to get **the robot** out of the yard.	25%	25%
Shared in the situational context	Can you hand me **the pepper mill**, please?	55%	10%
Modifiers of the noun	For example, **the introduction** *of noise barrier conditions next to a proposed residential development* can increase environmental satisfaction . . .	5%	40%
Inferable from a previous noun	*Our text adventure game* contains a fixed set of places, such as a meadow, house, or desert, and a fixed set of things, such as a door, key, or flower. **The player** navigates the world and interacts with things . . .	5%	15%
Other (e.g. idioms, generic reference)	. . . and **the word on the street** is that CBS Sports wants to hire Al Michaels.	10%	10%

conversation but only 10% in academic writing. Modifiers of the noun account for 40% in academic writing but only 5% in conversation. These differences are not surprising since people in conversation share the physical setting but rarely have the need for highly specific or technical noun phrases, while academic writing circumstances are just the opposite. Knowing this corpus analysis can help teachers explain the definite article and answer questions more thoroughly. Without this kind of information, teachers are often left answering questions about articles with an unsatisfying "*The* just sounds right there." They are less likely to give their students practice with the most common reasons they will need to produce definite articles.

Differences in these two registers concerns more than just small grammar features. Another difference involves the kind of grammatical complexity each has (Biber, Gray and Poonpon 2011). Casual speech tends to be complex in its use of clauses. There are often many clauses in a sentence, and they are often embedded. The following sentence example from the spoken category of COCA has an adverbial clause and a *to*-infinitive clause used within a *that*-complement clause:

> She said [that (when she saw David Perry]) he actually jumped behind a palm tree and tried (to conceal himself)]. (COCA)

The noun phrases in the spoken sentence are simple; the longest is *a palm tree*, and many are pronouns. Academic prose, on the other hand, tends to have simpler clause structure but complexity in phrases, especially in noun phrases. For example, the following sentence from academic prose is just one clause, but it has a noun phrase with two prepositional phrase modifiers, one embedded inside the other, and another noun phrase with two adjectives as modifiers:

> The use [of mobile computer vision (for assistive technology)] imposes *particular functional constraints*. (COCA)

Stressing the differences in the structural complexity of the two registers, Biber, Gray and Poonpon (2011) note that the phrasal structures are less explicit about meaning and thus are likely one reason that novice readers find professional academic prose challenging. They suggest that the dense use of noun phrase structures is the highest level of academic writing mastery; in contrast, most evaluation of ESOL writing uses complex clause constructions as a sign of increased proficiency.

It is probably clear even from these two examples that EAP teachers can learn valuable information from corpus work to make their teaching more EAP focused. In addition, any teachers who want their students to be prepared for comprehending or engaging in conversation outside the classroom also need to take the register differences into account. Conversation typically expands the use of some features from their prescriptive uses in textbooks. For example, Table 3.2

describes the use of past tense for politeness in offers. Other verb forms also figure in politeness or indirectness in conversation. For example, Carter and McCarthy (2006: 710) note the use of the progressive and perfect aspects to soften utterances (e.g. *I was hoping . . . , I'm wondering . . . , I've been wanting . . .*). Being less direct is important in softening the face-threatening nature of many interpersonal interactions.

A particularly illustrative example of corpus research about grammar in conversation concerns the word *though*. It is traditionally covered in ESL textbooks as a way to make an adverbial clause of contrast; for example, *Though it was cold, I went swimming* (Azar and Hagen 2009: 407). A typical list of connectors for showing contrast and concession includes *but, however, on the other hand, in contrast, while, whereas, yet, even so, nevertheless, in spite of, although, even though* (Thewlis 2007: 185). Coverage like this leaves out an important role of *though* in conversation.

In conversation, *though* is far more common as a contrastive linking adverbial at the end of a sentence (Conrad 1999). It conveys a sense of concession and so is a less direct way to signal disagreement than more direct contrast connectors like *but* or *however*. A typical example is as follows:

> A: *And—and some of these also prove that, you know, you can never underestimate the American public's laziness.*
> B: *Yes.*
> A: *I mean everything is instant. You know, technology—*
> B: *Well, convenience is good **though**.* (COCA)

The use of *though* (along with the discourse marker *well*) downplays the disagreement here, conceding speaker's A point about the American public's laziness while bringing up the counterpoint that convenience is good. Conrad and Biber (2009: 82) uses an example from a conversation where speaker B obviously disagrees with a friend about a call during a football game, but still softens the disagreement with *though*:

> [Watching a football game, discussing a penalty call]
> A: *Oh, that's outrageous.*
> B: *Well, he did put his foot out **though**.*

Consider the different impact of the statement if speaker B had said, *But he did put his foot out.*

Conversation also uses some features that have traditionally not been covered in grammar books at all—including discourse markers (e.g. *well, okay, like*), minimal responses (e.g. *yeah, no problem, oh really?*), and other structurally incomplete utterances (e.g. *me too, how about you?, nice shirt!*). Such features do not occur in written texts, but they are regular features in fluent conversation and serve important functions in regulating interactions. Further details on these and other features are in Biber et al. (1999), Conrad and Biber (2009: units 48 and 49), and Carter and McCarthy (2006).

Some teachers consider the different grammar features of conversation to be unworthy of attention in classes. They argue that they will teach only accurate standard written English to their students on the grounds that prescriptively correct English can be used anywhere while using informal features appropriately is harder. Such a belief, however, denies the important role that conversational grammar features play in face-to-face interactions, especially with friends. Friends do not expect to interact in fully explicit, prescriptively correct English; instead, using forms associated with casual English is a way of expressing closeness. Furthermore, if students are in a country where English is widely spoken, they will hear the typical forms used in conversation and need at least receptive proficiency with them.

Before corpus research became common, differences between speech and writing could be covered with examples. It is only with the publication of corpus-based studies of grammar that the complexity of conversational grammar and the prevalence of speech-writing differences has become clear. Reported speech, the expression of attitudes and judgments, modal verbs, and a host of other topics show striking differences between speech and writing, and well-trained grammar teachers need to take these into account. (See the Essential Reading list at the end of this chapter for sources with further details on speech and writing.)

D. Integrating Grammar and Vocabulary

Another contribution of corpus linguistics has been to reveal many strong connections between grammar and word choices. Traditionally, ESOL students were taught grammar and vocabulary as distinct components of language. Corpus analyses show, however, that English users do not randomly combine grammatical structures with all possible words. There are many connections between our choices in grammar and vocabulary. In fact, corpus work includes an area called lexico-grammar (*lexico-* from lexical—related to vocabulary or words).

One kind of lexico-grammatical research that is useful to teachers concerns which words are used within a particular grammatical feature. For example, when you are teaching phrasal verbs, knowing which phrasal verbs are the most common is helpful (see Gardner and Davies 2007; Liu 2011). Similarly, in the second section of this chapter, the example investigation of common passive voice verbs was a lexico-grammatical analysis.

Another useful type of lexico-grammar study investigates which words are used in combination with a grammatical construction. For example, studies have investigated verbs that take gerunds and verbs that take infinitives. It is not surprising that these constructions are bewildering to students. Some verbs take one kind of complement and not the other, some can take either but have a clear meaning difference, and some can take either but have very subtle, if any, meaning differences:

Infinitive *to*-clause only:	*I hope to go.*	**I hope going.*
Gerund *ing*-clause only:	**I keep to eat chocolate.*	*I keep eating chocolate.*
Both, but meaning difference:	*I stopped to check my messages.*	*I stopped checking my messages.*
Both, little or no difference:	*We began to argue about grammar.*	*We began arguing about grammar.*

So many verbs can take one, the other, or both complements; it is hard to know where to focus instruction. Along with other factors (such as what meanings your students are likely to need to express), it is helpful to know the most common verbs in different registers, as displayed in Table 3.4.

Analyses like those in Table 3.4 help to give a framework to think about a difficult teaching topic. Seeing frequency information can also alert the teacher

TABLE 3.4 Most Common Verb + Infinitive and Verb + Gerund Combinations (condensed from Conrad and Biber 2009: 97–101)

Grammar Structure and Register	Meaning Category	Common Verbs in the Construction and Example Sentence
Verb + infinitive— Academic prose, fiction, newspaper writing, and conversation	Want or need	*hope, like, need, want, want NP, wish* I don't really want to be here.
	Effort	*attempt, fail, manage, try* The information failed to cheer them up.
	Begin or continue	*begin, continue, start* The aircraft began to lose height.
	"Seem"-verbs	*appear, seem, tend* Lisa seemed to like him a lot.
Verb + gerund— Conversation and fiction writing	Begin, continue, or end	*begin, get (NP), keep, keep on, spend time, start, stop* She keeps saying she wants to go to Florida.
	Remember or think	*remember, think about, think of* It makes me think of being sick.
	Hear, see, or other sense	*hear NP, see NP* They heard the door opening.
Verb + gerund— Academic writing	Describe a process or report research	*be used for (passive), be achieved by (passive), involve* Chlorine is widely used for disinfecting water.

to remember to teach something that might otherwise be forgotten. For example, an EAP teacher might want to give extra emphasis to the passive verb + gerund constructions (*be used for* and *be achieved by*). In conversation classes, I never thought to include the phrasal verb *keep on* with verb + gerund practice before I saw the corpus-based list. It is also possible for teachers to extend this list by using COCA to see what verbs are common as the gerunds or infinitives (e.g. *keep on going, keep on doing*).

Findings of lexico-grammatical studies can also be taken as evidence that some language is better practiced as chunks rather than as analyzed grammatical features. For instance, corpus research has found that these verb + preposition combinations are especially common in academic writing (see further Conrad and Biber 2009: 41):

account for	*consist of*	*depend on*	*occur in*
allow for	*contribute to*	*differ from*	*refer to*
belong to	*deal with*	*lead to*	*result in*

Since many of these combinations defy logic (why *result in* rather than *result to*?), addressing them as chunks is likely a helpful strategy. In addition, the list is another reminder that advanced students may need structures recycled in the curriculum from new perspectives. Verbs and prepositions are usually covered in early levels of language instruction, but these combinations are useful for the more advanced skill of academic writing.

Applying Corpus Linguistics in Your Own Teaching

Helping students use grammar appropriately and effectively is more challenging than simply teaching what is structurally accurate. With so many factors already important for effective teaching, the need to apply findings from corpus linguistics, too, might feel overwhelming. However, a variety of approaches are possible, and even a small time commitment can have substantial benefits in more effective grammar coverage in your courses. Here I introduce three suggestions.

1. Look for textbooks that incorporate information from corpus analyses.

One time-saving way to incorporate corpus linguistics into your teaching is to use a grammar textbook that integrates information from corpus investigations. In recent years, more have gradually become available. Some—like *Real Grammar* (Conrad and Biber 2009)—are designed to serve as a supplement to a comprehensive textbook. *Real Grammar* presents analyses simplified from the *Longman Grammar of Spoken and Written English* and, although designed for students, can serve as a simple reference for teachers, too. Another approach is to consider a corpus-informed series. These books apply findings of corpus research in comprehensive textbooks. They usually consider corpus analyses in formulating their presentations of grammar and also have some sections with overt reporting of corpus findings. The *Grammar and Beyond* series has "Data from the Real World" sections that provide information and practice with items found in corpus analysis. For instance, a unit that covers simple past and time clauses includes practice with the use of time clauses without main clauses to answer questions in conversation—e.g. "When did you start studying English? After I got my job at the museum" (Reppen 2012: 57). The *Clear Grammar* series emphasizes lexico-grammar information from corpus studies; for instance, the phrasal verb unit in *Clear Grammar 3* reports the top 10 phrasal verbs in English from a published corpus study (Folse 2015: 5). The *Viewpoints* series—for high intermediate and advanced levels (e.g. McCarthy, McCarten and Sandiford 2014)—also adds some frequency analysis information in Language Notes for teachers. Both *Grammar and Beyond* and *Viewpoint* also use information from a learner corpus analysis to warn against common errors.

Unfortunately, it is sometimes difficult to tell exactly how corpus information has been used in textbooks even when it is advertised. Many other factors also make textbooks effective, so corpus information cannot be the only criterion in choosing a textbook. It is thus helpful for teachers to have corpus-based references to consult, too—as described in the next suggestion.

2.   Use published corpus research to discover how grammar features are typically used.

Most teachers do not have the time, resources, or desire to conduct extensive corpus studies on their own. Luckily, numerous published sources provide useful information from corpus analyses.

The most important resource for grammar teachers is a comprehensive corpus-based reference grammar. A reference grammar covers many grammar features in one book, so teachers can look up information about the use of almost any feature. Two especially useful references referred to throughout this chapter are the *Cambridge Grammar of English* (Carter and McCarthy 2006) and the *Longman Grammar of Spoken and Written English* (Biber et al. 1999). The books have different strengths. For example, the *Cambridge Grammar* has an easy-to-use A–Z section that covers frequent, multifunctional words and their uses (e.g. *about, come/go, ok*) and is written in language that an advanced ESL student can understand. The *Longman Grammar* is for teachers and researchers; its greatest strengths lie in the numerous quantitative findings for grammar features in four registers. Both books cover features of conversation.

Some teachers find corpus-based reference grammars dauntingly large or do not believe they will learn anything useful from them. Let me share the experience of two teachers in an intensive English program. Working in an EAP program, they were particularly interested in features of academic writing. Although most people use reference grammars for looking up specific information, they decided to read the 1,200-page *Longman Grammar of Spoken and Written English* chapter by chapter, focusing on the frequency and function of features in academic prose. Over about nine months, with a few breaks, they read a chapter per week, took notes on a shared document, and then met to discuss the information together. Both reported finding the investment worthwhile:

> There are things in there [the *Longman Grammar*] that I probably never would have learned about if I had continued to only learn by searching for specific information. Also, the interpretations of the data were so helpful in reshaping how I think about academic prose and the choices writers make.
>
> *(D. Smith, personal communication, April 29, 2015)*

> The whole process was incredibly informative. I learned a ton, not only about what grammar is present in academic writing, but also why it is used. By the end of our project, I felt like I had a better grasp on why we write in academic contexts, and how we express these ideas. Before we had embarked on this project, I owned the *Longman Grammar*, but I was a bit intimidated by the size and the level of detail. Now, I refer to it fairly regularly when trying to understand the context in which we might use a particular grammatical feature.
>
> *(L. Spitzer, personal communication, April 29, 2015)*

Of course, not all teachers can commit the time to a project of this magnitude. Even a smaller project with a larger group can be helpful, though. Consider meeting with a group of grammar teacher colleagues. If each person reads about the use of one grammar feature and shares information at the meeting, everyone can go away with a greatly expanded knowledge of grammar with just a small time investment.

In addition to corpus-based reference grammars, many published articles cover information about use patterns for specific grammar features. Even a simple search on the Internet or in an article database using terms like *corpus*, *study*, and the name of the feature will identify publications.

3.   Try your own corpus searches.

Even if you do not do extensive corpus research, conducting your own corpus searches can be a helpful addition to your teaching skill set. A corpus search can be a quick way to get additional examples of a grammar feature in typical contexts. It can provide data for supplementary activities you design. It can reveal lexico-grammatical relationships that may not be covered in the textbook. A search also sometimes reminds you of aspects of grammar you otherwise forget about. For example, I was working on a verb + gerund versus verb + infinitive activity, using *stop to* + verb and *stop* + verb-*ing* to illustrate meaning difference. *Stop to smoke* versus *stop smoking* is an easy example, but I wondered what else people stop to do and stop doing. A quick search with COCA showed me that, in the spoken category, *stop* + -*ing* is regularly used with negatives in speech, especially with *talking* but also with other verbs; for example, *she won't stop talking* and *you never stop being a parent*. Of course, I know negatives are possible in English, but it simply hadn't occurred to me to use them in examples until I looked at the corpus.

Table 3.5 contains a short list of corpora that are available for searches on the Internet or that can be downloaded for free and analyzed with the free concordancing software package AntConc. Details about each corpus and how to access it are included on the websites. These corpora are a good place to start exploring corpora on your own. To get started, here are some searches to try with COCA for features that have been covered in this chapter. They will introduce you to three different ways to search with the COCA interface.

TABLE 3.5 A Short List of Corpora and Software for Trying Searches on Your Own

American and British English	
COCA—Corpus of Contemporary American English	http://corpus.byu.edu/coca/
BNC—British National Corpus	http://corpus.byu.edu/bnc/ or http://www.natcorp.ox.ac.uk/
MICASE and MICUSP—Michigan Corpus of Academic Spoken English and Michigan Corpus of Upper-level Student Papers	http://quod.lib.umich.edu/m/micase/ and http://micusp.elicorpora.info/
World Englishes and English as a Lingua Franca	
GloWbE—Corpus of Global Web-based English	http://corpus.byu.edu/glowbe/
ICE—International Corpus of English	http://ice-corpora.net/ice/
VOICE—Vienna-Oxford International Corpus of English	http://www.univie.ac.at/voice/
ELFA—English as a Lingua Franca in Academic Settings	http://www.helsinki.fi/englanti/elfa/elfacorpus
Free Corpus Analysis Software to Use with Corpora That You Download or Compile Yourself	
AntConc Laurence Anthony, the developer of AntConc, has numerous helpful YouTube tutorials for getting started with AntConc.	http://www.laurenceanthony.net/software/antconc/

1. Compare the use of *though* in COCA's academic and spoken categories.
   a. Under DISPLAY, choose CHART. Type *though* for the SEARCH STRING WORD(S).
   b. Every other setting should be at its default. Click on SEARCH.
   c. When bars appear for the categories, click first on ACADEMIC and look at the lines. Is *though* more often a subordinator making an adverbial clause or the linking adverbial *though*?
   d. Then click on the SPOKEN bar. Do you see more or fewer uses of *though* as a linking adverbial?
   e. Are your findings the same as those in subsection C of this chapter? Remember, the COCA spoken category is unscripted radio and TV, but the findings in this chapter were from conversation. Do you think you see differences in *though* that might be due to the difference in registers?
2. Investigate *call* in the passive voice in other speech.
   a. Under DISPLAY, choose LIST. SEARCH STRING WORD(S): is|are [vvn] This search string means "either *is* or *are* followed by a verb participle form." You will not see passives with intervening adverbs (e.g. *is often called*), but this is an easy search to start with. You can add intervening passives as you develop your search skills.
   b. Every other setting should be at its default. Click on SEARCH.
   c. When you see the list of items, click on *is called* and *are called* to see the concordance listings. Do you see many examples of *call* used for naming terms as in the class sessions described in the second section?
3. Investigate whether *differ* occurs with many other prepositions besides *from* in academic writing.
   a. Under DISPLAY, choose KWIC. SEARCH STRING WORD(S): [differ] By using the square brackets around *differ*, you tell COCA to include all forms of differ (e.g. *differs, differed*).
   b. In SECTIONS, highlight ACADEMIC.
   c. Look at the concordance lines. They will be alphabetized by the first word to the right. Is *from* a common preposition after *differ*? Do you see other prepositions or other words that might deserve coverage as a chunk for EAP students? (Notice that the colors show different grammatical classes—e.g. verbs, prepositions, adverbs. The colors can help students see patterns in grammar, too.)

Conclusion

Once they get to know corpus linguistics, many teachers also want to introduce it to their students. Using corpus tools with students can help increase learner autonomy as students analyze patterns in language use for themselves. These teaching techniques are beyond the scope of this chapter, but helpful advice is in publications about data-driven learning and discovery learning (e.g. Sripicharn 2010;

Gavioli 2005: chapter 5), as well as in items in the Essential Readings list at the end of this chapter.

Whether or not you choose to make corpus linguistics overt in your own teaching, I hope this chapter has at least convinced you of its importance for our understanding of grammar. Other teachers have commented that once they learn about corpus linguistics and see what it can tell them about language use, it is difficult to remember ever having a purely structural view of grammar. As one participant in a corpus seminar reported years after the seminar:

> In some ways, it's hard for me to say when I'm using CL [corpus linguistics] and when I'm not because I feel like it's influenced me so much in the way I think about language, and that influences what I do in the classroom.
>
> *(Lachenmeier 2006: 49)*

Discussion Questions

1. Think of your own experience learning a second language. Was grammar presented as structural accuracy, or were patterns of use included? Did you ever wonder how native speakers of the language chose between alternatives or why they were saying things you didn't recognize? If the teacher had told you more about grammar for conversation vs. academic writing, do you think you would have felt overwhelmed, or would it have been useful?
2. Imagine you are teaching a high intermediate grammar course in an ESL setting where students can interact with native speakers outside of class or in an EFL setting where students read texts in English outside of class. Are there grammar features covered in this chapter that you would cover for receptive skills (for comprehending the use of the feature)? Would you investigate other features in a corpus to see whether receptive practice would be useful?
3. Discuss the extent to which you agree with teachers who claim that teaching prescriptively correct English is the best thing to do. Refer to points in this chapter for evidence or in making counterpoints.
4. Many factors that influence grammar choices are covered in this chapter (see Table 3.2). Which factor do you think is most important for a grammar teacher to know about? Why? If your answer is "it depends," explain what it depends on.

Essential Reading

The following two books will provide ideas for corpus searches you can do on your own or with students, as well as give guidance in activity and materials planning.

Bennett, G. (2010). *Using corpora in the language learning classroom.* Ann Arbor: University of Michigan Press.

Reppen, R. (2010). *Using corpora in the language classroom.* Cambridge: Cambridge University Press.

This article provides a condensed version of some of the issues covered in this chapter looking at how the field of grammar teaching was poised for change in the year 2000.

Conrad, S. (2000). Will corpus linguistics revolutionize grammar teaching in the 21st century? *TESOL Quarterly, 34,* 548–560.

All grammar teachers should look through at least one of these corpus-based resources:

Biber, D., Johansson, S., Leech, G., Conrad, S., & Finegan, E. (1999). *Longman grammar of spoken and written English.* Harlow, UK: Pearson Education.
Alternatively, you could consider the shorter student version:
Biber, D., Conrad, S., & Leech, G. (2002). *Longman student grammar of spoken and written English.* Harlow, UK: Pearson Education.
Carter, R., & McCarthy, M. (2006). *Cambridge grammar of English: A comprehensive guide.* Cambridge: Cambridge University Press.

If you haven't already, visit at least two of the websites in Table 3.5 and learn about the corpora. For corpus linguistics, familiarity with well-known corpora is as important as familiarity with certain publications.

References

Azar, B., & Hagen, S. (2009). *Understanding and using English grammar* (4th ed.). White Plains, NY: Pearson Education.

Biber, D., & Conrad, S. (2009). *Register, genre, and style.* Cambridge: Cambridge University Press.

Biber, D., Conrad, S., & Cortes, V. (2004). "If you look at . . .": Lexical bundles in university teaching and textbooks. *Applied Linguistics, 25,* 371–405.

Biber, D., Conrad, S., & Leech, G. (2002). *Longman student grammar of spoken and written English.* Harlow, UK: Pearson Education.

Biber, D., Conrad, S., & Reppen, R. (1998). *Corpus linguistics: Investigating language structure and use.* Cambridge: Cambridge University Press.

Biber, D., Conrad, S., Reppen, R., Byrd, P., & Helt, M. (2002). Speaking and writing in the university: A multi-dimensional comparison. *TESOL Quarterly, 36,* 9–48.

Biber, D., Gray, B., & Poonpon, K. (2011). Should we use characteristics of conversation to measure grammatical complexity in L2 writing development? *TESOL Quarterly, 45,* 5–35.

Biber, D., Johansson, S., Leech, G., Conrad, S., & Finegan, E. (1999). *Longman grammar of spoken and written English.* Harlow, UK: Pearson Education.

Biber, D., & Reppen, R. (2002). What does frequency have to do with grammar teaching? *Studies in Second Language Acquisition, 24,* 199–208.

Carlisi, K. (2008). *Grammar Connection 3.* Boston: Thomson Heinle.

Carter, R., & McCarthy, M. 2006. *Cambridge grammar of English: A comprehensive guide.* Cambridge: Cambridge University Press.

Conrad, S. (1999). The importance of corpus-based research for language teachers. *System, 27,* 1–18.

Conrad, S. (2000). Will corpus linguistics revolutionize grammar teaching in the 21st century? *TESOL Quarterly, 34,* 548–560.

Conrad, S., & Biber, D., with Daly, K., & Packer, S. (2009). *Real grammar: A corpus-based approach to English.* New York: Pearson Education.

Danielson, D., & Porter, P. (1990). *Using English, your second language* (2nd ed.). Englewood Cliffs, NJ: Prentice Hall Regents.

Davies, M. (2008–). *The corpus of contemporary American English: 450 million words, 1990–present.* Available online at http://corpus.byu.edu/coca/

de Klerk, V. (2006) *Corpus linguistics and World Englishes: An analysis of Xhosa English.* London: Continuum.

Folse, K. (2015). *Clear grammar 3* (2nd ed.). Ann Arbor: University of Michigan Press.

Frazier, S. (2003). A corpus analysis of *would*-clauses without adjacent *if*-clauses. *TESOL Quarterly, 37*, 443–466.

Gardner, D., & Davies, M. (2007). Pointing out frequent phrasal verbs: A corpus-based analysis. *TESOL Quarterly, 41*, 339–359.

Gavioli, L. (2005). *Exploring corpora for ESP learning.* Amsterdam: John Benjamins.

Gilquin, G., & Granger, S. (2010). How can data-driven learning be used in language teaching? In A. O'Keeffe & M. McCarthy (Eds.), *The Routledge handbook of corpus linguistics* (pp. 359–370). London: Routledge.

Lachenmeier, E. (2006). The impact of teacher training in corpus linguistics. Unpublished master's thesis. Portland State University, Portland, Oregon.

Larsen-Freeman, D. (2002). The grammar of choice. In E. Hinkel & S. Fotos (Eds.), *New perspectives on grammar teaching in second language classrooms* (pp. 103–118). Mahwah, NJ: Erlbaum.

Liu, D. (2011). The most frequently used English phrasal verbs in American and British English: A multicorpus examination. *TESOL Quarterly, 45*, 661–688.

McCarthy, M. (2015). The role of corpus research in the design of advanced level grammar instruction. In M. Christison, D. Christian, P. Duff, & N. Spada (Eds.), *Teaching and learning English grammar* (pp. 87–102). New York: Routledge.

McCarthy, M., McCarten, J., & Sandiford, H. (2014). *Viewpoint teacher's edition 2.* New York: Cambridge University Press.

Nesselhauf, N. (2004). Learner corpora and their potential for language teaching. In J. Sinclair (Ed.), *How to use corpora in language teaching* (pp. 125–152). Amsterdam: John Benjamins.

O'Keeffe, A., & McCarthy, M. (Eds.) (2010). *The Routledge handbook of corpus linguistics.* London: Routledge, chs. 3–8.

O'Keeffe, A., McCarthy, M., & Carter, R. (2007) *From corpus to classroom.* Cambridge: Cambridge University Press.

Reppen, R. (2012). *Grammar and beyond—level 2.* Cambridge: Cambridge University Press.

Sripicharn, P. (2010). How can we prepare learners for using language corpora? In A. O'Keeffe & M. McCarthy (Eds.), *The Routledge handbook of corpus linguistics* (pp. 371–384). London: Routledge.

Thewlis, S. (2007). *Grammar dimensions 3* (4th ed.). Boston: Thomson Heinle.

4

GRAMMAR IN STUDENT BOOKS VS. GRAMMAR THAT STUDENTS NEED

Which Grammar to Include, Which Grammar to Omit

Keith S. Folse

Introduction

Hundreds of grammar books exist for our ESL/EFL learners today. While some larger works are designed to serve as grammar references, the vast majority are student course books, often appearing as part of a three- or four-volume grammar series, with each book targeting a predetermined list of grammar points deemed appropriate for learners at a specific proficiency level (e.g., beginning, intermediate, upper intermediate, advanced). Unfortunately, course time constraints sometimes necessitate omitting certain grammar points because teachers simply cannot cover all of the material in the books. In this chapter, we look at how and why teachers would intentionally choose to teach certain grammar points while excluding others. We examine the relationship between student needs and grammar course content by considering one teacher's experiences teaching grammar in three different ESL/EFL programs with three different student groups with contrasting ultimate learner goals—writing better academic papers, passing a high-stakes exam, and improving personal conversational skills in English. We will learn how to analyze a textbook's list of grammar points and then read about recent applications of corpus linguistics research techniques that can help us make better informed decisions about which grammar points to emphasize as well as those to skip in our lessons. The main focus of this chapter is on the important connection between learner needs and the grammar content that might be selected for that course. In sum, learner needs should drive not only our grammar classes but also the whole curriculum.

Reasons to Teach Grammar

Why are we teaching grammar? I hope your answer to this question is strongly connected to the answer to this question: Why are our students studying grammar? While learner needs are at the heart of most second language (L2) teaching methods today, there were many times during the history of L2 teaching when simply mastering a list of grammatical or lexical items was everyone's goal, often resulting in students who could translate things or pass a multiple-choice exam but were not actually able to use the language. Another way to say this is that students learned *about* the language but did not actually learn the language. They might be able to demonstrate linguistic competence but not communicative competence.

In her outstanding chapter "Grammar Teaching: Research, Theory, and Practice," Ur (2011) explains why grammar is often the pivotal course in the curriculum of most ESL programs, as well as how grammar has been viewed historically in various teaching methods in the past century or so. Sometimes grammar has been promoted, almost worshipped, in our field, but other times grammar has been completely shunned. Despite the often predictable swings of the pendulum in acceptable L2 pedagogy, grammar has continued to be central to the teaching of foreign languages. As Ur (2011) aptly summarizes the situation: "[I]n spite of the current promotion of communicative and task-based methodologies by ministries of education worldwide, grammatical explanations and exercises continue to be prominent both in course books and in the classroom practice of teachers in school-based foreign-language courses" (507).

Longtime teacher and popular textbook writer Betty Azar (2009), from whose grammar books many teachers have taught and in fact learned about grammar, sums up this rather tumultuous history in English language teaching as follows:

> Our field has seen tremendous changes since 1965, when language teaching was shifting away from grammar. Fortunately, we have shifted back (though some of us never stopped teaching grammar, much to our students' benefit and delight). With both research and teaching outcomes on its side, grammar is now recognized by most in the field as an essential component in balanced programs of second language instruction.
>
> *(v)*

Many teachers and students alike believe that we study grammar solely to avoid errors. While better accuracy could in fact be one of the results of grammar instruction, there are two overarching general reasons to teach grammar to adults. One is to help students express their ideas in English. The other is to do so while helping them avoid common errors. Thus, one reason deals with a positive proactive sense, while the other deals with avoiding a negative situation.

The positive sense enables students to say something. For example, if you are going to make oatmeal cookies, you need to buy flour, oatmeal, and sugar, so you might talk about how *much* flour to buy, but in the actual recipe, you would talk about how *many* cups of flour to add. This grammar point of when to use *how many* and when to use *how much* is called *count and noncount nouns*. In some languages, there is only one word to ask about quantity, e.g., *combien* in French, so here we are teaching students how to express this idea in English by using *how many* for count nouns and *how much* for noncount nouns. (See Folse 2009: 152–160, for teacher-friendly practical information on this grammar point.)

The negative sense starts with the idea that English learners are highly likely to make certain errors with a grammar point. For example, we expect English learners to make any of the following errors:

1. *There are 20 student in my class.* (an incorrect plural form)
2. *Computer has mouse and keyboard.* (a missing article with a singular count noun)
3. *I have a lot of homeworks for tomorrow.* (a plural form of a noncount noun)
4. *I have a homework to do now.* (singular article with a noncount noun)

(Folse 2009)

In my experience, adult learners like seeing these error examples because they can see the gap between what they are producing and what they should be saying. However, some teachers object quite strongly to grammar materials that have errors printed on the page. My rebuttal to these teachers is that our learners *are* in fact making these errors and it is useful to have these pointed out to learners. Sometimes learners cannot hear a difference between what they are saying and what they should be saying; other times learners simply do not know that what they are saying is not the correct form. In either of these situations, adult learners appreciate having someone point out this gap. A teacher or a textbook pointing out common errors can make learners aware of their errors and therefore more likely that second language learners will attempt to correct them and avoid fossilization. In brief, learners cannot correct something if they do not realize in the first place that it is wrong.

Another very important reason that we teach grammar involves adult students' expectations. Adults, unlike children, come to our classrooms with a complete set of life experiences, learner strategies, and classroom expectations that young learners do not have. Adults want rules that will help make sense of the linguistic chaos they may see in their new language, and they want relevant examples—and *lots* of them—given in language that they can understand. Many adult learners like the comfort of seeing language presented in nice, neat boxes in course books such as those presented so succinctly in the *English Grammar* series by Betty Azar and Stacy Hagen or in *English Grammar in Use* by Raymond Murphy.

In addition, adult learners want correction. While some have debated the value of error correction, particularly in writing (Ferris 2011; Truscott 1996), ESL students expect their written work to be corrected. In a detailed survey of 100 ESL students in freshmen composition classes, Leki (1991) found that students wanted their composition teachers to correct *all* errors in their written assignments. Similarly, in a survey of 418 ESL students, Chenoweth, Day, Chun, and Luppescu (1983) found that students viewed the correction of spoken errors as not just helpful but actually necessary. The fact that learners want their errors to be corrected does not mean that corrections are necessarily a good thing; this issue is a separate research issue. However, it is abundantly clear that adult learners expect corrections. Despite all of the academic debate on the ultimate value of error correction, the bottom line is that our adult learners do want to be corrected.

In all teacher decisions about what to teach, when to teach it, how to teach it, how to practice it, and even how to test it, we should always keep our focus clear: learner needs. Learner needs should run the show. The real language needs of our learners should always be the foundation for every classroom decision we make. Therefore, it behooves all of us to know who our students are and why they are studying English.

The Varying Language Needs of Real Students

In many teacher training courses, there is often a one-size-fits-all approach when it comes to the contents of a grammar course, pronunciation course, or writing course, for example. However, different students have different language needs, and this most certainly includes grammar needs. In this section, I offer concrete examples from some of the types of L2 programs in which I have taught during my career. Though I have taught a wide range of different kinds of students—both ESL and EFL, both adults and children, both academic and nonacademic, most of my ESL teaching has been at intensive English programs at a college or university in the United States. These students wanted English for academic purposes (EAP) and had two pressing needs. One need was related to a standardized test, while the other was related to their ability to actually use the language in an academic course.

First—at least in the students' minds—they needed to pass a high-stakes exam such as the Test of English as a Foreign Language (TOEFL) or the International English Language Testing System (IELTS). As a result, students often like to practice English through example TOEFL or IELTS questions. For instance, if I at any time wanted to get a student's immediate and undivided attention, all I had to do was say that the item currently being practiced on the board was likely to appear on the TOEFL, and most students would give me their undivided attention.

To meet my learners' needs here, I had to know all about TOEFL and IELTS. I had to find out what kind of language issues might be covered in these exams and what the assessment items might look like. To make sure I could meet my students' needs here, I studied released items from both exams, bought and worked through practice exams in published books, and interviewed numerous students after they had taken these exams.

Second—again in the students' view but perhaps first from the teachers' point of view—students needed language that would help them in their academic classes. Because their language needs were academic English in general, we focused on better compositions or faster reading of material typically found in college text-books. For composition, we covered some of the most common errors students typically made in writing, e.g., verb tenses, articles, and prepositions. For reading, we covered sentence structure, including clauses and reduced clauses. While this focus on the language that students would actually need to write or read English is clearly the one that teachers emphasize—and for good reasons—it is important for all of us teachers to remember to put ourselves in our students' shoes. By doing so, we can all better understand why our students clearly tend to focus on their more immediate need to pass TOEFL or IELTS, since for them, not doing so could completely eliminate their need for future academic English in the first place.

In contrast to these students in an EAP program at a U.S. college or university, my students in Saudi Arabia were not interested in academic English. They were young officers in the Saudi Arabia National Guard who had been selected to receive one year of paid leave to learn English in Saudi Arabia before going to Lackland Air Force Base in Texas (again on paid leave) to receive military training in English provided they first could pass the American Language Course Placement Test (ALCPT) in our English program in Saudi Arabia. Once again, these students also had two different kinds of language needs. Their first need was to pass an exam in Saudi Arabia. After passing the test, however, their need was to be able to function in their training programs in the United States, so they also had an English for Specific Purposes (ESP) need. However, on many occasions, students' questions and attention in class were uniquely limited to their concerns about the ALCPT, which were largely vocabulary and very basic grammar, while they completely ignored their future need to listen and speak in their military training.

Though the following anecdote happened some 30 years ago, I distinctly remember it because it so profoundly impacted how I viewed what the term *learner needs* really means in the real world—and by real world here, I mean in our students' real world. In *Vocabulary Myths* (Folse 2004), I tell the story of a seemingly simple question that a student posed to me in class one day in Saudi Arabia about the difference between the words *dictionary* and *encyclopedia* (85–87) and my attempt to answer the student's question.

"Folse, what means encyclobedia? Encyclobedia—same-same dictionary?" (Folse 2004: 86). At this point in my career, I had five years of EAP teaching experience but none with ESP students. I started my lengthy explanation with, "Well, no, not exactly. You see, an encyclopedia is. . . ." As any good teacher, I used level-appropriate language as well as pertinent examples. When I had finally finished, the students conferred in Arabic for a few moments, and then the original asker smiled and proclaimed, "Yes, same-same."

Internally, I sighed, frustrated that my explanation seemed to have fallen on deaf ears. Though I felt deflated at the time, however, that changed just a few weeks later when I was finally able to see questions on the ALCPT for the first time, many of which tested simple synonyms. I realized that if the word *encyclopedia* did appear on the ALCPT, it would most likely occur in a simple multiple-choice item that merely required my students to match *encyclopedia* with another word such as *book* or *dictionary*. I learned a very valuable lesson here about knowing my students' actual language needs. In this case, my students clearly had a better grasp of what they needed to know about the word *encyclopedia* than I did. In other words, to teach to my students' actual language needs, my answer to the student question of "Encyclobedia (because Arabic has /b/ but no /p/)—same-same dictionary?" should have started with "Yes" followed by some simple elaboration. My students were never going to use an encyclopedia; they just needed that word for the exam because passing that exam was the ticket to their future military training in the United States and a promotion in their jobs upon returning to Saudi Arabia. This anecdote taught me firsthand that teachers do not always know what is best and underlined the point that learner needs should drive the curriculum and lesson planning.

In stark contrast to my EAP students at the university or ESP students in the military program, many students enroll in an English course simply to be able to speak better English. When I taught at a language school in Japan, for example, our students were coming for *ei-kai-wa*, or English conversation. In many cases, students attended classes for self-improvement of their English, not because of some external pressure such as TOEFL or another exam.

In perhaps the biggest paradigm shift of my teaching career, I had to learn to teach less and provide more practice due to the unique class time constraints and varied student needs. While my EAP and ESP classes met five or more hours per week, my English conversation classes met only once a week for 75 minutes, meaning I had less than one-third of my usual teaching time. In addition, students' needs were quite different. My *ei-kai-wa* students were adults with three main goals: (1) to improve their English speaking and listening skills through exposure and practice, (2) to learn about American culture, and (3) to socialize with like-minded Japanese. It is extremely important to note that these goals are not very time-sensitive because they are not driven by an external goal with a looming deadline.

Given these student needs, I had to adjust my teaching to be 90% practice with perhaps 10% input, including (possibly) a new grammar point. Each week's class was the source of the new grammar point, the source of the subsequent input (i.e., rich comprehensible input that was pregnant with many examples of the target grammar), the source of student practice, and the source of student output or production. This EFL scenario was completely different from what I had experienced teaching in an ESL or intensive L2 setting.

In my EAP classes in an intensive program in an ESL setting, my goal was not complete student mastery of the grammar point being taught. I anticipated that my students in an ESL setting would be exposed to English outside my class, which would allow them to notice the features that I had taught them, much as Schmidt's story of how being made aware of certain linguistic features of Portuguese during his classes (Schmidt 1990; Schmidt & Frota 1986) then allowed him to notice these features daily as he lived in Brazil. In an ESL setting, Schmidt's Noticing Hypothesis (Leow 2013; Schmidt 1993) has more chance to be effective because the students should be immersed in or at least exposed to the target language a great deal. In an EFL setting, however, students usually lack such exposure to the target language, thus requiring the classroom to be the main source of everything—teacher input and student output.

In each of the teaching scenarios I have described in this section, the grammar focus was different according to student needs, which is how we should approach teaching not just grammar but everything in our English classes. Note the similarities and differences among the three groups as outlined in Table 4.1.

Grammar Points Typically Taught in Grammar Books

The purpose of this chapter is to discuss which grammar points teachers should or should not teach. Wherever you teach and no matter what your students' ultimate goals with English are, your class most likely has a course book that has been assigned. Therefore, it is important to have a solid understanding of which grammar points are typically covered in books. Despite the large number of grammar books available on the market today, there is tremendous overlap among these books in the overall grammar syllabus that they cover. For example, you will see the same verb tenses presented in pretty much the same sequence no matter which grammar series you are using: simple present, simple past, present progressive, future,

TABLE 4.1 Examples of How Three Different Programs Teach Grammar

Students/Teaching Setting	Grammar in the Program	Student Grammar Needs
International ESL students in an intensive EAP program in the United States	Students attended five hours of class daily, with one class dedicated solely to grammar.	Students focused heavily on grammatical accuracy, especially for academic writing.
Saudi military students in an EFL program in Saudi Arabia	Students attended six hours of class daily; lessons included grammar points and vocabulary but emphasized listening over other skills.	Students were taught certain grammar points but were tested more on listening and vocabulary.
Japanese adult students in an EFL conversation program in Japan	Students attended 75 minutes of class once a week; class focused solely on improving conversation.	Students learned grammar for certain linguistic conversational functions, e.g., *do/does* to ask yes/no questions or *could* to express possibility. Classes focused heavily on speaking and listening.

past progressive. These grammar points also tend to be the same by proficiency level, so that the grammatical items covered in lower-intermediate-level Book A by Publisher X are remarkably similar to, if not exactly the same as, what is covered in lower-intermediate-level Book B by Publisher Z. Therefore, as you strive to answer the question of which grammar is covered in which course books, you should focus on two issues: the target student proficiency level of the course book and the grammar points in that book.

Almost all language programs have multiple proficiency levels. Upon entering a language school or program, students take a placement test that identifies the level in which the students should study. At the intensive English program at my current university, our ESL program offers four levels: beginning, intermediate, high intermediate, advanced. At another intensive program where I used to teach, they had these four levels: beginning, lower intermediate, upper intermediate, advanced. The labels may vary, but the intended audiences are very similar.

Because publishers want to sell books, savvy publishers have one and often several grammar series in their catalog, each consisting of three or four books. This number is not a random occurrence. Publishers are reacting to market conditions, and these market conditions dictate offering one grammar book for each of the levels, which is abundantly clear in Table 4.2.

TABLE 4.2 Grammar Books by Publisher and Number of Levels

Publisher	Title	Levels
Cambridge	*Grammar in Use* (3rd ed.) (Murphy 2009)	3
	Grammar and Beyond (Reppen et al. 2012)	4
Longman	*My Grammar Lab* (Foley and Hall 2012)	3
	Focus on Grammar (3rd ed.) (Schoenberg et al. 2011)	5
	Grammar Practice (3rd ed.) (Walker and Elsworth 2007)	4
	Next Generation Grammar (Cavage et al. 2013)	4
National Geographic Cengage Learning	*Grammar in Context* (5th ed.) (Elbaum 2010)	4
	Grammar Explorer (Mackey et al. 2014)	3
Oxford	*Elements of Success* (Ediger et al. 2014)	3
	Grammar Sense (2nd ed.) (Bland et al. 2012)	4
University of Michigan Press	*Clear Grammar* (2nd ed.) (Folse 2010, 2012, 2014a, 2014b)	4

Now that we have seen that the number of books offered by publishers is based on the number of proficiency-level courses taught in most English programs, we will turn our attention to the grammar points that are covered in these books. It is important to examine these grammar points in two very distinct, important ways: vertically and horizontally.

A vertical analysis would include listing all of the grammar points taught from the lowest book to the most advanced book in any one series. Creating such a list—even for one series—would give you a good understanding of what a grammar course could include.

This listing could then be compared to a listing from one or more other publishers' series. Comparing two of them would demonstrate that there really is not a lot of variety in the overall list of possible grammar points. To be certain, variety exists between two series, but overall the similarities greatly outweigh any individual differences. In general, there is a consensus about the grammar points in a vertical listing of grammar points for English learners.

What would one series' grammar list look like? Table 4.3 lists the grammar points covered in the second edition of *Clear Grammar*, a four-volume series by the University of Michigan Press (Folse 2010, 2012, 2014a, 2014b). These grammar points are typical of those covered in other publishers' series as well. In addition, notice how a review of grammar points as well as recycling of verb tenses from one level to the next are included. These two pedagogical features are also common to most publishers' grammar series. Recycling previously taught grammar provides necessary reinforcement in the language acquisition process. Even though students may seem to have learned a grammar point, whenever a new grammar point is introduced, some students will backslide on the previous learned item, which is a natural part of interlanguage, which is the ebb and flow of mastering any feature of a second language (Selinker 1972).

While a vertical analysis entails a listing of all possible grammar points throughout one grammar series, a horizontal analysis necessitates comparing the grammar points taught by two or more books at the same proficiency level. In other words, we want to see to what degree the same grammar points are covered at a certain proficiency level, e.g., beginning. Table 4.4 is a horizontal analysis for two grammar books at the beginning level but from different authors and different publishers.

A comparison of the two books' tables of contents shows a strong overlap in grammar points covered. Although both books are for the same proficiency level, *Grammar in Context 1* is substantially longer than *Clear Grammar 1*—by 40%, in fact, with a difference of 133 pages, which includes two more units. All of the grammar points in *Clear Grammar 1* are covered in *Grammar in Context 1*. The grammar points taught in *Grammar in Context 1* but not in *Clear Grammar 1* include frequency adverbs, object pronouns, modals, infinitives, comparatives and superlatives, and tag questions. All of these grammar points are covered in book 2 or 3 in the *Clear Grammar* series. While a horizontal analysis of these two books

TABLE 4.3 Vertical Listing of Grammar Points in One ESL Textbook Series

Book/Proficiency Level	Unit: Grammar Points
Clear Grammar 1 (2nd ed.) (Folse 2010) (beginning proficiency)	1: Simple Present Tense of *Be* 2: Possessive Adjectives and Demonstrative Words 3: Simple Present Tense 4: Descriptive Adjectives 5: Past Tense of *Be* 6: Past Tense of Regular and Irregular Verbs 7: *Wh-* Questions 8: Present Progressive Tense 9: Count and Non-Count Nouns 10: Prepositions: *at, on, in* 11: *Be Going To* + Verb 12: Review of Verb Tenses from Book 1
Clear Grammar 2 (2nd ed.) (Folse 2012) (low intermediate proficiency)	1: Review of Verb Tenses (simple present, present progressive, *be going to*) 2: Articles 3: Irregular Past Tense Verbs 4: Present Perfect Tense 5: Adverbs of Frequency 6: Nouns Used as Adjectives 7: Object Pronouns 8: Past Progressive Tense 9: *One* and *Other* 10: Possessive 11: Comparatives and Superlatives of Adjectives 12: Modals
Clear Grammar 3 (2nd ed.) (Folse 2014a) (upper intermediate proficiency)	1: Phrasal Verbs 2: Infinitives and Gerunds 3: Participial Adjectives: *-ing* vs. *-ed* 4: Prepositions after Adjectives, Verbs, and Nouns 5: Passive Voice 6: Adjective Clauses 7: Adverbs 8: Connectors 9: Review of Verb Tenses 10: Review of Units 1–9
Clear Grammar 4 (2nd ed.) (Folse 2014b) (advanced proficiency)	1: Subject-Verb Agreement 2: Word Forms 3: Past Perfect Tense 4: Conditionals 5: Adverb Clauses 6: Noun Clauses 7: Reduction of Adjective and Adverb Clauses, Including Appositives 8: Past Modals 9: Review of Verb Tenses 10: Review of Units 1–9

TABLE 4.4 Horizontal Analysis of Grammar Points in Two Beginning-level Books

Unit	Grammar in Context 1 (5th ed.) (Elbaum 2010) 464 pages; 14 units	Clear Grammar 1 (2nd ed.) (Folse 2010) 331 pages; 12 units
1	Present Tense of *Be* *This, That, These, Those*	Simple Present Tense of *Be*
2	Simple Present Tense	Possessive Adjectives; Demonstrative Words
3	Frequency Words with the Simple Present Tense Prepositions of Time	Simple Present Tense
4	Singular and Plural *There + Be +* Noun; Articles and Quantity Words	Descriptive Adjectives
5	Possession Object Pronouns Questions About the Subject	Past Tense of *Be*
6	Present Continuous Tense	Past Tense of Regular and Irregular Verbs
7	Future Tenses—*Will* and *Be Going To;* Comparison of Tenses	*Wh-* Questions
8	Simple Past Tense	Present Progressive
9	Infinitives; Modals; Imperatives	Count and Non-Count Nouns
10	Count and Non-Count Nouns; Quantity Words	Prepositions: *At, On, In*
11	Adjectives; Noun Modifiers; Adverbs	*Be Going To* + Verb
12	Comparatives; Superlatives	Review of Verb Tenses from Book 1
13	Auxiliary Verbs with *Too* and *Either;* Auxiliary Verbs in Tag Questions	
14	Verb Review	

shows some differences in content, these differences would not exist in a vertical analysis of all four books in both series. Therefore, we find no grammar points in Book 1 of *Grammar in Context* or *Clear Grammar* that are unique to only one of the series. The point we should note here is that a grammar series tends to follow a more or less stable list of grammar points, which is very good news for ESL/EFL teachers, especially those new to the field, because it makes it easier for us to become familiar with a relatively finite list.

Before we talk about which grammar points deserve more of your teaching time, I would like to point out that these grammar points are not limited to just grammar books. Lessons in conversation books may also be organized around grammar points, as seen in Table 4.5.

TABLE 4.5 Analysis of Grammar Points in a Conversation Book

Unit	World English 1 (2nd ed.) (Chase, Milner, and Johannsen 2015)
1	Review of Present Tense: Be; Be + Adjective (+ Noun); Possessive Adjectives
2	Review: Simple Present Tense; Prepositions of Time; Adverbs of Frequency
3	Possession; Imperatives; Should for Advice
4	Count and Non-count Nouns: Some and Any; How Much and How Many with Quantifiers: Lots of, a Few, a Little
5	Present Continuous Tense; Stative Verbs
6	Simple Past Tense; Simple Past Tense of to Be
7	Verbs with Direct and Indirect Objects; Irregular Past Tense; Sensory Verbs
8	Future Tense: Be Going To Will for Predictions and Immediate Decisions
9	Comparatives; Superlatives
10	Modals (Could, Ought To, Should, Must); Have To; Questions with How
11	Present Perfect Tense; Present Perfect Tense vs. Simple Past Tense
12	Real Conditionals (Also Called the First Conditional)

The fact that grammar is such an integral component of conversation books and courses may surprise many who are under the very mistaken impression that conversation classes are just about speaking and who believe the myth that being a native speaker alone qualifies a person to teach English conversation. Just because you speak the language does not in any way suggest you are able to do a good job explaining it to a non-native speaker. The truth is that all ESL/EFL teachers need to know English grammar well. In fact, it is well documented through surveys of both ESL and EFL students that native speaker teachers are unsurprisingly perceived to be poor at explaining grammar (Benke and Medgyes 2005; Han 2005; Walkinshaw and Oanh 2014). Teachers cannot be good at explaining what they do not know; explicit knowledge of English grammar is a requisite for being able to explain this to a student.

Looking at Table 4.5 may give the very wrong impression, however, that this particular conversation book focuses only or even primarily on grammar. In actuality, nothing could be further from the truth. Good conversation books often have an integrated skills approach in which each unit has many different areas of focus with the ultimate goal of improving the learner's overall proficiency level in English. This particular series focuses on at least eight different areas: communicative functions (e.g., asking for information, describing occupations), grammar, vocabulary, listening, speaking and pronunciation, reading, writing, and understanding video clips.

To help you better understand the possible role of grammar in a conversation book, it would be helpful for you to see the Scope and Sequence for one of the units in *World English 1* (2nd ed.) (Chase, Milner, and Johannsen 2015). In Table 4.6, you can see these different areas and how they are all related to the unit theme of "People." One of the first things that any good teacher will do when faced with a new book is read the introductory section, which is often called "To the Teacher" and includes a Scope and Sequence, so spending time deciphering this information is a valuable teacher task.

Grammar Points to Teach, Grammar Points Not to Teach

At this point, we have explored at length a list of possible grammar points through a vertical analysis, so we now come to the real question that most teachers face. Given that we all have class time limitations, we cannot possibly cover everything in our course books, so we have to make decisions about what to teach and what not to teach.

Sometimes teachers have no control over the contents of their course. Sometimes there is a program-wide syllabus that dictates what to teach. In some programs, the course syllabus even stipulates when to teach a certain grammar point, e.g., present perfect tense in week 5.

Other teachers have more control over the content and sequencing of content in their classes. For these teachers, decisions about what to teach should be based entirely on learner needs, keeping in mind that these needs can vary greatly, as we saw earlier in this chapter, from passing a standardized English exam to being able to converse in English better.

So how do we determine which grammar points our students need? In some cases, it is rigidly dictated by our school's or program's syllabus, and we as teachers cannot deviate from what has been proscribed. For example, the teacher may receive a syllabus listing the grammar textbook and which specific chapters should be covered in the term (if not all are being covered), sometimes even in which order they should be covered. In some cases, teachers are allowed to choose which

TABLE 4.6 Scope and Sequence for Unit 1 of *World English 1* (2nd ed.) (Chase, Milner, and Johannsen 2015)

Unit	Topic	Unit Goals	Grammar	Vocabulary	Listening	Speaking and Pronunciation	Reading	Writing	Video Journal
1	People	• Meet people • Ask for and give personal information • Describe different occupations • Describe positive and negative parts	Review of present tense: *Be*; *Be* + adjective (+ noun); Possessive adjectives	Occupations Countries Nationalities Descriptive adjectives	Focused listening: Personal introductions	Asking for and giving personal information Contractions: -'m, -'re, -'s	National Geographic: "People from Around the World"	Writing about people's occupations and nationalities	National Geographic: "The Last of the Woman Divers"

grammar points to teach or not teach. In this scenario, the teacher could conduct some sort of needs analysis in the first class meeting. Common ways to gather this data include giving the students a pretest on the grammar points in the book or having the students produce a writing sample that the teacher can analyze for frequent or important errors.

A valid reason not to teach a grammar point is that the particular grammatical structure is not common either in English in general or in the type of English interactions in which your students are most likely to take part. In considering the value of dedicating limited classroom instructional time to a grammar point, good teachers are guided by these questions: "Will my learners ever have to use this grammar point? If they have to use it, how will they most likely need to use it? In writing? In speaking? In an informal email? In a job interview?" In other words, good teachers take learners' needs into account as they determine not only the grammar points to teach but also how much classroom time to allocate for each grammar point.

Let's consider an academic writing course. Which grammar points would we teach? More importantly, which would we choose not to teach? And why? Once again, the answers to these curriculum questions depend first and foremost on learner needs. In her excellent overview of grammar points that are so infrequent that they should not be taught in an academic writing course, Hinkel (2013) presents grammar points that are essential in academic writing as well as those that are rare in academic writing. While verb tenses, for example, are an important part of any grammar course to complement an academic writing course, Table 4.7 outlines nine grammar points that Hinkel suggests do not merit instructional time.

Now that we have looked at structures that are common as well as those that are uncommon in academic writing, let's consider the grammar issues in spoken English. Simply put, spoken grammar refers to the linguistic patterns that occur frequently in natural spoken language. Some of these patterns are more obvious to English speakers, while others are not.

An obvious example of a spoken English grammar pattern is the use of *gonna* + VERB for future actions. In spoken English, the words *going* and *to* are reduced

TABLE 4.7 Grammar Points Not Frequent in Academic Writing (Hinkel 2013)

1. Future perfect tense
2. Future perfect progressive tense
3. Past perfect tense
4. Past perfect progressive tense
5. Passive in some tenses (future perfect, future progressive, present progressive, past progressive, past perfect, past perfect progressive)
6. Subjunctive in noun clauses
7. The modal *must* for obligation
8. The modals *may* for permission
9. Inversion of subject-verb after sentence-initial negatives

only when followed by an action. Therefore, the grammatical pattern is *gonna* + VERB, so people say, "I'm gonna call her," never "I'm gonna Miami."

A much less obvious example of a spoken English grammar pattern is the use of the word *though* at the end of a spoken clause. Traditional grammar books, which are designed for written language, teach that *though* is used exactly as *although*, which would mean that *though* would occur at the beginning of a dependent clause or as the connector between two clauses; for example, the website of ESL Lounge Student (http://www.esl-lounge.com/student/grammar-guides/grammar-advanced-5.php) offers this rule and two examples: "**Though** is used exactly as **although** is used. *Though it rained, we played tennis. OR We played tennis though it rained.*" However, I think most English speakers would find that these examples sound contrived and not normal. In spoken English, the word *though* appears at the end of an utterance and has a meaning more like *but* or *however*. These two examples from the website for Teaching ESL to Adults (http://www.esl-tutor.com/2007/06/using-though-at-end-of-sentence.html) sound much more natural: *He's a rotten husband. He's good to his children, though. . . . She drives too fast. She's never gotten a speeding ticket, though.*

McCarthy and Carter (1995) explain the differences between written and spoken English, as well as the problems of using written language to teach spoken language. They point out that written English has historically been viewed as "correct" English, whereas spoken English has been viewed as somehow corrupt, incorrect, or even vulgar. Their point is not to criticize the grammar commonly found in written English, such as the use of *whom* in the object position in a sentence (e.g., **Whom** *did you see?* vs. **Who** *did you see?*) but rather to make the point that we need to present our learners with various options in expressing an idea and that these options depend on many factors, including whether the learner is writing a formal academic paper or speaking informally to a peer or acquaintance.

Table 4.8 lists several features found only in spoken English (Timmis 2005). These features do not occur in written language and are perhaps therefore rarely, if ever, presented in any ESL book because most ESL/EFL books, even those supposedly teaching speaking or conversation, rely exclusively on written language as their basis. However, if we are teaching a speaking class or conversation class, then, yes, we need to take into account these grammar points that are in fact more

TABLE 4.8 Features of Spoken English (Timmis 2005)

Feature	Example
Heads	*Most of my high school friends, we used to do that.*
Tails	*They asked for more money, the workers.*
Ellipsis	*Want to go now?*
Flexible word order	*That was when you arrived, I think, wasn't it?*

common in spoken language. Once again, learners' needs should control the content of our courses.

These real language examples illustrate that grammar can vary between two genres such as academic writing (Hinkel 2013) and informal conversation (Timmis 2005). Therefore, ESL/EFL practitioners need to identify grammar points that are relevant to our students' proficiency level, mode of communication, and ultimate language goals. In the next section, we will look at a small action research study that can easily be replicated by any teacher who is interested in better matching learners' needs with the relevance of a given grammar point.

An Action Research Study of the Usefulness of Allocating Textbook Space and Instructional Time to the Future Perfect Tense

Since the verb is an essential part of all English sentences, one of the most common ESL/EFL grammar points to teach is how to use the appropriate verb tense. English has 12 verb tenses, so a vertical analysis of most grammar series will show 12 lessons for this general topic, with one lesson for each verb tense. However, the 12 verb tenses differ greatly in their frequency of use, so more attention should be given to some tenses while other tenses merit less attention—or perhaps no attention—in a grammar syllabus based on actual learner needs.

Which of the 12 verb tenses in English are the most frequent and which are the least frequent? To the best of this writer's knowledge, no study has determined a frequency ranking hierarchy of the 12 verb tenses in samples of written or spoken English. Some work has been done, however, comparing pairs of verb tenses. In their corpus study, Biber and Reppen (2002) found, for example, that the simple present tense occurs in conversation more than 20 times as often as the present progressive tense, thereby suggesting that teachers and materials developers teach simple present tense before present progressive tense.

An example of a verb tense that might not merit a dedicated lesson in a grammar book or conversation book is future perfect tense (Hinkel 2013). This tense consists of the modal *will* plus the auxiliary verb *have* plus the past participle form of the verb. Examples include *will have launched, will have been,* and *will have passed.* To determine the utility of teaching this tense, we need to determine its frequency in general English.

To extrapolate a rough idea of the relative frequency of the future perfect tense, I performed a simple search as part of an action research project (Burns 2015) regarding the word *will* using the Corpus for Contemporary American English (COCA) (Davies 2008–) and examined its usages there. This well established corpus consists of more than 450 million words from five different types of language: unscripted conversation, fiction, popular magazines, newspapers, and academic journals. Because of its size, range of search options, and free access, COCA is one of the most frequently used search tools for questions about current English usage.

TABLE 4.9 Frequency of Four Usages of the Word *Will* in a Random Sample from COCA

Usage of Will	Examples	Raw Count/500	Frequency Percentage of Will Usages
Simple future tense	*will become*	485	97.0%
Future progressive tense	*will be watching*	12	2.4%
Future perfect tense	*will have increased*	3	0.6%
Future perfect progressive tense	*will have been taking*	0	0.0%

The word *will* is the 33rd most common word in general English according to the General Service List (Bauman n.d.; Gilner 2011; West 1953). However, I now wanted to know how it is being used. How often is it part of future perfect tense?

In this simple example of action research, I carefully examined a randomly generated list of 500 examples of the word *will* in COCA without controlling for using the five different types of English housed in the corpus, i.e., the search involved what we might call general English. Table 4.9 clearly shows that the most common verb tense associated with the word *will* is simple future, e.g., *will become*. Future perfect tense examples are extremely rare (less than 1% of the usages of the word *will*) in actual usage, and classroom instructional time should reflect this limitation as well. In sum, ESL/EFL students will almost never encounter the future perfect tense, so why would a teacher spend limited and valuable classroom time on this tense?

Conclusion

In this chapter, we reviewed some of the important reasons to teach grammar, and we saw how the language needs of students, particularly their grammar needs, can vary tremendously according to the type of program and the students' goals. Because limited classroom time seems to be universal, teachers should determine which grammar points merit more and less instructional time, but their informed decisions should be solidly based on learner needs.

We also analyzed, both vertically and horizontally, a list of grammar points often covered in grammar books as well as conversation books. We found that despite differences in program settings and book publishers, there is great overlap in the list of grammar points covered in most ESL/EFL textbooks. We also saw that the grammar important for one skill may not be the same as that for other skills, e.g., academic writing vs. conversation/speaking.

Finally, we looked at the results of one simple action research project regarding the low relative frequency of the future perfect tense and concluded that this tense does not merit instructional time.

Research should use corpus linguistics analyses to examine the saliency and usefulness of many of the other grammar points commonly taught in ESL/EFL classes. For too long, we have blindly relied on publishers to tell us what we should teach when in fact teachers, curriculum writers, and materials developers should be making these decisions based on our learners' actual needs.

Sample Activities and/or Suggestions for Teaching

1. Have students conduct action research in which they determine the frequency of active voice, passive voice, and intransitive verbs in a 5,000-word sample from one subject area (e.g., history). Share the results in discussion groups.
2. Have students complete a vertical analysis of the grammar points taught in the grammar books used at the nearest ESL/EFL program.
3. Have students complete a horizontal analysis of the grammar points taught in two or three grammar books from different publishers but at the same proficiency level.
4. Have students compile an annotated bibliography of 15–20 articles related to the topic of this chapter.

Discussion Questions

1. Summarize the types of courses the author taught and how the students' language needs were varied. Discuss the language needs of students that you have taught. Can you come up with language needs that might be different from those discussed in this chapter?
2. What is the main message of this chapter for classroom teachers? How would prescriptive grammarians and descriptive grammarians disagree with the author's message?
3. Not including verb tenses, what are five grammar points that you think do not warrant much instructional time? Explain your choices. Offer a concrete plan for verifying one of your decisions using corpus linguistics.
4. What are some of the reasons a grammar series might include a review of verb tenses?

Essential Reading

Azar, B. (2007). Grammar-based teaching: A practitioner's perspective. *TESL-EJ, 11*(2). Available online at http://tesl-ej.org/ej42/a1.html

Biber, D. (1988). *Variation in speech and writing*. Cambridge: Cambridge University Press.

Ellis, R. (1998). Options in grammar teaching. *TESOL Quarterly, 32*(1), 39–60.

Ferris, D. (2011). *Treatment of error in second language student writing* (2nd ed.). Ann Arbor: University of Michigan Press.

Folse, K. (2009). *Keys to teaching grammar to English language learners: A practical handbook*. Ann Arbor: University of Michigan Press.

Hinkel, E. (2004). Tense, aspect and the passive voice in L1 and L2 academic texts. *Language Teaching Research, 8*(1), 5–29.

Hinkel, E. (2013). Research findings on teaching grammar for academic writing. *English Teaching, 68*(4), 3–21.

Tarone, E., Dwyer, S., Gillette, S., & Icke, V. (1998). On the use of the passive and active voice in astrophysics journal papers: With extensions to other languages and other fields. *English for Specific Purposes, 17*(1), 113–132.

Truscott, J. (1996). The case against grammar correction in L2 writing classes. *Language Learning, 46*(2), 327–369.

References

Azar, B. (2009). Foreword. In K. Folse (Ed.), *Keys to teaching grammar to English language learners: A practical handbook* (pp. v–vi). Ann Arbor: University of Michigan Press.

Bauman, J. (n.d.). *About the General Service List*. Available online at http://jbauman.com/aboutgsl.html

Benke, E., & Medgyes, P. (2005). Differences in teaching behaviour between native and nonnative speaker teachers: As seen by the learners. In E. Llurda (Ed.), *Nonnative language teachers: Perceptions, challenges and contributions to the profession* (pp. 195–215). New York: Springer.

Biber, D., & Reppen, R. (2002). What does frequency have to do with grammar teaching? *Studies in Second Language Acquisition, 24*, 199–208.

Burns, A. (2015). *Perspectives on action research*. Cambridge: Cambridge University Press.

Chase, B., Milner, M., & Johannsen, K. (2015). *World English 1* (2nd ed.). Boston: National Geographic Cengage Learning.

Chenoweth, A., Day, R., Chun, D., & Luppescu, S. (1983). Attitudes and preferences of ESL students to error correction. *Studies in Second Language Acquisition, 6*(1), 79–87.

Davies, M. (2008–). *The corpus of contemporary American English: 450 million words, 1990–present*. Available online at http://corpus.byu.edu/coca/

Elbaum, S. (2010). *Grammar in context* (5th ed.). Boston: National Geographic Cengage Learning.

Ferris, D. (2011). *Treatment of error in second language student writing* (2nd ed.). Ann Arbor: University of Michigan Press.

Folse, K. (2004). *Vocabulary myths: Applying second language research to classroom teaching*. Ann Arbor: University of Michigan Press.

Folse, K. (2009). *Keys to teaching grammar to English language learners: A practical handbook*. Ann Arbor: University of Michigan Press.

Folse, K. (2010). *Clear grammar, Book 1* (2nd ed.). Ann Arbor: University of Michigan Press.

Folse, K. (2012). *Clear grammar, Book 2* (2nd ed.). Ann Arbor: University of Michigan Press.

Folse, K. (2014a). *Clear grammar, Book 3* (2nd ed.). Ann Arbor: University of Michigan Press.

Folse, K. (2014b). *Clear grammar, Book 4* (2nd ed.). Ann Arbor: University of Michigan Press.

Gilner, L. (2011). A primer on the General Service List. *Reading in a Foreign Language, 23*(1), 65–83.

Han, S.-A. (2005). Good teachers know where to scratch when learners feel itchy: Korean learners' views of native-speaking teachers of English. *Australian Journal of Education, 49*, 197–213.

Hinkel, E. (2013). Research findings on teaching grammar for academic writing. *English Teaching, 68*(4), 3–21.

Leki, I. (1991). The preferences of ESL students for error correction in college-level writing classes. *Foreign Language Annals, 24*(3), 203–218.

Leow, R. P. (2013). Schmidt's Noticing Hypothesis: More than two decades after. In *Noticing and second language acquisition: Studies in honor of Richard Schmidt* (pp. 11–23). Manoa: National Foreign Language Center, University of Hawai'i at Manoa.

McCarthy, M., & Carter, R. (1995). Spoken grammar: What is it and how can we teach it? *ELT Journal, 49*(3), 207–218.

Schmidt, R. (1990). The role of consciousness in second language learning. *Applied Linguistics, 11*(2), 129–158.

Schmidt, R. (1993). Awareness and second language acquisition. *Annual Review of Applied Linguistics, 13*, 206–226.

Schmidt, R., & Frota, S. (1986). Developing basic conversational ability in a second language: A case study of an adult learner of Portuguese. In R. R. Day (Ed.), *Talking to learn: Conversation in second language acquisition* (pp. 237–322). Rowley, MA: Newbury House.

Selinker, L. (1972). Interlanguage. *International Review of Applied Linguistics, 10*, 209–231.

Timmis, I. (2005). Towards a framework for teaching spoken grammar. *ELT Journal, 59*(2), 117–125.

Truscott, J. (1996). The case against grammar correction in L2 writing classes. *Language Learning, 46*(2), 327–369.

Ur, P. (2011). Grammar teaching: Research, theory, and practice. In E. Hinkel (Ed.), *Handbook of research in second language teaching and learning* (Vol. 2, pp. 507–522). New York: Routledge.

Walkinshaw, I., & Oanh, D. (2014). Native and non-native English language teachers: Student perceptions in Vietnam and Japan. *SAGE Open.* doi: 10.1177/2158244014534451

West, M. 1953. *A general service list of English words.* London: Longman, Green and Co.

5

FUNCTIONAL APPROACHES TO TEACHING GRAMMAR IN THE SECOND LANGUAGE CLASSROOM

Anne Burns

Introduction

English language teachers all over the world grapple with the challenge of teaching grammar, including the questions of whether to teach it and how it should be taught. One of the reasons is that many different approaches to teaching grammar have been proposed over time, and each brings with it a particular perspective on what grammar teaching involves. These perspectives range from arguing for various effective approaches for incorporating grammar to avoiding the teaching of grammar at all (e.g. Krashen 1981; Prabhu 1987). Krashen distinguished between 'acquisition' and 'learning' and argued that language acquisition takes place through exposure to comprehensible input. This argument implied that language proficiency is acquired naturally and that as long as teachers provide the necessary input, acquisition would inevitably follow. Prabhu recommended a 'strong' version of communicative language teaching, asserting that it was only by communicating that learning could take place. Both of these positions questioned the need for grammar teaching and error correction—and even discouraged it.

Over the years, this "zero option" view (Ellis 1994: 653) of grammar teaching has been overtaken by research showing conclusively that the teaching of grammar has a positive effect on language development (e.g. Ellis 2006; Norris and Ortega 2000). As a result language teaching has, as Larsen-Freeman (2003: 20) aptly puts it, moved away from the questionable position that:

> [w]hat works well in the natural environment is what should be adhered to in the language classroom. The assumption is that it is our job to create the natural conditions of acquisition present in the external environment . . . [I]nstead what we want to do as a language teacher is . . . to improve upon natural acquisition, not emulate it . . . [and to] accelerate natural learning.

Teachers still, however, face many possibilities and dilemmas when adopting an approach to grammar instruction. Two major types of grammatical focus have been shown to have a positive effect on language learning. The first, Focus on Form (sometimes referred to as FonF) "involves briefly drawing students' attention to linguistic elements in context as they arise incidentally in lessons whose overriding focus is on meaning or communication", which means that grammar could be taught during an activity or reactively after the activity or both (Long 2000: 185). In this approach, the teacher would be likely to identify particular items that are causing problems for the learners. Focus on FormS (or FonFS), on the other hand, is a more traditional approach that involves teaching preselected linguistic items that are sequenced and introduced through structured activities, such as drills, pattern practice and opportunities to practise these forms. In this approach, teaching would be more likely to be organized around a grammar-based syllabus that means working from grammar structures to grammar use, with activities or tasks being inserted from time to time to promote practice.

Against this background of recent debates on grammar acquisition, the discussion in this chapter takes a functional approach to the teaching of grammar. It sees grammar in language learning as primarily concerned with social interaction and the creation of meaning. In order to situate this approach within other concepts about grammar and grammar teaching, I first provide a brief account of different perspectives that have influenced language teaching.

Formal and Functional Approaches to Grammar and Grammar Teaching

Over time, two major perspectives on the teaching of grammar relate to seeing grammar in either formal (prescriptive) or functional (descriptive) terms.

A *formal (logical) approach* to grammar goes back as far as Aristotle, who "saw language as a set of constituent classes: syllables, affixes, articles, nouns, verb conjunctions and so on, with rules for their combinations" (Derewianka 2001: 243). Later grammarians, such as Ben Johnson, began to codify, or formalize the grammar of English based on descriptions of classical Latin and Greek that were available only in written form, and established a tradition of scholarly grammars of English by linguists such as Jespersen and Sweet that has lasted to the present time. Approaches to teaching grammar for language learning based on formal perspectives (which are still alive and well today in classrooms all over the world) are therefore concerned with language as a system of rules, that can be separately identified and taught in a predictable sequence. 'Grammar translation' and 'structural' approaches (Bloomfield 1933; Fries 1945) adopt a strong concern for accuracy, error correction and language analysis. While grammar translation focused on written sentence-level grammar, structural grammar incorporated an interest in promoting oral production. It focused on pattern practice, which was believed, given enough reiteration, to lead eventually to fluent language production habits.

A grammar translation approach is the way I remember learning French as a foreign language at high school. The teacher would use a textbook in which each lesson was presented in a fixed format that would consist of:

- Grammar: Presentation of new grammar structures and revision of those introduced in a previous lesson.
- 'Lecture': A short reading passage in French containing many examples of the new items and revised items.
- Exercises: A series of exercises including (a) comprehension questions related to the 'lecture', (b) practice of the grammar by manipulating different items, (c) translation of individual sentences from English to French or vice versa.
- Vocabulary: Lists of vocabulary items presented for revision or preparation for the next lesson.

There were also some signs of the influence of structural grammar in these lessons, however, as there was sometimes an attempt to encourage 'free writing' or to engage students in thinking about how to construct a short and familiar interaction, such as the following:

> Compose a little shopping scene. A boy (or a girl) comes into a shop to buy some article. The child and the shopkeeper have the usual sort of conversation:
> Jean: *Bonjour, Monsieur.* [Good morning, sir.]
> Le Marchand: *Bonjour, mon petit, qu'est-ce que vous desirez?* [And so on . . .]
> [Good morning, my dear, what would you like?]

These kinds of approaches were underpinned by a 'building block' view, which saw language learning as a linear process of acquiring one structure after another, based on repetition and habit formation. From the 1960s, Chomsky's concept of transformational-generative grammar confronted these assumptions:

> It seems to me impossible to accept the view that language behavior is a matter of habit, that it is slowly acquired by reinforcement, association and generalization.
>
> *(Chomsky 1966: 43)*

He proposed a distinction between competence (the innate ability of humans to acquire the language they speak by drawing on universal language rules) and performance (the language actually produced by a speaker). Chomsky's interest was in competence, the underlying mental systems used by an 'idealized' native speaker to generate language structures. Performance was viewed as "somewhat degenerate and untidy when compared with the idealised competence" (Derewianka 2001: 251). His views represented a major challenge to structuralist theories that language consisted of observable surface structures. Chomsky claimed that, rather than rehearsing language structures, acquisition involved "language in use", an active creative process of drawing on innate rules to generate language production. Chomsky's ideas, however, did not translate easily into language teaching, and in fact he himself claimed they did not have relevance to language programs. Their value lay in seeing the language learner as an active generator of hypotheses about language use rather than an absorber of grammatical structures, and they also promoted the concept that errors were a positive indication that hypothesizing about how language works was taking place.

In the middle of the twentieth century, however, further strands of thinking emerged, based on the idea that language use was a form of social action. Hymes argued that:

> [t]here are rules of use without which the rules of grammar would be useless.
>
> *(Hymes 1971: 278)*

Hymes coupled the notion of 'communicative' with 'competence', arguing that if speakers are to use language effectively, grammatical knowledge needed to be complemented by other kinds of knowledge like the communicative setting, the participants, purposes, channel of communication and topics. Canale (1981) outlined Hymes's notion of communicative competence as including sociolinguistic competence (knowing how to express meaning appropriate to purpose, audience and context), discourse competence (selecting, sequencing and managing language to express meaning effectively), strategic competence (using strategies to compensate for breakdown in communication), as well as linguistic competence (using grammar correctly to express one's message). A major shift that emerged from these arguments was to change the emphasis in instructional situations from teaching grammatical structure to teaching communicative skills, a shift that also led to further developments in considering the backgrounds and profiles of learners, their language learning needs, their purposes for learning and the kinds of interactions they wished to engage in. A major outcome of this shift in thinking was the emergence of communicative language teaching with its interest in grammar as it relates to use through discourse and text, in other words the functional uses of authentic language. This change in orientation placed greater emphasis on descriptive grammars that could illuminate how language is actually used in naturalistic written and spoken communication. As Celce-Murcia (1990: 146) expressed it, what was required was "an interactive model of grammar and discourse, one that demonstrates the necessity and importance of both levels of language to the language learning process and to the attainment of communicative competence".

Systemic Functional Linguistics: A Social Theory of Grammar

One such functional approach to grammar is systemic functional grammar (Halliday 1978, 1994). Halliday conceives of language as a social semiotic (a meaning-making system that is socially motivated). The model of grammar he developed focuses on the relationships between the social purposes for which people use language and the grammatical resources of their linguistic repertoire, on which they draw to communicate. His description of language consists of three *metafunctions* through which different kinds of meanings are created:

- *Ideational* metafunction: Language to create meaning about experiences of the world (personal, workplace, imaginative and so on).
- *Interpersonal* metafunction: Language to express relationships with others (novice, expert, friend, spouse and so on).
- *Textual* metafunction: Language to construct cohesive and coherent stretches of spoken and written text appropriate to the purpose and context.

The notion of text in a functional approach relates to "any stretch of language which is held together cohesively through meaning" (Feez 1998: 4) and which has a particular social purpose in a particular context. A complete text can consist of single words, such as *Hi!* (spoken in passing to an acquaintance) or *Exit* in a shopping centre or railway station, or it can consist of lengthy interactions, such as an extensive casual conversation, or a political speech, or extended pieces of writing such as a romantic novel or a workplace memo. A functional approach examines how speakers convey meaning through extended discourse rather than through single utterances or sentences, which have tended to be a common unit of analysis in many grammar classes. In a functional approach, teachers and learners can analyze the structure, organization and development of texts more systematically using different aspects of the grammar.

Systemic functional approaches explain language in terms of a system of choices, rather than as a set of structures. In other words, SFL is interested in the *potential* of the language system to create meaning in a particular social context. The choices made will vary across different strata or levels of the language: semantic (meaning), syntactic (lexico-grammatical features—vocabulary, grammar and morphology) and phonological (sounds and symbols that convey language). The way in which language users make choices from their repertoire of potential language use depends on a set of *register variables*—the dimensions of a context that combine to create meaning for different purposes and audiences and through different modes of communication. The register variables are described by Eggins (2004: 90) as:

- Field: What the language is being used to talk about (the topic/concepts).
- Tenor: The role the language is playing between the interactants (relationships/status).
- Mode: The role the language is playing in the interaction (spoken/written).

TABLE 5.1 Grammatical Sources for Field

Verbs (processes)	• Action (*pick up, walk*)
	• Relating (*be, have*)
	• Thinking (*reflect on, think about*)
	• Communicating (*whisper, disagree*)
	• Feeling (*calm down, buck up*)
Nouns and nominal groups (participants)	• Noun (*house*)
	• Nominal group (*the nice old house*)
Prepositional and adverbial phrases (circumstances)	• Circumstance of time (*on Monday*)
	• Circumstance of place (*at the movies*)
	• Circumstance of manner (*untidily*)

TABLE 5.2 Grammatical Sources for Tenor

Type of clause	• Declarative (*I'd like a cup of coffee.*)
	• Interrogative (*Can I have a cup of coffee?*)
	• Imperative (*Give me a cup of coffee.*)
Modality (expressions of low to high probability or tentativeness)	• Verbs (*I might go. I will go*)
	• Adverbs (*I'll possibly go. I'll definitely go*)
	• Nouns (*There's a chance I'll go. There's a certainty I'll go.*)
	• Adjectives (*It's unlikely I'll go. It's definite that I'll go.*)

TABLE 5.3 Grammatical Sources for Mode

Thematic structure of the clause (the starting point of the message)	• Theme (the starting point of the message—given information: *On Thursday . . .*)
	• Rheme (the rest of the message—new information: *we went to the movies.*)
Links between parts of text	• Conjunctions (*and, but, so*)
	• Pronouns (*I, we, them*)

Grammatically, each of these three variables is reflected through different sources in the language. Field is indicated in choices of content that reflect the topic. Grammatical items include those shown in Table 5.1. The grammar of tenor—how writers and speakers negotiate the interpersonal aspects of a text—is created by the grammatical features shown in Table 5.2. Finally, mode is reflected grammatically in the elements shown in Table 5.3.

Register and Grammar

In the following texts, the topic of communication is the same—an invitation to a birthday party. But consider how the register varies according to the different purposes and audiences the producers of the text have in mind, as well as the distance from the receivers of the text in time and space:

Text 1

Hi gorgeous, Remember! my birthday's on 12th. fancy coming over to my place for a bite to eat? A x

Text 2

Hi Linda, I'm wondering if you received the invitation for my birthday party on 12 June? If you would like to join us for lunch you'd be most welcome. Hope to see you then. Anne

Text 3

Dear family and friends
    You are cordially invited to attend a luncheon party in honour of Anne's birthday on 12th June, 2015. It will commence at 12:30 at 16 Frances St, Bingham. Please RSVP by 5 May, 2015 for catering purposes. We very much look forward to seeing you on the day.

We can see that across the texts, the relationships between the participants varies from a very personal, close and possibly intimate contact in Text 1 to more distant, formal and generic contacts in Texts 2 and 3. Text 1 suggests communication between very close friends or perhaps romantic partners, while Text 2 implies a relationship between less close acquaintances or perhaps work colleagues. Text 3 addresses a general audience that incorporates relationships that are possibly close or more distant and therefore must send a general message that includes different levels of social contact. These sets of relationships affect the way the writers of the text make selections from the lexico-grammatical resources they have at their disposal in order to create the meaning. Text 1 uses very informal lexis to construct the message, addressing the receiver as *gorgeous*, issuing a direct command (*Remember!*), referring to a known location (*my place*), making assumptions about shared knowledge (*the 12*th) and using an informal and formulaic expression to express the activity they will share (*a bite to eat*).

The lexico-grammar of Text 2 reflects the more formal relationship between Linda and Anne. Because the writer cannot assume the same level of familiarity as in Text 1, the reminder of the event is hedged through a polite expression of modality (*I'm wondering if . . .*), and the event is spelled out explicitly (*my birthday on 12 June*). The writer uses the modal form *would*, conveying the message that the receiver has a choice whether to act on the invitation. Text 3 opens with a speech act of invitation (*you are cordially invited*), expressing a generalized message to a group of people, with other 'prestige' choices of lexis such as *attend*, *luncheon party*, *in honour of*, *commence*, *for catering purposes* being selected to suggest a formal occasion. Drawing language learners' attention to the notion of register can help them to understand how register variation in their linguistic choices is related to what is culturally and socially relevant in different textual contexts.

Another notable aspect of these three texts is the mode of communication. Although all three texts are written—we can imagine the first being a text message, the second an email and the third a formal written invitation—the first is distinctly 'spoken-like' in style, while the second and third are more 'written-like'. Taking the idea of mode further, we can consider in more detail the differences between spoken and written language that can be taken into account when teaching grammar for speaking and listening or reading and writing.

Relationships Between Spoken and Written Language

Halliday (1985: 45) notes that although spoken and written language are related to each other, "the kinds of meanings that are transmitted in writing tend to be somewhat different from the kinds of meanings transmitted in speech". Having a sense of what these differences are, and therefore where it is important to assist students with different kinds of grammar knowledge, is valuable information for language teachers. Broadly speaking, speech and writing typically serve different social purposes and are intended for different kinds of audiences. Speakers and writers draw on a common repertoire of linguistic resources but use them in different ways. To illustrate some of the differences typical of speech and writing, compare the following texts. Both texts deal with the same topic—the experience of studying in a master's course through distance learning. In Text 4, the speaker is describing her experience to some of her colleagues.

Text 4

I was working in Turkey at the time. . . um I was lucky enough to have one of my colleagues doing the same program . . . started at the same time as me so we . . . er . . . used to get together regularly. . .um sometimes as often as twice a week and would get together and compare our findings and . . . er because our learning styles were different as well, we, well we compensated for one another . . . .

Text 5 expresses the same information in a written version.

Text 5

I was then employed in Turkey where, fortunately I was able to collaborate with a colleague who commenced the program simultaneously. We held regular weekly meetings to compare findings. Because our learning styles were different, we complemented each other.

TABLE 5.4 Spoken and Written Language: Typical Features

Spoken Language	Written Language
Basic unit is the clause (*utterance*).	Basic unit is the sentence.
Clauses are linked by conjunction (*and, but, so* etc.) to build the text.	Clauses are linked by subordination (*who, which, when* etc.) to build the text.
Frequent use of formulaic chunks (*I was lucky enough*)	Little use of formulaic language
Informal language preferred (*we used to get together*)	Formal language preferred (*commenced*)
Range of noticeable performance effects (hesitations, pauses, repeats, false starts, incompletion) (*er . . . um . . . we, well we*)	Few/no noticeable performance effects
Frequent use of ellipsis (omission of grammatical elements, *started at the same time*)	Little use of ellipsis
Frequent use of personal pronouns (*I, we*)	Little use of personal pronouns

There are some noticeable differences in the way that the lexis and grammar 'package' the meaning in these two texts. Speakers must generally construct speech spontaneously in 'real time' and therefore their utterances show particular patternings of language use that are different from written texts. Table 5.4 summarizes some of the key differences between spoken and written language and illustrates them from Texts 4 and 5. It needs to be stressed, however, that these differences *typify* the differences; speech and writing may be more or less spoken-like or written-like depending on the sociocultural context, the topic, the relationships between speaker/writer and listener/reader and the distance in time and space from the phenomena, events or actions that are the focus of meaning.

The Mode Continuum

A useful way of thinking about the relationships and differences in the way grammar and lexis vary across texts is the idea of a spoken and written continuum (Figure 5.1).

Most spoken   **Most written**
(Language accompanying action)   (Language as reflection)

FIGURE 5.1 Spoken and Written Continuum (Hammond et al. 1992)

Language accompanying action occurs where interaction is immediate and there is the least physical distance between the participants in the communication, such as in watching sports, sharing games, constructing something. This kind of language is highly context-dependent. Here is an example of this kind of interaction, where the speakers are in the kitchen doing some cooking together (all texts adapted from Hood et al. 1996; see also Feez 1998).

Text 6

S1: That's OK.
S2: OK, how much?
S1: All of it, the lot . . . the whole lot
S2: Like err . . . this?
S1: Yeah, now just work it in . . . softly . . . softly . . . not too fast . . . or it won't work.

We can see that this spoken text is made up of rapid speaker turns, where there are questions, responses and feedback. The speakers rely on the social and physical context and their relationships within that context to make the language meaningful. They do not need to explicitly refer to different things or items in the context as it is obvious to them what they are. Therefore, there are inexplicit references, such as *that*, *it* and *this,* to the physical actions and items. The speakers use incomplete clauses, and there are repetitions, hesitations and everyday colloquial expressions, like *the lot*. Moving along the continuum might mean encountering a text more like this next one.

Text 7

Add seasoning and briskly beat the mixture. Beat the egg whites until they hold firm peaks. Fold them into the mixture. Pour it into a buttered souffle dish.

Text 7 is clearly a recipe, a written text typically found in cookery instructions. However, in this text, the objects in the process are explicitly referenced, *seasoning*, *mixture, peaks* and so on. Because this is a procedure or instructional text, the verbs clauses are imperative, for example, *beat, fold*, to indicate the processes that must be carried out. The key messages are linked together by conjunctions, *and*, *until*. Moving even further towards the written end of the continuum, we might encounter a text such as this:

Text 8

The addition of the beaten egg whites provides the necessary aeration to enable the souffle to rise.

Here, we see a much more formal and technical text whose purpose is an explanation of the cooking process aimed at a specialist or professional audience. Rather than being presented as verbs in imperative form, the actions are transposed into nouns—or *nominalized*—which creates more prestige, technical and formal language, *addition, aeration*. The messages expressed in the text are linked through verbs rather than conjunctions, *provides, to enable*.

Of course, there is no clear dividing line between texts that are spoken and those that are written, as the dashed lines in Figure 5.1 indicate. For example, a political speech or a news item may be spoken but is very likely to have been prepared as a written text rather than produced spontaneously. Alternatively, a text message might be created through writing but could be more typical of something that is spoken or created 'on the run' as in Text 4. However, the concept of the mode continuum is useful in grammar instruction as teachers can use it to identify where different forms of language production may be required from their students. For example, teachers could begin with the concrete language used to undertake an action or describe a situation. They can then help students to shift the grammar along the continuum towards creating the more abstract texts that are important in academic writing. Working on reference and nominalization are two areas, for example, where a teacher could assist students in improving texts.

Reference

When students are practising texts about events or people that are distant in time or space from the immediate context, it is important to ensure that they have the vocabulary to label these items fully (e.g. *egg whites, mixture*). They also need to then know how to refer back to these items by using pronouns (*them, it*). By practising the use of reference they can begin to learn to link parts of the text together to create a cohesive whole.

Nominalization

Nominal groups—for example, *the addition of the beaten egg whites, the necessary aeration* from Text 8—represent actions, not through verbs, but as things through noun phrases. In spontaneous speech, it is more likely that these actions would have been constructed as verbs, that is, *add* and *aerate*. Halliday (1994) refers to this process of expressing actions as nouns as nominalization. Once actions have been expressed as nouns, the speaker or writer can manipulate the meaning. First, the noun group can be expanded to make the expression of meaning more intricate and complex: *the timely addition of the fluffy beaten egg whites; the timely and prompt addition of the fluffy lightly beaten egg whites* and so on. Second, the people doing the action can be removed from it: *the necessary aeration* does not identify who is doing the aerating.

The Concept of Genre

Martin (2001: 155) defines genre as a "staged, goal-oriented social process":

* Staged in that there are recognizable stages in the unfolding of texts.
* Goal-oriented in that texts have the goal of creating meaning.
* Social in that texts are created to achieve a social purpose.

In other words, genres are typical configurations or arrangements of text patterns that emerge (and change) over time in a cultural/social context. They are socially purposeful and created in order to achieve particular types of meaning (that is, they are functional in that context). For language teachers, understanding the notion of genre, particularly the genres that are commonly used in academic contexts, can provide a basis for program planning. The following two written texts are about New Year celebrations in Australia and in Vietnam. As you read the texts, think about the ways that they differ and how the lexico-grammar is used to construct the different stages of the text.

Text 9

On New Year's Eve my flatmates and I decided to go to the city to watch the fireworks. We caught the train at about 3 o'clock in the afternoon because we wanted to get a good spot under the Harbour Bridge. We took our picnic basket filled with enough food to get us through to twelve o'clock.

It was beautiful watching the night move in over the harbour and everyone was feeling very festive. At midnight the fireworks started and they were fantastic. Balls of light burst over the water and at the end a rain of white light fell from the bridge.

It took us so long to get home that we thought we might stay in a hotel next year and go home the following day.

Text 10

Tet is the Vietnamese New Year. It is an important festival in Vietnam. It is celebrated during the full moon which can be any time from late January to mid-February.

The Vietnamese from all over the country return to their parents' home bringing food and gifts. During Tet the people are expected to repay debts, correct mistakes and remember their ancestors. It is a mixed time of happiness and noise and seriousness and quiet.

People put peach blossom in their homes and decorate the rooms with coloured paper. They cook sticky rice and make cakes. Fireworks light up the sky every night between the old year and the New Year and people visit the temples. Tet is a time for people to remember the past and enjoy the present.

(de Silva Joyce and Burns 1999: 83)

Text 9 is in the form of a *recount* of personal experience of the events and the writer's reaction to them. Its structure and grammar differ in various ways from Text 10, which is a *report* of the generalized nature of people's experience within a particular culture (Table 5.5).

The notion of genre not only sheds light on typical grammatical patterns in different types of texts. It also highlights how genres have recognizable ways of unfolding—their generic structure—and that different stages in the text exhibit different grammatical patterns. In Table 5.6, which shows the generic structure of a recount and a report, the symbol ^ means 'is followed by', and an element enclosed in parentheses () indicates that it is optional in the structure.

TABLE 5.5 Grammatical Features of Texts 9 and 10 (de Silva Joyce and Burns 1999: 84)

Recount	Report
Text opens with an orientation to the event, including: • Prepositional phrase (circumstance) of time *On New Year's Eve.* • Prepositional phrase (circumstance) of place *into the city.*	Text opens with a general classification statement, including: • Relational verb (relational process) *Tet is the Vietnamese New Year.*
Text uses past tense: • To refer to previous personal experience.	Text uses present tense: • To refer to habitual social experience.
We caught the train at about 3 o'clock in the afternoon because we wanted to get a good spot . . .	*People put peach blossom in their homes and decorate the rooms with coloured paper. They cook sticky rice and make cakes.*
Action verbs (material processes) dominate: *Balls of light burst over the water and at the end a rain of white light fell from the bridge.*	Linking verbs (relational processes) dominate: *Tet is the Vietnamese New Year. It is an important festival in Vietnam.*
Noun groups refer to specific people: *my flatmates and I.*	Noun groups refer to general categories of people: *During Tet the people are expected to repay debts, correct mistakes and remember their ancestors.*

TABLE 5.6 Generic Structure for Recount and Report (adapted from Macken-Horarik 2002: 21)

Genre	Purpose	Generic Structure	Description of Stages
Recount	Retells events in a temporal sequence to inform or entertain	Orientation^Record of events^(Reorientation)	Orientation: Information about situation (who, what, why, where, when) Record of events: Events in time sequence Reorientation: Events brought back to present
Report	Describes recurrent natural, social, environmental situations by classifying them and describing their characteristics	General statement/ classification^Description of aspects^Description of activities	General statement: Information about topic Description of aspect: Lists/elaborates qualities or features Description of activities: Describes behaviours/ functions/uses

The Teaching-Learning Cycle

Cummins and Man (2006: 807) argue that:

> [t]o develop proficiency in academic English, students need systematic scaffolding and instruction to deal with longer texts, structurally more complex sentences, more subject specific new vocabulary, less visual material and more creative and critical higher order thinking skills.

In order to provide such systematic scaffolding in the teaching of texts, a teaching-learning cycle is often used in a genre-based and functional approach to teaching grammar. The cycle aims to scaffold and support learning through various stages as learners work towards understanding and producing a particular spoken or written text. In this cycle, texts are explored in terms of their social and cultural, as well as their functional and linguistic, purposes. The classroom talk that occurs between teacher and learners is a crucial aspect of: (1) building knowledge, skills and understanding; (2) learning the language needed to successfully control the text; (3) learning about the language and how it works in the text.

The cycle outlined in Figure 5.2 (Hammond et al. 1992) is one that was adapted from earlier work by Callaghan and Rothery (1988). The cycle consists of four interrelated phases that progressively build towards a knowledge base that allows learners to gain greater control of the target text type or genre.

Building Knowledge of the Field involves exploring and developing cultural knowledge in relation to the text. This could mean making cultural comparisons

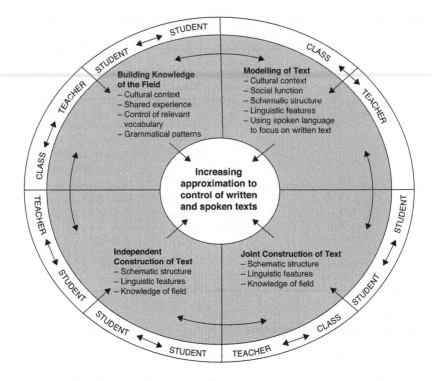

FIGURE 5.2 The Teaching-Learning Cycle

of texts; developing knowledge of key contexts where such texts are produced; understanding their purposes within those contexts; considering the kinds of relationships that might be involved between those who use the texts; researching information on the content; and developing key language skills (e.g. vocabulary) required to produce and negotiate the target texts. The *Modelling of Text* stage involves the teacher in providing sample texts of the target genre so that learners can build up knowledge of their purpose in the cultural and social context, the generic structure and text staging, the key vocabulary and the patterns of the grammatical structures.

At the *Joint Construction of Text* stage, the teacher spends time working collaboratively in the classroom with the learners to co-construct a text related to the target genre. This stage typically involves drawing on the learners' new knowledge of text models to help them to construct a similar text. It is also a stage where teachers might diagnose what further work needs to be done to consolidate the language skills learners need to have in order to manage the text. The final stage, *Independent Construction of Text*, occurs when learners reach a point where they have enough knowledge to work independently on construction of the text. In a spoken text, it means being able to take up appropriate roles as a speaker and/or listener, to handle the vocabulary and grammatical structures required to produce the text and to facilitate the flow of the text by using effective discourse strategies such as turn-taking, backchanneling, clarification requests and other features that prevent breakdown of communication.

The model is cyclical in nature, which means that it is not meant to be used in a lockstep sequence but as a conceptual framework for planning the processes of genre-based pedagogy. Potentially, teachers could begin a unit of work on a particular genre at any point in the cycle. For example, asking intermediate learners to first construct a text independently can be a form of needs analysis that allows teachers to diagnose how well learners can already manage a text or what areas the teacher needs to explicitly teach. The key to using the cycle is to see it not as a prescriptive teaching approach but more as a means of scaffolded guidance and support for learning that will lead to successful achievements for learners.

Putting the Teaching-Learning Cycle into Action: A Practical Example

To provide an example of how a teacher could work with the idea of genre, text and grammar and use the teaching-learning cycle, consider the following text written by a low-intermediate-level adult ESL student (de Silva Joyce and Burns 1999: 118). The student's aim was to write a letter of complaint to a real estate agent asking for a problem to be fixed in their house. The teacher began the cycle by asking the students in her class to compose the letter using their existing language knowledge. In this way she could begin by diagnosing where they were in their grammatical knowledge of the text and how able they were to create the text by themselves.

Text 11: Independent Construction

Dear Mr _____

I don't know how many time I should inform 'this' to you. 'This' is '*something wrong*' on the roof of my rent bathroom and rent flat it on _____Avenue. Tilp 99999999.

Last night from 2 am until writing this letter (morning) again water still drift flow through that roof.

Yours_____

We can see that the text produced by the student shows that he has not fully achieved the goal of producing a letter of complaint. In some ways, he manages to give a clear picture of the problem in his flat, and he expresses his frustration with the situation by underlining parts of the letter. His spelling skills are also quite well developed. However, he does not have the appropriate control of grammar and vocabulary or adequate knowledge of interpersonal resources in the grammar to be able to express his message clearly enough that it will be taken seriously. The letter revealed to the teacher that the student did not have good knowledge of the generic structure of a letter of complaint, of how to format such a letter in English and of the relevant grammar and vocabulary. The teacher decided to *build knowledge of the field* in relation to the purpose, audience, language and structural features by discussing the following questions with the students (adapted from Paltridge 2001):

- For what purpose is this kind of text written?
- Who would write this type of text?
- What is the text meant to be about?
- What is the setting or context of the text?
- Who is the intended audience?
- What is the relationship between the writer and the audience?
- Who is likely to read this text?
- What sort of information would the reader expect to find in the text in order to deal with the problem?

Having raised the students' awareness of the social purpose and context for writing such a text, the teacher then decided to show the students a *model* text of a letter of complaint, such as the following one (Hammond et al. 1992):

Text 12

25 Brighton Boulevard
Leasington, NSW 2066

29th November

The Manager
Streetwood Homes
21 Scott Street
Leasington, NSW 2066

Dear Sir/Madam

I am writing about the stove in my flat. Two elements aren't working and it is very difficult for me to cook a meal.

I have twice reported this problem to you (10th November and 24th November) and nothing has been done about it.

This problem is urgent and I would appreciate it if you could arrange to have the stove fixed immediately.

Yours sincerely

TABLE 5.7 Generic Structure and Grammatical Patterns of a Letter of Complaint

Address/date	25 Brighton Boulevard Leasington, NSW 20662 9th November The Manager Streetwood Homes 21 Scott Street Leasington, NSW 2066	Reference to specific participants
Salutation	Dear Sir/Madam	Formulaic expression for correspondence
Identification of complaint	I am writing about the stove in my flat. Two elements aren't working and it is very difficult for me to cook a meal.	• Reference to specific participants, items and actions • Use of present tense
Justification of complaint	I have twice reported this problem to you (10th November and 24th November) and nothing has been done about it.	• Reference to specific participants, items and actions • Use of present perfect tense
Demand for action	This problem is urgent and I would appreciate it if you could arrange to have the stove fixed immediately.	• Reference to specific participants • Use of modality and politeness marker
Signature	Yours sincerely	Formulaic expression for correspondence

The teacher then worked with the students to analyse the generic structure of the text and the grammatical features (Table 5.7) and provided various activities for the students to practise them.

In the next stage of the cycle, *joint construction*, the teacher asked the students to form groups and to select their own problem to focus on in their joint letter of complaint. She then asked the groups to share their letters with the class so that they could receive feedback from her and the rest of the students. Here is part of the discussion that emerged at this stage.

Text 13

Teacher:	Now a lot of you have written your letter. So let's just see what you wrote. You started with . . .
Steven:	Dear Sir
Chen:	Or Madam
Teacher:	Alright Dear Sir/Madam. Now Sara's group wrote a good letter. How did you start Sara?
Sara:	I'm writing about a broken window in my flat.

Teacher:	All right, that's enough to start with. (Writes Sara's sentence on the board.) All right, that's the first part. Now what did you say next?
Sara:	Could you please?
Teacher:	Could you please?
Sara:	Get someone to fix it
Teacher:	To fix it?
Students:	Immediately . . . as soon as possible . . .
Teacher:	As soon as possible, or immediately. Did you say because . . . ?
Sara:	Because I am afraid . . .
Tony:	Because it is cold . . .
Teacher:	All right, so there are lots of reasons. Because the flat is cold or because I am worried about . . .
Sara:	About someone coming in
Teacher:	About burglars
Sara:	Yeah, burglars

After the text was concluded through this kind of discussion and joint creation, the students entered the *independent construction* stage of the cycle. The teacher showed the students a picture of a leaking sink under which was the statement, "The plumber came to fix the sink but it is still leaking". She asked the students to write their own letters setting out this problem and requesting it to be resolved. Since the students had by now received quite extensive scaffolding through the discussion of the context and purpose of the text, as well as the modelling and joint construction conducted in class, they were in a much better position to achieve a more successful outcome. Here is an example of a letter produced by the same student who had written Text 11.

Text 14

The Manager
41 Tumbarumba Crescent
Interdel Realty
Heckenburg, 2168
21 Scott St
Liverpool
30–11

Dear Sir/Madam
    I am writing about my sink. The plumber fixed it and now it is leaking again.
    The problem is urgent and I would appreciate it if you would arrange to have the sink fixed immediately because the water is overflowing.
    Yours sincerely

This cycle of work dealt with an issue that was of concern to these adult students. As the teacher moved through the cycle, she drew on a range of activities and tasks, all the time keeping the goal and outcome of the lesson in mind. Some of the activities had a strong teacher focus where she led the lesson and the discussion; at other points, she stepped back, and the lesson became more student-centered. The tasks she selected aimed to build up the students' knowledge of purpose, context, genre and grammar and to provide support for the students as they increased their knowledge. Her ultimate goal was to provide enough support for the students to work independently. She used the teaching-learning cycle as a flexible framework to organize the sequence of the activities so that she could reach this goal.

Conclusion

Adopting a functional approach to teaching grammar enables teachers to use a whole text perspective and to view language as a communicative resource whose goal is to create meaning. A functional perspective sees language as a set of interrelated systems through which users of the language draw on different types of grammatical resources to express ideas about a topic, to negotiate interpersonal aspects of language use and to produce stretches of language (text) that are cohesive and coherent within the context.

Discussion Questions

1. To what extent does a formal 'grammar translation' approach (as explained in the example from the French textbook) form part of your language learning experiences? What are the possible advantages of this approach? What are the possible disadvantages? Think about these two questions from both the teacher's and the student's points of view. Which approach do you prefer to adopt in your teaching?
2. Identify a spoken or written text you would like your students to use more effectively.
   a. What is the text about (the field)?
   b. What are the relationships between the speaker/listener or writer/reader (the tenor)?
   c. What kind of text (face-to-face, email, short message service, telephone call, academic essay) is being created (the mode)?
   d. What features of the grammar and the generic structure lead you to your conclusions?
3. Use the text from question 2 or select a different text you would like your students to use.
   a. What is the purpose of the text (e.g. inform, narrate, recount, give instructions)?
   b. How does the text begin in order to achieve this purpose?
   c. How does the text proceed? What different stages can you identify?
   d. How does the text end?
   e. What grammatical features do you notice at each stage of the text?

4. How could you use the teaching learning cycle with your students? Think about different activities that you could introduce at each point in the cycle to help them develop their skills in both spoken and written grammar.

Essential Reading

Butt, D., Fahey, R., Feez, S., & Spinks, S. (2012). *Using functional grammar: An explorer's guide* (3rd ed.). South Yarra, Victoria: Macmillan Education Australia.

Hyland, K. (2004). *Genre and second language learning.* Ann Arbor: University of Michigan Press.

Jones, R. H., & Lock, G. (2010). *Functional grammar in the ESL classroom. Noticing, exploring and practicing.* London: Palgrave Macmillan.

Larsen-Freeman, D. (2003). *Teaching language: From grammar to grammaring.* Boston: Thomson/ Heinle.

Schleppergrell, M. (2004). *The language of schooling: A functional linguistics perspective.* Mahwah, NJ: Erlbaum.

Thompson, G. (2004). *Introducing functional grammar.* London: Arnold.

References

Bloomfield, L. (1933). *Language.* New York: Henry Holt.

Callaghan, M., & Rothery, J. (1988). *Teaching factual writing: A genre-based approach.* Report of the DSP Literacy Project. Sydney: Metropolitan East Region, NSW.

Canale, M. (1981). From communicative competence to language pedagogy. In J. Richards & R. Schmidt (Eds.), *Language and communication* (pp. 2–27). London: Longman.

Celce-Murcia, M. (1990). Discourse analysis and grammar instruction. *Annual Review of Applied Linguistics, 11,* 135–151.

Chomsky, N. (1966). Linguistic theory. In R. J. Mean (Ed.), *Language teaching: Broader contexts: Northeast Conference on the Teaching of Foreign Languages; Reports of the Working Committees* (pp. 43–49). Wisconsin: Monaska.

Cummins, J., & Man, E. Y. (2006). Academic language: What is it and how do we acquire it? In C. Davison & J. Cummins (Eds.), *Part 2, International handbook of English language teaching* (pp. 797–810). New York: Springer.

Derewianka. B. (2001). Pedagogical grammars: Their role in English language teaching. In A. Burns & C. Coffin (Eds.), *Analysing English in a global context* (pp. 240–269). London: Routledge.

de Silva Joyce, H., & Burns, A. (1999). *Focus on grammar.* Sydney: National Centre for English Language Teaching and Research.

Ellis, R. (1994). *The study of second language acquisition.* Oxford: Oxford University Press.

Ellis, R. (2006). Current issues in the teaching of grammar: An SLA perspective. *TESOL Quarterly, 40*(1), 83–107.

Eggins, S. (2004). *An introduction to systemic functional linguistics* (2nd ed.). London: Continuum.

Feez, S. (1998). *Text-based syllabus design.* Sydney: National Centre for English Language Teaching and Research and New South Wales Adult Migrant English Service.

Fries, C. C. (1945). *Teaching and learning English as a foreign language.* Ann Arbor: University of Michigan Press.

Halliday, M. A. K. (1978). *Language as social semiotic: The social interpretation of language and meaning.* London: Arnold.

Halliday, M. A. K. (1985). *Spoken and written language.* Geelong, Australia: Deakin University Press.

Halliday, M. A. K. (1994). *An introduction to systemic functional grammar* (2nd ed.). London: Arnold.

Hammond, J., Burns, A., Joyce, H., Brosnan, D., & Gerot, L. (1992). *English for social purposes.* Sydney: National Centre for English Language Teaching and Research.

Hood, S., Solomon, N., & Burns, A. (1996). *Focus on reading.* Sydney: National Centre for English Language Teaching and Research.

Hymes, D. (1971). On communicative competence. In J. Pride & J. Holmes (Eds.), *Sociolinguistics* (pp. 269–293). London: Penguin.

Krashen, S. (1981). *Second language acquisition and second language learning.* Oxford: Oxford University Press.

Larsen-Freeman, D. (2003). *Teaching language: From grammar to grammaring.* Boston: Thomson/ Heinle.

Long, M. H. (2000). Focus on form in task-based language teaching. In R. H. Lambert & E. Shohamy (Eds.), *Language policy and pedagogy* (pp. 179–192). Amsterdam and Philadelphia: John Benjamins.

Macken-Horarik, M. (2002). "Something to shoot for": A systemic functional approach to teaching genre in secondary school science. In A. Johns (Ed.), *Genre in the classroom. Multiple perspectives* (pp. 17–42). Mahwah, NJ: Erlbaum.

Martin, J. R. (2001). Language, register and genre. In A. Burns & C. Coffin (Eds.), *Analysing English as a global language* (pp. 149–166). London: Routledge.

Norris, J., & Ortega, L. (2000). Effectiveness of L2 instruction: A research synthesis and quantitative meta-analysis. *Language Learning, 50*(3), 417–528.

Paltridge, B. (2001). *Genre and the language learning classroom.* Ann Arbor: University of Michigan Press.

Prabhu, N. S. (1987). *Second language pedagogy.* Oxford: Oxford University Press.

PART II
Strategies and Techniques

6

GRAMMAR PRACTICE

Penny Ur

Introduction: Grammar Practice—What Is It?

Practice can be defined roughly as 'doing something repeatedly in order to get to do it better'. In grammar practice, learners have repeated opportunities to understand and/or produce grammatical forms and meanings of the target language under more or less controlled conditions; the goal is that they should be able later to do so correctly in their own free written or spoken production.

Most teachers, if asked to describe what grammar practice is, would immediately identify the term as referring to conventional exercises, such as the following:

Write the verb in the past.

1. John _____ Mary. (meet)
2. I _____ my sister some money. (give) (or transformation)

Write what Sam said using reported speech.

1. Betty: "I'm living in London." Betty said . . ..
2. Sam: "I have never seen it." Sam said . . . (or sentence expansion)

Write full sentences in the present perfect, using the words given.

1. I can't find my bag. (someone/steal/it)_____
2. Jessie isn't here. (she/not/arrive/yet)_____

The purpose of such exercises is to get learners to create correct sentences using a specified grammatical feature, and they are normally preceded by explanations of rules or forms presented by the teacher or the textbook. Each item is *discrete* (separate, decontextualized) and has one right answer.

However, the term can also be applied to procedures that allow rather more open responses, providing learners with opportunities to use the grammar to make meanings. For example, learners can look at a picture and suggest what *is going to* happen or use guessing games to practice the 'yes/no' interrogative form. In these cases also, a major aim is to get learners to formulate correct sentences using the target rule or grammatical form in order to get them to practice it; but there is also creative and meaningful language use (Ur 2009).

In this chapter the term *activities* will be used to cover both types of practice procedures. I shall return to issues relating to the optimal use, or possible combination, of these types in a later section.

Does Grammar Practice Work?

There is considerable controversy in the literature over the question of whether grammar practice does in fact achieve the goal defined at the beginning of this chapter. Some feel it does and that it is an essential component of language teaching and learning in the context of a formal course of study. Others have reservations, and some would go so far as to condemn it as useless and banish it altogether from the language teaching classroom. We shall look later at these different approaches within the various language teaching models, but first let us examine the main arguments, based on theoretical models, research, and practice.

Arguments in Favor

Skill Theory

The theoretical rationale for the use of practice in grammar teaching is provided by *skill theory*, which is based on the distinction between declarative and procedural knowledge. *Declarative* knowledge is conscious 'knowledge that. . .': facts or ideas that can be articulated in words, such as a theory, a description of a situation, event or process, a definition, a categorization. *Procedural* knowledge is tacit 'knowledge how. . .'; it is expressed in physical or verbal performance but not articulated; for example: knowing how to swim, drive a car, play a musical instrument or use acceptable grammar in our mother tongue.

In the learning of a skill within a formal instructional situation, the process typically begins by an instructor defining the behavior to be mastered in declarative terms. In driving, for example, this might start with, 'Make sure the gear is in neutral, put the key in the ignition. . .' and so on. The learner then performs the actions. However, he or she will become skilled at doing these actions only if he or she practices: while initially bearing in mind the instructions, he or she performs the actions again and again until they become proceduralized and later highly *automatized*: performed smoothly and swiftly without conscious thought.

In terms of grammar practice, the declarative stage is provided by the grammar explanation provided by the teacher or textbook, and proceduralization is implemented through grammar exercises. DeKeyser has famously described the proceduralization-through-practice process in language learning as 'engaging in the target behavior—or procedure—while temporarily leaning on declarative crutches' (DeKeyser 1998: 49). The process results in eventual automatization, so that the learner can produce the target grammatical features accurately and appropriately in his or her own production without thinking about it: he or she has *implicit* knowledge of these features.

The Power Law of Practice

Research on practice in various fields shows that the ability of a learner to perform the target skill quickly, fluently and correctly increases proportionately to the number of opportunities he or she has to practice (Anderson 2000). Each practice event produces improvement but at a decreasing rate: so the more proficient the learner, the less improvement is produced by each subsequent practice activity, until a ceiling is reached at which further practice produces little or no improvement. This is either because the learner has fully and successfully automatized the target skill or because he or she has reached a point at which some inaccurate aspect of performance has become *fossilized* and is difficult to change. The fossilization phenomenon goes some way towards explaining why practice does not always make perfect; other reasons will be discussed later. It should be noted that even after the performer has reached a ceiling, he or she normally continues to practice in order to prevent deterioration.

Transferred to the field of grammar, this means that a learner needs to practice the foreign language grammar until he or she is able to produce it appropriately and effortlessly, and his or her regular use of it thereafter, whether productively or receptively, in fluent discourse in fact functions as further practice, enabling maintenance of this ability in the long term.

Expertise

The ultimate goal of language learning is that the learner should become an *expert language user*—a term increasingly used in the literature to describe the performance of both native and non-native fully proficient speakers of a language (e.g. Seidlhofer 2006). The research on expertise in general relates to a variety of types of skilled practitioners: chess players, for example, doctors, musicians and so on. What unites them is a very high standard of proceduralized knowledge that enables them to perform routine actions or verbal production rapidly and automatically, freeing up their attention to address nonroutine issues.

Recent research indicates that the key factor in the achievement of expert levels of performance is the amount of what is called 'deliberate practice' (Ericsson 2006). The expert—sometimes with and sometimes without the guidance of an instructor or trainer—deliberately practices his or her professional activity, focusing on those areas that are seen as needing improvement. In order to reach the highest levels of performance, an enormous number of hours of such practice is needed: probably several thousand.

If we translate this description to language learning, then in our first language we are practicing it continuously as we grow up, through interpersonal interaction and later through reading. This is not 'deliberate practice', in the sense that it is not focused on specific items, but it is certainly practice in the sense of repeated engagement with target forms and meanings that leads to improvement. It is obvious that when we learn our first language, we easily reach and exceed the required number of hours of practice—which explains, in terms of expertise theory, why we are experts in our implicit knowledge of L1 grammar. The learner of an additional language, however, will have to make do with a fraction of this time; opportunities for engagement with the language are often limited to three or four hours' study a week in a 30-week academic year; even if this study continues over several years of schooling, it is easy to see that an average learner will not get the massive opportunities for practice that would ensure expertise. This fact may go some way towards explaining the fact that many such learners do not achieve high levels of successful automatization in the use of grammar. But the claim that practice improves performance remains valid.

Research on Grammar Learning

The research on the effectiveness of grammar practice specifically within second language acquisition studies is relatively sparse. The fact that this has been little researched is, in my view, due to two main reasons. One is the fact that the use of practice is so widespread (see the next section) and so basic a component of classroom teaching that it is not seen as an interesting topic for research. Other comparable topics are effective language explanation, or the use of homework in language learning—important for teachers but not attractive to researchers. The other is that since the communicative approach—specifically, task-based language teaching—is today in general favored in the literature on language teaching, 'grammar practice' as such is seen as unfashionable and unworthy of investigation. Be that as it may, the evidence available varies, depending to some extent on the stance of the researcher. Ellis (2002a), for example, produces evidence based on studies of his own in the 1980s showing that learners who did accuracy-focused exercises on a particular grammatical form did not learn it well. However, by and large, researchers have found value in repetitive practice (e.g. Lyster and Sato 2013), particularly if it is meaningful (Larsen-Freeman 2009). Studies contrasting receptive and productive practices have found overall positive outcomes for one or both (DeKeyser 1997; DeKeyser and Sokalski 1996; Erlam 2003; Salaberry 1997).

Use by Teachers in Classrooms

Grammar practice in general is very widely used in language classrooms. The most commonly used exercises are ones that focus on accuracy ('get it right!'), as in the first three examples shown at the beginning of this chapter; books based on this type of practice, such as Murphy (2009), are popular worldwide.

Most coursebooks include a substantial component of conventional grammar exercises (Nitta and Gardner 2005). It is likely that most teachers use grammar practice exercises in their lessons (Phipps and Borg 2009) and that most students expect it and feel that it helps (Brown 2009). Interestingly, according to the last two studies mentioned, many teachers use such exercises even when they claim to believe that more communicative procedures are more effective. This is certainly partly due to student pressure but also possibly due to their *espoused beliefs*—what they explicitly claim to believe—being different from their *beliefs in action*—what they really feel is true, as betrayed by the way they behave (Argyris and Schoen 1974). Their beliefs in action may well include a tacit but firm conviction that grammar practice aids learning.

The fact that grammar practice is widely used by experienced practitioners (including myself) in classrooms worldwide cannot be summarily dismissed on the grounds that teachers are uninformed, unthinking or overly conservative (as claimed, for example, by Skehan 1998: 94). It is more likely that their belief that grammar practice 'works' is rooted in professional judgment based on extensive classroom experience and reflection.

Arguments Against

Lack of Transfer in Practice

The main obvious objection to the use of practice is the undeniable phenomenon, familiar to most experienced teachers, that even after extensive practice in a target grammatical feature, students frequently continue to make mistakes in the same feature in their own production. The conclusion has been drawn by some methodologists that practice itself is in principle ineffective: skill theory does not apply to language learning, and practice is useless as a contributor to proceduralized, implicit knowledge of grammar. See, for example, the description of the Input hypothesis, later in this chapter, for theoretical models that are clearly premised on this assumption.

This conclusion, however, is not inevitable and may lead to throwing the baby out with the bathwater. The fact that some students continue to make mistakes after practice does not invalidate the fact that others do not or that those who initially make mistakes later improve, very possibly as a result of further practice. In other words, a more plausible conclusion is that practice is likely to work well but that its function is to produce gradual improvement rather than immediate perfection.

The reason for the phenomenon of lack of transfer is, in my view, not that practice is in itself totally ineffective as a means of helping students learn grammar; it is rather because (a) the expectation that practice will lead to immediate perfection is unrealistic; (b) in the context of a formal course of study we cannot provide enough of it (see the preceding 'Expertise' subsection); and (c) that the kind of grammar practice commonly provided (as in the examples shown at the beginning of this chapter) is not conducive to such transfer, in that it requires students to focus on the formation of correct sentences rather than offering them opportunities to use the grammar to create meanings.

The Input Hypothesis

The *input hypothesis*, associated with the name of Stephen Krashen (Krashen 1982), makes a distinction between the *acquisition* and *learning* of language. Learners *acquire* implicit, intuitive knowledge of the language, which is immediately available for correct and appropriate use in output; they consciously *learn* language rules or items through (usually teacher-initiated) presentation and practice. An important corollary of this distinction is that the one cannot transfer to the other: items taught explicitly cannot move into the acquisition system by way of practice and automatization. The only way students can really acquire language is through extensive exposure to comprehensible input, at a level slightly above where they are at the moment ('$i + 1$').

The hypothesis allows a minor place for practice exercises based on the application of explicit rules but only in order to help learners monitor their own output when they have time and attention to spare for conscious self-correction. In other words, it explicitly denies the process that is the basis of skill theory: the creation of implicit knowledge through practice.

On the whole, the input hypothesis in its strong form has not been supported by research and has not been popular in classrooms, but it has had considerable influence in the development of the communicative approach. Proponents of task-based language teaching also see the main source of grammatical knowledge as deriving from the use of language in genuine communication, rather than from conscious teaching of rules and practice.

The Teachability Hypothesis

The teachability hypothesis is based on the research finding that learners acquire grammatical structures in a new language in a more or less invariable order (Pienemann 1989), which, it is claimed, cannot be changed by order of teaching.

When, therefore, the teacher introduces and provides practice in a new grammatical structure, it will be learned and become implicit, procedural knowledge only if the learner is at the right developmental stage. In such cases, practice may accelerate learning, but it cannot induce learners who are not at the appropriate developmental stage to learn a new feature if they are not ready for it.

However, it is difficult, if not impossible, for a teacher in the course of teaching a class to do the tests necessary to find out at what developmental stage each student is; and in any case in any normal class, different students will be at different stages, so that the theory that new structures should be taught at the appropriate moment is impracticable. The conclusion therefore would be, as stated by Ellis (2002b: 163): 'teaching implicit knowledge through production practice is unlikely to work unless it so happens that the instruction coincides with the learner's state of readiness—a condition that is virtually impossible to meet'. In other words, practice is in most cases fairly useless.

There has, however, been research showing that teaching a structure even if it is well ahead of the learners' stage of development can lead to improvement (Spada and Lightbown 1999), and recently the hypothesis itself has been challenged by research indicating that the use of specified teaching procedures, including practice, can override the natural order of acquisition and allow learners to acquire new structures in an order determined by the teacher (Zhang and Lantolf 2015).

The Implementation of Practice in Some Major Models of Language Teaching

The role of grammar practice depends on the overall method or specific grammar teaching model adopted. *Method* can be defined as 'a coherent set of learning/teaching principles rooted in clearly articulated theories of what language is and how it is learnt, which is implemented through specified types of classroom procedures' (Ur 2013: 468). Some of the items in the following list are indeed methods according to this definition (grammar translation, for example); others are generalized processes or sequences of procedures relating specifically to grammar teaching (consciousness raising, for example).

Grammar Translation

In *grammar translation*, grammatical rules are explicitly defined, and practice aims at implementing them in focused discrete-item exercises, which are typically based on sentence completion, matching, true–false, multiple choice or translation. Exercises are normally written rather than performed orally. The assumption is that rules learned and repeatedly practiced in this way will then be used correctly in the student's own speech and writing. Today a modified form of grammar translation is used in many (possibly most) classrooms worldwide, often referred to as a 'traditional' methodology, where both rules and practice are regularly employed but translation only rarely.

Consciousness Raising

The process of *consciousness raising*, proposed by Ellis (2002a), includes teaching of explicit grammar rules by inductive or deductive means. Grammar exercises may be done, but their function is to raise awareness of the rules, not to practice in order to proceduralize. The underlying rationale is that if a student is ready, according to the teachability hypothesis, to acquire a grammatical feature, he or she will do so anyway, through exposure to natural communicative language; if he or she is not ready, then practice will not help. Consciousness raising may, however, help learners to notice the grammar in input and thus accelerate the process of acquisition (the latter term is used here similarly to its definition within the input hypothesis).

Presentation-Practice-Production (PPP)

The PPP sequence that is used in many textbooks and classroom processes includes three stages: a new grammatical structure is first explained (Presentation), then practiced through focused exercises (Practice) and finally produced by students in their own written or spoken output (Production) (Ur forthcoming). As in grammar translation, the underlying assumption, linked to skill theory, is that practice will lead to automatization and the ability to produce grammatical structures correctly in students' own unassisted output. It is associated with traditional methodologies and often condemned by proponents of task-based language teaching as ineffective.

Focus on Form (FonF)

This model of grammar teaching is associated with the communicative approach: in particular, task-based language teaching. Grammatical features are taught not proactively according to a grammatical syllabus but reactively, in response to needs arising in the course of performance of a communicative task. Very frequently, such reactive treatment of grammar is based on a student error. It may consist of a brief explanation aimed at awareness raising and the presentation of added examples; in some cases, it may also include focused practice exercises (Shak and Gardner 2008). In recent research, Valeo and Spada (forthcoming) relate to the possibility of 'isolated' as well as an 'integrated' focus on form: occasional work on a grammatical feature detached from a communicative task, as well as within it.

Interim Summary and Conclusions

In general, the consensus seems to be that there is a place for grammar practice in language teaching, though its functions and level of effectiveness in different situations are under discussion.

We may distinguish at least three different—though in practice overlapping—functions for such practice. The first is the obvious one of converting declarative to procedural knowledge, in a conventional PPP model; students practice in order to become more skilled and accurate in their use of grammar. The second is perhaps less obvious: practice not clearly based on pretaught explicit rules. Proceduralization through practice does not always depend on the existence of a preceding, or underlying, declarative form of the target knowledge. The 'declarative crutches' may have been thrown away even before full automatization has been achieved; at advanced stages in the learning of grammar, the learner may be usually getting it right without recalling the explanation but needs to continue practicing in order to be able to retrieve the target forms more readily and rapidly where appropriate: in other words, to become more fluent. In some cases, the declarative form may not have existed at all; the learner may be practicing the target grammatical form on the basis of examples and analogy and a vague awareness of 'what sounds right'—but needs plenty of practice in order to become fluent. The third function is close to what Ellis (2002a) defines as 'consciousness raising': the very performance of a grammar exercise at the early stages may help the learner understand the rule and how it is applied, even before proceduralization processes kick in.

In order to fulfill any of these three functions, a practice activity may occur within the lesson either as part of a traditional model of explanation followed by practice or as an occasional reactive focus on form.

In the first case, grammar is taught deliberately and proactively, usually based on an explicit grammatical syllabus laid out in the course materials. The unit of the textbook, or the teacher in a lesson, proclaims openly that a specific grammatical feature will now be taught, explains how it works and what it means (sometimes in the students' mother tongue), and then requires the students to do exercises implementing what they have learned. In some cases, the explanation may be preceded by the reading of a text specially written to provide a number of examples of the target structure (as in, for example, Davis, Rimmer, Lloyd, and Day 2011). Samples taken from this text may be used by the teacher in the course of the explanation.

In the case of focus on form, there is normally no grammatical syllabus, and any texts used are not composed deliberately to provide examples of a grammatical feature. Attention to grammar grows out of the reading of an authentic or simplified text for comprehension or the performance of a communicative task either because a student makes an error, or because the teacher draws attention to it, or because it produces difficulty in comprehension or production. The teacher takes a temporary break from the main procedure and provides an explanation and some practice. Such practice may be very brief and minimal: the provision of a few more examples for students to hear or read, or the elicitation of such examples from students in response to cues. Or it may be more extended: there may be full accuracy-oriented exercises in a 'language focus' stage at the end of a communicative task. (Willis 1996). Note that the focus on form process, as originally envisaged by Long and Robinson (2002), is based on spontaneous, unplanned response of the teacher to a perceived need for attention to grammar within a communicative task. Later variations allow for the possibility of pre-planning (Ellis, Basturkmen, and Loewen 2002) and even occasional isolated focus on form detached from any communicative context (Valeo and Spada, forthcoming).

The advantage of the traditional model is that it ensures that the main gram-matical structures are taught systematically, which is important particularly at the early stages of learning, accords with the expectations of many students and pro-vides a feeling of organized, solid progression. The disadvantages are, however, that its use tends to focus students' attention on the production of accurate forms rather than on the use of the grammar for creating or understanding meanings, and there is a danger that grammar teaching, including practice, can take over a large propor-tion of a course in the shape of 'grammar lessons', at the expense of learning other important aspects of language use: vocabulary, for example, or fluency in the use of spoken and written language. Conversely, the focus on form model is less sys-tematic and may be less acceptable for students who prefer a more organized, graded approach to grammar learning. However, it does provide them with the experience of encountering and using the grammar feature in genuine communi-cative contexts and focuses on meaningful use.

There is no reason, of course, why these two ways of integrating grammar practice into a lesson should be mutually exclusive. It seems sensible to include both, as indeed suggested by Ellis (2015): to teach some basic grammatical struc-tures systematically through planned, proactive explanation and practice but also to take 'time out' from communicative tasks or text comprehension activities, in order to pay attention to salient grammatical features and to provide opportunities for relevant practice.

The bottom line is, then, that grammar practice may contribute to students' knowledge of grammar through any of these modes of use. The question remains: what are the factors that can increase its effectiveness in improving student perfor-mance? In particular, what can be done to facilitate the transfer of grammatical knowledge attained through practice activities to learners' own independent out-put? The rest of this chapter will be devoted to some responses to this question in the shape of practical guidelines and examples relating to the design and use of grammar practice activities.

The Design of Grammar Practice Activities

The first requisite is to design grammar practice activities so that they provide for optimal learning outcomes and do not waste time on 'busy' but irrelevant occupa-tion or on repetition that is boring or unhelpful. The following descriptions of design criteria for effective grammar exercises are updated and expanded versions of lists previously published in Ur (2009, 2012).

Validity

The concept of *validity* is commonly applied to tests: it means that the testing tool used does in fact test what it claims. Some listening tests, for example, are invalid, in that the learners actually spend more time reading a large amount of text in the form of multiple-choice questions than they do listening and is to that extent a test of reading, rather than listening, comprehension. The same criterion can be applied to grammar practice: it needs to be valid in the sense that the learners, while doing it, are mainly focused on engaging with the target grammar and do not spend too much of their time trying to understand surrounding text (reading comprehension) or looking up words they do not understand (vocabulary).

Quantity

The main function of practice is to engage the learner in repeated reception or production of the target form. Broadly speaking, the more opportunities there are for such engagement within a practice activity—the greater the *quantity* of practice—the more learning will take place. As suggested in the 'Expertise' subsection and confirmed by researchers on language practice (DeKeyser 2007: 292), thorough automatization of much English grammar probably demands a good deal more quantity of practice than we can possibly provide in the classroom and is likely to be completed only when the learner is 'practicing' further in real-life language use after the end of the formal English course. This means classroom practice is probably a necessary but not sufficient condition for ultimate automatization and that the more opportunities for practice we can provide in the classroom, the better: hence the importance of the aspect of quantity in activity design. This is clearly linked to the previous item: if the activity is invalid, then the number of instances of the target feature will be reduced. But even if it is valid, the activity may still lack quantity if the practice procedure is very short, based on a small number of instances, if it does not ensure participation of the majority of learners in the classroom or if it involves a high proportion of puzzling-out or other time-wasting 'busy' work.

Success Orientation

One of the most difficult ideas for many teachers to accept, in my experience, is that the goal of practice is for the learners to perform the task successfully and correctly, not to make mistakes and be corrected. In a sense, this is the converse of the 'garden-path' strategy, according to which students are actually induced to make mistakes resulting from overgeneralization of a rule, in order that they may be corrected and learn from the correction (Herron 1991). Certainly being corrected will raise students' awareness of a grammatical point, and may be a useful preliminary to practice—but it will not directly contribute to proceduralization.

Proceduralization takes place as a result of doing something right and being aware that it is right, again and again. A good practice exercise should therefore be presented when the teacher is fairly sure that learners have declarative knowledge of the target material, or familiarity with previously learnt exemplars; and it should be designed to optimize opportunities for successful performance. There should also be regular positive confirming feedback: this is usually from the teacher but can also appear as part of a computerized grammar exercise.

Heterogeneity

A good practice activity should be available for students to do successfully at a variety of levels. Most conventional exercises are designed to be done at a single level: there is a series of isolated cues with predetermined correct answers, such as those shown at the beginning of this chapter. If these are too easy for more advanced students, they will not get practice at a level appropriate for them and may get bored. Lower-level students, on the other hand, may not be able to perform at all or may get the answers wrong (see the 'Success Orientation' subsection). Activities should be designed, therefore, to provide choice and flexibility, so that learners at different levels can engage with them and benefit from the practice. This can be done by various strategies: by providing open-ended cues, with a range of possible correct student-initiated responses at different levels; by allowing students to choose which items they respond to from a number of possibilities; or by designating a set of easy items as compulsory and supplying further and more difficult ones as optional extras (for more detail on these strategies, see Ur 2012: 276–280).

Interest

The arousal and maintenance of learner interest is, of course, important in principle, for any part of the lesson, in any subject. The reason why we need to pay particular attention to it in the design of grammar practice activities is that the aspects of quantity and success orientation are likely to lead to the design of activities that are very repetitive and that provide little challenge in the production of acceptable responses—that are, in short, in danger of becoming boring. The design of such activities therefore needs to include features that will raise interest. Some examples of such features are:

- **Meaningfulness**: The production of meaningful responses rather than just correct samples of grammar.
- **Visual materials**: The use of relevant pictures or other graphic material, whether print or digital.
- **Open-ended questions**: Cues that have no one predetermined answer but invite a range of possible responses that are unpredictable and may be original and/or humorous.

- **Personalization**: Opportunities to create responses that relate to students' own opinions, tastes, experiences or cultures.
- **Higher-order thinking**: Tasks that require students to think critically or creatively rather than just recall or identify.
- **Tasks with content outcomes**: The production of outcomes other than just production of correct sentences—for example, a story, a set of priorities, a solution to a problem.
- **Game-like activity**: The use of game-like challenges such as guessing, recalling from memory, brainstorming, brainstorming within a time limit, team competitions.

Accuracy-Focused and Meaning-Focused Grammar Practice

The distinction between mechanical, meaningful and communicative grammar practices was made some years ago by Paulston and Bruder (1976) and has been adopted by various writers since. DeKeyser (1998) stresses communicative practice and denies the usefulness of mechanical, on the grounds that mechanical exercises involve the manipulation of forms without any relating to meaning and therefore cannot contribute to the proceduralization of grammar for meaningful use.

An example of a mechanical exercise follows:

Write the past tense of the verbs in the following sentences:

1. We (go) _____ to town.
2. She (give) _____ him some money.
3. I (come) _____ here yesterday.

The learner can, assuming he or she knows the target grammatical forms, do the exercise without understanding the sentences and, indeed, theoretically may not bother to read them at all but just fill in the blanks with the required past tenses. In my experience, however, most students do in fact read and understand the sentences. (The ones who do not are usually the very bright ones, who quickly realize that they don't need to do so in order to succeed in getting it all right!) But the main point here is not whether students do or do not understand the meanings; the point is that they do not *attend* to them: they are focusing on producing correct forms.

A more useful distinction is, therefore, that between *accuracy-focused* and *meaning-focused* exercises: in the former, the attention of the learner is mainly on identifying or creating correct forms, as distinct from the latter, wherein their attention is on understanding or creating meanings. Note that the difference is one of degree; these are not absolute, mutually exclusive categories. So we may have an exercise where learners are focusing very much on accurate form, as in the preceding example; we may have ones where they are focusing on both accuracy and meaning; and we may have ones where the focus is mainly on meaning, while keeping an eye, as it were, on the formation of correct sentences or phrases.

By way of illustration, see the following five examples of grammar practice activities, which progress from a primary focus on accurate forms in Exercise A to overriding focus on meaning in Exercise E.

A. *Write correct sentences, using the comparative form of the adjective given and adding* than.
   1. A kilometer is _____ a centimeter. (long)
   2. A dog is _____ a mouse. (big)
   3. Meat is _____ vegetables. (expensive)
B. *Write correct and true sentences, using the comparative form of* **one of** *the adjectives given and adding* than.
   1. A kilometer is _____ a centimeter. (long, short)
   2. A dog is _____ a mouse. (big, small)
   3. Meat is _____ vegetables. (expensive, cheap)
C. *Write sentences that express your own opinion, using the comparative form of the adjectives given.*
   1. Biology/literature (interesting, boring)
   2. Computers/books (important, useful)
   3. Pizza/hamburgers (nice, healthy)
D. *Write sentences comparing these two things, using the comparative form of adjectives. Write two different sentences for each item.*
   1. London/Madrid

   _____

   _____

   2. I/my friend

   _____

   _____

   3. Elephants/crocodiles

   _____

   _____

E. Compare and contrast the characters of Elinor and Marianne in Jane Austen's *Sense and Sensibility.*

The function of Exercise A is simply to get learners to apply rules about the formation of the comparative of adjectives to specific adjectives. It can be done without understanding meanings, but it does fulfill an important function. Learners cannot usually start to proceduralize grammar on the basis of declarative knowledge of a rule until they are confident that they know they are applying the rule correctly to specific words or sentences, and the importance of this type of exercise is that it gives them opportunities to do just that, with no other objectives to distract them (see the third function of practice suggested under 'Interim Summary and Conclusions' above). Once a learner feels 'I know how to do it', he or she can then move to the next stage of getting to do it better, faster, more fluently: that is, to proceduralize.

However, to continue doing such very accuracy-focused exercises will not in itself contribute to learners' ability to use the grammar in their own production. It will only enable them to do more, similar exercises correctly. They will be able to apply the rule successfully *when they have time and attention to devote to conscious formulation of sentences.* When they are focusing on communicative meaning in their own speech, they cannot normally do this very easily; unless and until the grammar is fully automatized, they are likely to continue to make errors.

The answer is, as Johnson (1997) suggests, progressive form defocus: that is to say, to provide students with opportunities to use the grammar in situations where they are attending less and less to the creation of correct forms and more and more to the creation of meanings.

If we look at Exercise B, we can see that it is impossible to do it without engaging with the meanings of the sentences and application of real-world knowledge. The objective is still explicitly the production of sentences that use the comparative of adverbs correctly, but this can be done only through awareness of what the resulting sentences will mean.

Exercise C goes one step further: it does not supply the 'skeleton' sentences, but only the key lexical items that the learners can use. They have to write out the sentences themselves—again in order to make meanings. They are still required to use the target forms, but in this case the meanings not only have to be true, they also have to be personally relevant and there is an element of choice; they can choose which adjective they wish to use and can express their own personal opinions or tastes.

Exercise D also requires the creation of meaningful sentences, but it is less controlled, in that it does not supply possible adjectives: the learner has to think up his or her own adjectives in order to create meanings that may express either fact or opinion. In many cases, exercises like this result in half-humorous or original ideas that embody the playful use of language (Cook 2000; Bell 2012). Note that a parallel task could be to supply the adjectives but not the nouns: so that you might supply the adjective *comfortable* and challenge students to express opinions about the comparative comfort of anything they like: homes, chairs, modes of transport, for example. Again, this is likely to result in interesting and sometimes funny suggestions.

Exercise E is clearly communicative, in that it is a real academic assignment, with no overt suggestion that the target grammatical feature should be used. The nature of the task, however ('Compare and contrast') makes it very likely that the comparative will be used purposefully and meaningfully. Hopefully by this time the student has had plenty of experience in exercises like the previous ones in creating meanings using the target grammar and is likely to be able to use it appropriately in the present context.

The progression from focus on accuracy to focus on meaning carries with it other types of development: from controlled to free and from decontextualized to contextualized. In Exercise A, the student has no choice at all what to write, the correct answers are predetermined. In B and C, he or she does have minimal choices to make. In D, there is minimally guided sentence construction and completely free writing of a full text. As regards contextualization: all the Exercises A through D are based on discrete items: separate, apparently decontextualized sentences. But if you try doing them, you will find that in C and E, you are starting to create mental pictures of the situations you are describing in your sentences: in other words, you are creating 'mini contexts' for each statement you make. And any writing done in response to the task shown in the final exercise is obviously within the context of the novel under discussion.

The main point I am trying to make here is that the importance of including intermediate types of practice (exemplified here by Exercises B–D) in materials or lesson plans devoted to grammar teaching. Very accuracy-focused exercises like the first one, however many are done, cannot on their own lead to good learning of the target grammar in the sense of creating automatic knowledge that will be expressed in the student's own production of speech or writing. It is vital to provide also opportunities for students to get used to performing tasks that require them to make or understand meanings while maintaining an underlying sensitivity to the proper use of grammatical forms.

Note also that these intermediate types of practice also score higher on some of the design criteria for effective practice previously described than do the conventional types of exercise exemplified in Exercise A. They are clearly more interesting to do; Exercises C and D provide opportunities for more than one response to each item and therefore are likely to produce more quantity of practice; and Exercise D enables students to produce more, or less, difficult sentences, depending on what vocabulary they employ, thus making the task available for use at different levels of proficiency.

Conclusion

Practice does not 'make perfect' (indeed, no single language teaching technique does that), but grammar practice activities—if they are well designed and induce students to understand and produce original meanings as well as create acceptable grammatical forms—can in most teaching situations make a substantial contribution to students' ability to use the target grammar correctly and appropriately in their own output.

This does not mean that we should spend more than a small proportion of our total lesson time on grammar practice. The learner needs to be doing other things as well in order to master the target language through a formal course of study: learn and practice vocabulary, for example, communicate through the spoken language in fluency activities, read extensively, compose original written texts . . . and more. The challenge facing the language teacher—and, indeed, the materials writer—is to identify all those procedures that can facilitate good language learning and to combine them in a way that will afford optimal learning opportunities to students with a variety of learning styles in different learning contexts. All I am claiming here is that when our aim is to learn the grammar of a language, practice should be numbered among such procedures.

Discussion Questions

1. Can you define *grammar practice* in your own words? Compare your definition with the one given in this chapter.
2. What are the main advantages and disadvantages of grammar practice as facilitating the acquisition of target language grammar?
3. Have a look at a local language teaching textbook. What kinds of grammar practice activities are used? Can you suggest how they might be improved?
4. How much grammar practice would you/do you use in your own classroom? What kinds of activities would you/do you use?

Essential Reading

DeKeyser, R. (Ed.). (2007). *Practice in a second language: Perspectives from applied linguistics and cognitive psychology*. Cambridge: Cambridge University Press.
Ellis, R. (2002). Methodological options in grammar teaching materials. In E. Hinkel & S. Fotos (Eds.), *New perspectives on grammar teaching in second language classrooms* (pp. 155–179). Mahwah, NJ: Erlbaum.
Johnson, K. (1997). *Language teaching and skill learning*. Oxford: Blackwell.
Ur, P. (2009). *Grammar practice activities* (2nd ed.). Cambridge: Cambridge University Press.

References

Anderson, J. R. (2000). *Learning and memory: An integrated approach* (2nd ed.). New York: Wiley.
Argyris, C., & Schoen, D. A. (1974). *Theory in practice: Increasing professional effectiveness*. San Francisco: Jossey Bass.
Bell, N. (2012). Comparing playful and nonplayful incidental attention to form. *Language Learning, 62*(1), 236–265.
Brown, A. V. (2009). Students' and teachers' perceptions of effective foreign language teaching: A comparison of ideals. *The Modern Language Journal, 93*(1), 46–60.
Cook, G. (2000). *Language play, language learning*. Oxford: Oxford University Press.
Davis, F., Rimmer, W., Lloyd, M., & Day, J. (2011). *Active grammar*. Cambridge: Cambridge University Press.
DeKeyser, R. M. (1997). Beyond explicit rule learning. *Studies in Second Language Acquisition, 19*(2), 195–221.
DeKeyser, R. (1998). Beyond focus on form: Cognitive perspectives on learning and practicing second language grammar. In C. Doughty & J. Williams (Eds.), *Focus on form in classroom second language acquisition* (pp. 42–63). Cambridge: Cambridge University Press.
DeKeyser, R. (Ed.). (2007). *Practice in a second language: Perspectives from applied linguistics and cognitive psychology*. Cambridge: Cambridge University Press.

DeKeyser, R. M., & Sokalski, K. J. (1996). The differential role of comprehension and production practice. *Language Learning, 46*(4), 613–642.

Ellis, R. (2002a). Grammar teaching—Practice or consciousness-raising? In J. C. Richards & W. A. Renandya (Eds.), *Methodology in language teaching* (pp. 167–174). Cambridge: Cambridge University Press.

Ellis, R. (2002b). Methodological options in grammar teaching materials. In E. Hinkel & S. Fotos (Eds.), *New perspectives on grammar teaching in second language classrooms* (pp. 155–179). Mahwah, NJ: Erlbaum.

Ellis, R. (2015). Taking the critics to task: The case for task-based teaching. *Proceedings of CLaSIC 2014*, Singapore. Available online at http://www.fas.nus.edu.sg/cls/CLaSIC/clasic2014/Proceedings/ellis_rod.pdf

Ellis, R., Basturkmen, H., & Loewen, S. (2002). Doing focus-on-form. *System, 30*(4), 419–432.

Ericsson, K. A. (2006). The influence of experience and deliberate practice on the development of superior expert performance. In K. A. Ericsson, N. Charness, P. J. Feltovich, & R. R. Hoffman (Eds.), *The Cambridge handbook of expertise and expert performance* (pp. 683–703). Cambridge: Cambridge University Press.

Erlam, R. (2003). Evaluating the relative effectiveness of structured-input and output-based instruction in foreign language learning. *Studies in Second Language Acquisition, 25*(4), 559–582.

Herron, C. (1991). The garden path correction strategy in the foreign language classroom. *French Review, 64*, 966–977.

Johnson, K. (1997). *Language teaching and skill learning*. Oxford: Blackwell.

Krashen, S. (1982). *Principles and practice in second language acquisition*. Oxford: Pergamon.

Larsen-Freeman, D. (2009). Teaching and testing grammar. In M. H. Long & C. J. Doughty (Eds.), *The handbook of language teaching* (pp. 518–542). Chichester, UK: Wiley.

Long, M. H., & Robinson, P. (2002). Focus on form. Theory, research and practice. In G. Doughty & J. Williams (Eds.), *Focus on form in classroom second language acquisition* (pp. 15–41). Cambridge: Cambridge University Press.

Lyster, R., & Sato, M. (2013). Skill acquisition theory and the role of practice in L2 development. In M. G. Mayo, J. Gutierrez-Mangado, & M. M. Adrián (Eds.), *Multiple perspectives on second language acquisition* (pp. 71–92). Amsterdam: John Benjamins.

Murphy, R. (2009). *Essential grammar in use*. Cambridge: Cambridge University Press.

Nitta, R., & Gardner, S. (2005). Consciousness-raising and practice in ELT coursebooks. *ELT Journal, 59*(1), 3–13.

Paulston, C. B., & Bruder, M. N. (1976). *Teaching English as a second language: Techniques and procedures*. Cambridge, MA: Winthrop Publishers.

Phipps, S., & Borg, S. (2009). Exploring tensions between teachers' grammar teaching beliefs and practices. *System, 37*(3), 380–390.

Pienemann, M. (1989). Is language teachable? Psycholinguistic experiments and hypotheses. *Applied Linguistics, 10*(1), 52–79.

Salaberry, M. R. (1997). The role of input and output practice in second language acquisition. *Canadian Modern Language Review, 53*(2), 422–451.

Seidlhofer, B. (2006). English as a lingua franca in the expanding circle: What it isn't. In R. Rubdy & M. Saraceni (Eds.), *English in the world: Global rules, global roles* (pp. 40–50). London: Continuum.

Shak, J., & Gardner, S. (2008). Young learner perspectives on four focus-on-form tasks. *Language Teaching Research, 12*(3), 387–408.

Skehan, P. (1998). A rationale for task-based instruction. In *A cognitive approach to language learning* (pp. 93–120). Oxford: Oxford University Press.

Spada, N., & Lightbown, P. M. (1999). Instruction, first language influence, and developmental readiness in second language acquisition. *The Modern Language Journal, 83*(1), 1–22.

Ur, P. (2009). *Grammar practice activities* (2nd ed.). Cambridge: Cambridge University Press.

Ur, P. (2012). *A course in English language teaching.* Cambridge: Cambridge University Press.

Ur, P. (2013). Language-teaching method revisited. *ELT Journal, 67*(4), 468–474.

Ur, P. (forthcoming). PPP: Presentation, practice, production. In *TESOL Encyclopedia of English language teaching.* New York: Wiley.

Valeo, A., & Spada, N. (forthcoming). Is there a better time to focus on form? Teacher and learner views. *TESOL Quarterly.*

Willis, J. (1996). A flexible framework for task-based learning. In J. Willis & D. Willis (Eds.), *Challenge and change in language teaching* (pp. 52–62). London: Heinemann.

Zhang, X., & Lantolf, J. P. (2015). Natural or artificial: Is the route of L2 development teachable? *Language Learning, 65*(1), 152–180.

7

GRAMMAR TEACHING AS CONSCIOUSNESS RAISING

Rod Ellis

Introduction

All forms of grammar teaching—whether of the explicit or implicit kind—aim at raising second language learners' consciousness of specific grammatical forms and the meanings that they convey. However, they assume different positions regarding what consciousness consists of and, crucially, what role it plays in language learning. Thus to better understand the role of consciousness in grammar teaching, it is necessary to first consider what is meant by 'consciousness' and what role it plays in language learning.

George Miller (1962) commented that 'consciousness is a word worn smooth by a million tongues'. Not surprisingly, then, much effort has gone into defining the term. Velmans (1991) noted that in the psychological and philosophical literature, it is possible to distinguish three senses of what it means to call a process 'conscious':

1. Consciousness of the process itself.
2. Consciousness of the result arising from the processing of language.
3. Consciousness entering into or causally influencing the process.

These three senses map onto the 'deconstruction' of consciousness in the work of Schmidt (1994, 2001), which has been so influential in second language acquisition research. Consciousness of the process itself corresponds to what Schmidt called 'noticing'. He argued that stimuli need to be consciously attended to for learning to occur. 'Noticing' was defined as the subjective awareness of an exemplar of a linguistic feature that occurs in the input that the learner is exposed to. Consciousness of the result arising from the processing of language corresponds to what Schmidt called 'understanding'—awareness of an underlying grammatical rule or generalization. 'Noticing' may or may not result in 'understanding'. Finally, Schmidt recognized that consciousness can causally enter into the process of using an L2 when learners make intentional use of their explicit knowledge. He referred to this as 'consciousness as control' (Schmidt 1994). Thus, while acknowledging that 'consciousness' remains a slippery concept, Velmans' tripartite senses of the term and their parallel in Schmidt's framework affords a basis for exploring grammar teaching as consciousness raising. Before setting out to do this, however, we must first consider to what extent and in what ways consciousness is involved in using and learning the grammar of an L2.

We must first acknowledge that much of language *use* does not involve consciousness. Velman, for example pointed that when we are reading, we might become aware of specific words or specific grammatical forms, but we have no awareness of the reading process itself. For example, we are not conscious of the regressions we make or of skipping parts of a sentence because we have understood its meaning without having to process every word. Schmidt also acknowledged that there is an important skill aspect to L2 use and that fluent speech draws on implicit/proceduralized knowledge without any conscious awareness. Learners, for example, may code-switch without awareness of what language they are using. When learners are on automatic pilot, they are conscious only of the meanings they are trying to convey, not of the linguistic forms they are using.

However, whether consciousness is involved in *learning* is a controversial matter. For Krashen (1981), what he called 'acquisition' is a purely subconscious, incidental process, distinct from 'learning', which is intentional and conscious. In other words, for Krashen none of Velman's three senses of consciousness are involved in 'acquisition'. There is some evidence to support this position. Studies by Williams and his co-researchers (e.g. Leung and Williams 2011; Williams 2005) indicate that learners can demonstrate knowledge of grammatical structures without any awareness of having learned them. Such studies, however, remain controversial as they rely on demonstrating a lack of consciousness in terms of Velman's (2) and (3) senses, and there remains the possibility that there was still consciousness in terms of his (1) sense (i.e. consciousness at the point of learning). For Schmidt, 'noticing' (but not necessarily 'understanding') is a prerequisite for any learning to take place as there is no such thing as completely implicit learning.[1] As he put it 'attention is necessary for the conversion of input to intake' (1994; 17). N. Ellis (2005) takes an intermediate position. For him, learning is initially a conscious process but subsequently the pattern recognition mechanisms of connectionist memory take over, and learning becomes implicit. In other words, learning an L2 involves both explicit (conscious) and implicit (subconscious) processes. If one agrees with Krashen, there is at best only a minor place for the teaching of grammar. However, from the perspectives of both Schmidt and N. Ellis, consciousness—and therefore grammar teaching in one

TABLE 7.1 Consciousness and Grammar Activities

Three Senses of Consciousness	Types of Grammar Teaching
Consciousness-as-noticing	1. Text enhancement
	2. Interpretation tasks
Consciousness-as-understanding	1. Grammar explanation
	2. Consciousness-raising tasks
Consciousness-as-control	1. Monitoring activities
	2. Text manipulation activities
	3. Text creation activities

form or another—have a clear role to play in language learning. In the conclusion section of this chapter, I discuss this role further.

In the following sections, I will examine different ways of teaching grammar in terms of Velmans' and Schmidt's senses of consciousness. In so doing, I am taking a very broad view of what grammar teaching consists of—that is, it is any attempt to facilitate the process of learning by inducing learners' consciousness of grammatical forms either in the input that they are exposed to or in their own output. Table 7.1 shows the different types of grammar activities I will discuss.

Consciousness-as-Noticing

Grammar activities directed at consciousness-as-noticing are input based. That is they assume that learning can take place simply by inducing learners to pay attention to specific grammatical forms as these occur in oral/ written texts or while learners are interacting in the L2. All of these activities involve a primary focus on meaning. That is learners are required to comprehend input but in the process of doing so also to attend to exemplars of whatever the grammatical target of the activity is. A key feature of these activities is that they aim to help learners construct a form-meaning mapping. In other words, they require learners not just to notice the form of a grammatical structure but also to comprehend the meaning that it conveys.

Text Enhancement

In a text enhancement activity, learners read or listen to a text that contains multiple exemplars of the same target structure that have been highlighted by bolding, italicizing, colouring or paraphrasing in a written text or by intonation and stress in an oral text. In the activity in Table 7.2, exemplars of the past passive have been bolded. Altogether, there are 12 exemplars of this structure. To focus primary attention on meaning, the students are asked to read the passage in order to answer a question. As they read, however, their attention may be drawn to the exemplars of the passive construction.

TABLE 7.2 A Text-Enhancement Activity

Read the story about Kiki. When you have finished reading, cover the story and see if you can remember what happened to Kiki.

Kiki **was raised** in the countryside. One day he was playing inside his house when there was a big earthquake. He **was knocked down** by the falling bricks. He **was trapped** in the house. It was very dark. Kiki was badly hurt and could not move. A little later Kiki's mom came back home. She saw the house **was destroyed and** knew her boy **was buried** inside. She shouted out to him but he could not hear her because he **was covered** with bricks. People came to help. Slowly, the bricks **were removed** and Kiki **was pulled** out of the wreckage. He **was carried** to the local hospital and **was put** in an emergency room for treatment. He **was given** special food to help him recover. He **was allowed** to leave the hospital after one month.

The research to date suggests that text enhancement activities can be effective in helping learners to notice the target feature, but they are not always so (Lee and Huang 2008). A number of factors influence whether noticing occurs. In part it depends on the nature of the target structure. Some structures are more salient than others. For example, the passive construction is relatively salient as it consists of two words (*was/were* + past participle). In contrast, the plural form is much less salient as it consists of a single morpheme attached to the end of a noun (-*s*). Learners may also be more likely to attend to a grammatical form that they have already partially acquired and/or that they have explicit knowledge of than to a completely new form.[2] The main constraint, however, is the learner's level of proficiency. Less proficient learners may struggle to engage in the dual processing involved—comprehending the meaning of the text and consciously attending to linguistic form—and are likely to prioritize meaning over form. Studies (e.g. Shook 1999; VanPatten 1990) have shown that if learners engage in the top-down processing required for comprehension, less noticing of specific forms occurs.

Even if learners do notice the target feature, they may not acquire it. Noticing affects intake but not everything that is taken in passes into long-term memory. Lee and Huang (2008) examined 20 studies that had investigated the effects of text enhancement on L2 acquisition. They reported an overall positive effect in tests administered shortly after the learners had completed reading the enhanced texts but acknowledged that this was quite small and that there were marked differences in the results of individual studies. Lee and Huang also reported that the benefits of the exposure tended to wear off over time.

The effectiveness of text enhancement as a consciousness-raising activity may depend on the extent to which learners are induced to attend to form. In Tolentino and Tokowicz (2014), for example, learners were shown pairs of contrasting sentences that were presented in sequence on a computer screen. The target structures were visually enhanced through colouring, the learners were told to pay close attention to the grammatical patterns, and they were required to say the contrasting sentences out aloud after hearing them. Tolentino and Tokowicz reported that this instruction was effective in enabling the learners to distinguish grammatical from ungrammatical sentences containing a structure that was completely new to them. The pedagogical implication of this study is that if text enhancement is combined with other techniques to ensure more explicit processing of the target structure, it can be effective.

Interpretation Tasks

An interpretation task aims to assist learners to identify the meaning realized by a specific grammatical structure in the input they are exposed to. The goal is what I have called 'grammar comprehension' rather than 'message comprehension' (Ellis 1995). An interpretation task consists of structured input—sentences or continuous text that can be understood only if learners succeed in processing the target form and its meaning. It is in this respect that interpretation tasks differ from text enhancement activities where the processing of the target structure may assist comprehension but is not essential for it. In an interpretation task, learners are not required to produce the target structure but only to demonstrate their understanding of it nonverbally (e.g. by selecting the appropriate picture or by performing an action) or, sometimes, by means of a minimal verbal response (e.g. saying 'yes' or 'no'). An example can be seen in Table 7.3, where the target structure is again past passive. In order to respond to each sentence correctly, learners cannot rely on their world knowledge (e.g. that dogs bite people rather than people bite dogs); they have to attend to the form of the verb and the use of *by* + noun.

The theoretical basis for interpretation tasks is that grammar learning is input driven rather than output driven, in other words, learners do not need to produce the target structure in order to learn it. VanPatten (1996) saw such activities as helping learners to overcome default processing strategies that prevent them from attending to grammatical features in the input and therefore from learning them. For example, the First Noun Principle states that learners will naturally assume that the noun preceding the verb is the agent of the verb. This principle prevents their processing of the grammatical forms in a passive construction where the first noun is not the agent. Thus, when hearing a sentence like, 'The dog was bitten by Mary',

---

TABLE 7.3 An Example of an Interpretation Task

Listen to the sentences. Who did the action? Was it Mary or the dog?

1. The dog was bitten by Mary.
2. Mary kicked the dog.
3. The dog was licked by Mary.
4. Mary stroked the dog.
5. The dog was sat on by Mary.
6. The dog bought Mary a collar.
7. Mary gave the dog a cuddle.
8. Mary barked at the dog.

---

they are likely to comprehend it as 'The dog bit Mary'. However, if they receive feedback indicating that they have interpreted such a sentence incorrectly, they are encouraged to attend closely to the form of the passive construction in subsequent sentences. One of the key features of interpretation tasks is that they encourage explicit processing of grammatical structures in the input—in other words, they evoke a high level of consciousness. In this respect, they differ from typical text enhancement tasks, and this may be why they have been found to be effective.

There are now a large number of studies that have compared the effects of instruction involving interpretation tasks and traditional production-based instruction. While the relative effectiveness of these two types of grammar teaching remains a matter of controversy (see for example DeKeyser and Prieto Botana 2015), there is clear evidence that interpretation tasks do assist learning. One lesson to take from this research, then, is that grammar teaching can usefully include such tasks. In Ellis (2002), I noted that published grammar teaching materials include relatively few interpretation tasks.

Consciousness-as-Understanding

Grammar activities directed at consciousness-as-noticing may or may not result in learners developing an understanding of the target feature. Their purpose is simply to induce attention to the feature to facilitate intake, but it would seem quite likely that at least some learners—perhaps those with higher language analytical ability—also inductively arrive at some kind of explicit rule that captures the general properties of the feature. Thus, text enhancement and interpretation tasks can be seen as also contributing to consciousness-as-understanding.

However, the activities we will now consider have as their primary goal the development of learners' understanding of grammatical features. That is, they are directed at the formation of explicit knowledge. Elsewhere (Ellis 2005), I have characterized explicit knowledge as conscious (i.e. learners know they have it), declarative (i.e. it is comprised of facts about the language), often vague and imprecise (i.e. the understanding that learners develop is often 'fuzzy'), available only in controlled processing (i.e. it can be accessed when learners have plenty of time but it is not readily available in fluent language use) and verbalizable (i.e. learners can verbalize what they know using technical and semi-technical metalanguage).

It is clear from this description that explicit knowledge is limited in a number of ways. Understanding a grammatical feature does not guarantee its use in free communication. Also, some grammatical structures are so complex that it is difficult to ensure that learners achieve a clear understanding of them. Nevertheless, explicit knowledge is of value to learners in a number of ways:

1. Explicit knowledge is important in some types of language use (e.g. careful writing). It facilitates the formulation of sentences when there is no time pressure and also can be used to monitor output.

2. To some degree, it may be possible to automatize explicit knowledge so that it can be used effectively in everyday communication.
3. Because explicit knowledge is abstract, it is not tied to the particular linguistic context in which it was acquired; it is flexible and can be applied in a variety of different contexts.
4. Knowledge of explicit grammatical rules can aid the processes involved in developing the kind of knowledge (i.e. implicit knowledge) needed for the everyday communicative uses of the language. For example, learners are more likely to notice exemplars of a grammatical structure in the input if they already have explicit knowledge of it.

Thus, a clear rationale exists for helping learners develop explicit knowledge of grammar. As shown in Table 7.1, this can be achieved through 'grammar explanation' (i.e. the direct presentation of grammatical information to learners) or by consciousness-raising tasks that guide learners to the self-discovery of rules and generalizations.

Grammar Explanation

Perhaps the most obvious way to help learners develop their explicit knowledge of grammatical rules is to simply provide them with descriptions of the rules. In Ellis (2002), I analysed six grammar practice books and found five of them opted for direct explicit description of rules. In contrast, contemporary general course books such as *Cutting Edge* (Cunningham and Moor 2005) and *New Headway* (Soars and Soars 2003) tend to avoid explanations of grammar points in the main body of each unit, relegating detailed descriptions to the supplementary material at the back of the books. In both types of books, however, there is a clear recognition that learners need access to explanations of grammar. Both types, too, link explanation to practice activities.

Explanations of grammar points can be pedagogic or scientific in nature. *Pedagogic* descriptions provide learners with simplified descriptions of grammar points (i.e. 'rules of thumb' that they can understand and apply easily). The problem here is that there is a tension between the need for 'truthfulness' (i.e. a rule should be true to how a specific grammatical feature figures in real language use) and 'simplicity' (i.e. a rule should be sufficiently simple for learners to understand it). *Scientific* descriptions aim at truthfulness. They provide full descriptions based on linguistic research to explain in detail the link between grammatical forms and the semantic/functional concepts the forms convey. The aim here is to develop what Lantolf (2007) called 'conceptually organized grammatical knowledge'.

By and large, grammar practice books and general course books favour pedagogic descriptions. Ur (1996) reflects the general position taken when she proposed that rule explanation should cover the great majority of instances of a grammatical structure that learners are likely to encounter and some obvious exceptions but should avoid too much detail. Fortune (1998), however, showed how such an approach can lead to problems. He analysed how six popular grammar practice books handled five grammatical structures (conditional sentences, the passive voice, verb forms to express future meaning, present simple vs. progressive, and countable and uncountable nouns). He reported considerable variation in the treatment of these structures and noted a tendency to oversimplification and misleading explanation. He gave an example from an intermediate-level textbook that explained how to use articles with countable nouns but ignored the zero article with uncountable nouns, which he suggested might lead learners to form a 'false dichotomy' between the indefinite and definite articles.

Lantolf (2007) questioned the usefulness of 'rules-of-thumb' drawn from pedagogic grammar. He commented that 'rules of thumb are not necessarily wrong, but they generally describe concrete empirical occurrences of the relevant phenomenon in a fairly unsystematic fashion and, as a result, fail to reveal deeper systematic principles' (36). He argued that learners need access to 'scientific concepts', a term he took from Vygotsky (1986). Lantolf also argued that the presentation of scientific concepts was best achieved by means of a 'material instantiation' rather than verbal description. In Neguerela and Lantolf (2006), this took the form of a 'Schema for the Complete Orienting Basis of Action' for presenting grammatical aspect in Spanish. It consisted of a flow chart that led the learners through a series of questions to help them understand when to use the preterite and imperfect tenses. In accordance with sociocultural theory, the students were asked to verbalize the Schema six times while carrying out a number of oral and written activities in order to internalize the information in the Schema fully. Neguerela and Lantolf collected students' verbal explanations of the grammatical structures at the beginning and end of the course. They reported that initially their explanations were simplistic and incomplete, reflecting the rules of thumb in the textbooks the students were familiar with. After using the flow chart and applying the information in practice activities, their descriptions were generally more coherent and accurate.

The question of whether grammar explanation should be based on pedagogic rules or scientific concepts is an interesting one. It is unlikely that there is a clear-cut general answer. For some learners—such as the university students in Neguerela and Lantolf's study—scientific explanations may be preferable. For other learners, however, pedagogic rules are desirable. Perhaps, too, we should accept that explicit knowledge of grammatical rules is itself a 'developmental' phenomenon. Learners may commence with some oversimplified rule but gradually refine this over time. What is needed is research that sheds light on what different kinds of learners do when confronted with grammatical explanations and the extent to which they successfully internalize them.

Consciousness-Raising Tasks

An alternative pedagogic approach to providing learners with ready-made explanations of grammatical rules is to design tasks that will help them work out the rules for themselves. I have been an advocate of this approach to consciousness-as-understanding (Ellis 1991, 1993). I argued that it encourages the self-generated analysis of the target language and helps to develop the analytical ability that we know is a key characteristic of the 'good language learner'. In other words, tasks that guide learners to discover how specific grammatical features function not only serve to develop their explicit knowledge of these features but also constitute a form of learner training by equipping them with the analytical skills that they can apply autonomously.

Table 7.4 provides an example of a consciousness-raising task. This is directed at helping learners discover the difference between ditransitive verbs like *give* that permit two patterns as in 'Mary gave her father a present' and 'Mary gave a present to her father' and verbs like *explain* that do not (i.e. '*Mary explained her father the problem' is not grammatical). Interestingly, learners are unlikely to find an explanation of this difference in a pedagogic grammar book. I have used this task with language learners in many different contexts. It has never failed to arouse their curiosity. After completing the task, they have proposed all kinds of spurious explanations of the difference, but on each occasion there has always been one learner who could finally come up with the correct explanation—namely, that it depends on the number of syllables in the main verb, with one-syllable verbs like 'give' taking both patterns and verbs with two or more syllables like 'explain' only the one pattern.[3] The task also leads to the recognition of another important aspect

---

TABLE 7.4 A Grammar Consciousness-Raising Task

A. *In the following sentences, why does 'give' have two grammatical patterns whereas* explain *has only one?*

She gave a book to her father. (grammatical)
She gave her father a book. (grammatical)
The policeman explained the law to Mary. (grammatical)
The policeman explained Mary the law. (ungrammatical)

B. *Say whether each of these sentences is grammatical or ungrammatical. Your teacher will check your answers.*

1. They saved Mark a seat.
2. His father read Kim a story.
3. She donated the hospital some money.
4. They suggested Mary a trip on the river.
5. They reported the police the accident.
6. They threw Mary a party.
7. The bank lent Mr. Thatcher some money.
8. He indicated Mary the right turning.
9. The festival generated the college a lot of money.
10. He cooked his girlfriend a cake.

C. *Work out a rule for verbs like 'give' and* explain.

1. List the verbs in part B that are like *give* (i.e. permit both sentence patterns) and those that are like *explain* (i.e. allow only one sentence pattern).
2. What is the difference between the verbs in your two lists?

---

of grammar, namely that the grammar of a language is not fixed but in flux. For example, for many native speakers, the sentence, 'She donated the hospital some money' is considered grammatical these days even though *donate* is a two-syllable verb. In contrast, native speakers are unanimous in rejecting '*They suggested Mary a trip on the river'. This can lead to a discussion about why *donate* is now functioning like *give* whereas *suggest* is not. Grammar consciousness-raising tasks can not only help learners construct their own explicit rules but also sensitize them to nature of grammar and to grammatical change.

There are some important questions to ask about consciousness-raising tasks. Do they result in learners constructing accurate rules? Are they motivating for learners? Are they suitable for all learners? A number of studies (e.g. Fotos and Ellis 1991; Fotos 1994; Mohamed 2001) have addressed these, but more research is needed. By and large, adult learners are able to construct accurate rules, and, in some studies, such tasks lead to better learning than direct grammar explanation. Learners do find consciousness-raising tasks interesting and sometimes prefer this way of learning grammar to direct grammar explanation. Probably, though, such tasks are not well-suited to all learners. Mohammed found they were effective with a group of intermediate-level proficiency learners but not with a group of lower-proficiency learners. Learners need a basic knowledge of the language before they can engage with consciousness-raising tasks. Also, such tasks may be ill-suited to younger learners or to learners with an experiential as opposed to analytical learning style. It is encouraging to note, however, that such tasks are becoming increasingly popular in mainstream course books such as *New Headway*.

Consciousness-raising tasks can be performed by learners working individually, but in much of the research that has investigated them, learners are asked to perform the tasks in pairs or small groups. The idea here—underscored by sociocultural theory—is that the collaborative talk that takes place when learners grapple with a particular grammatical feature promotes better understanding. Eckerth (2008), for example, investigated two L2 German consciousness-raising tasks—a text reconstruction task and a text repair task—where students worked in pairs to agree on a correct version of the texts given to them. He reported that these tasks resulted in patterns of talk very similar to that found in communicative tasks (e.g. there was a similar amount of speech production, and the learners made efforts to resolve misunderstandings and negotiate the correct forms). He showed how the learners worked together as they struggled to achieve a metalinguistic understanding of how the grammatical structures worked. Moreover, the learners were not just focused on formal accuracy but rather 'attended to the way in which form, meaning, function and context interact' (104). Consciousness-raising tasks, therefore, can serve a dual function; they help develop learners' understanding of grammatical features, and they can also provide opportunities for communicative practice where 'grammar' becomes a content to talk about.

Consciousness-as-Control

Both direct grammar explanation and consciousness-raising tasks are aimed at helping learners' development of explicit knowledge. They do not aim to practise use of the target features. I will now turn to consider the third way in which grammar teaching can be understood as involving consciousness—the conscious use that learners make of their explicit knowledge of grammatical features when engaging in production activities.

Production practice has two aims. The first is that by consciously drawing on their explicit knowledge in speech or writing, learners can produce output that is grammatically accurate. That is practice helps learners to exercise conscious control over use of their explicit knowledge. The second is that by practising the production of grammatical forms, learners will fully internalize them up the point where they can use them without conscious processing. Thus, the first aim is to assist the *use* of the L2 while the second is to facilitate *learning*, which for many teachers is the real purpose of grammar teaching. It is, however, uncertain whether the transformation from conscious to unconscious knowledge does take place. As Lightbown (2000) pointed out, practice does not make perfect, and there is plenty of evidence to show that even after plentiful practice, learners are often not able to deploy a target feature in communicative language use. Sometimes it can induce false learning as when learners overuse a heavily practiced feature (Lightbown 1983).

In Table 7.1 I distinguished three types of activities that involve consciousness-as-control—monitoring, text manipulation and text creation activities. I will now discuss each, pointing out in what ways consciousness is involved.

Monitoring Activities

Monitoring is a quintessentially explicit process where learners draw on their explicit knowledge of the L2 grammar to inspect their own production, identify errors and self-correct them. Krashen (1981) noted that monitoring requires (1) a focus on form, (2) explicit knowledge of L2 grammatical forms and (3) time to access this knowledge. It can occur both during the production process itself (i.e. learners can monitor as they speak or write), or it can occur after the production of a complete text (e.g. when learners edit their own writing). Clearly it is easier to monitor writing rather than speech as writing is not carried out in real time, and there is a 'product' that can be easily inspected. However, monitoring also takes place frequently while learners are speaking as they struggle (i.e. engage consciously) for accuracy.

Monitoring is an important process especially for language use but can also play a role in language learning. Here are some suggestions for how teachers can encourage it:

1. They can provide learners with a written text that contains errors in one or more grammatical structures, ask them to read the text, identify the errors and

correct them. Such an activity might usefully follow a consciousness-raising task as it provides an opportunity for the learners to apply the understanding they gained from the task and to refine it by working out how to correct errors they typically make. Such an activity also helps learners to refine their explicit knowledge.

2. In a speaking activity, the teacher can give a signal when a particular type of error is made (e.g. by tapping on a desk), thus inviting the learner to self-correct.

3. Lynch (2001) suggested getting learners to make a transcript of an extract from a recorded performance of an oral activity and then go through the transcript to identify and correct any errors that they noticed. The teacher then reformulates the corrected transcripts and asks the learners to compare their own transcript with the teacher's reformulation of it.

4. Lynch also describes an activity he called 'proof listening'. This involves three cycles based on replaying a recording of learners' performance of a task. First, the students who did the task review and edit their own performance. Second, the recording is replayed, and other students are invited to comment, correct or ask questions. Finally, the teacher comments on any errors that have been missed.

Learners may also need training to help them become effective monitors. Ferris (2002) proposed a procedure aimed at helping learners become skilful, independent editors of their own writing. This consisted of three basic stages: (1) teaching students to pay attention to errors, (2) training them to recognize different types of errors and (3) providing self-editing practice.

Monitoring activities make the link between learners' understanding of grammatical features (i.e. their explicit knowledge) and their conscious application of this in language use. It is therefore an important strategy for achieving accuracy in production. Monitoring can also assist language acquisition in a number of ways. Kormos (1999) suggested that uncertainty regarding whether an error has or has not been committed can motivate learners to notice the gap between their own spontaneous production and their explicit knowledge of what is grammatically correct. Self-correcting errors can also help the learner to rehearse an error-free solution to a particular problem in short-term memory, which can then be stored in long-term memory, contributing to the memory of target-like chunks. Finally, the self-repair that results from monitoring constitutes a form of 'pushed output', which Swain (1995) hypothesized can expand learners' linguistic repertoire.

There is, of course, a time to monitor and a time not to monitor. Learners also need to experience opportunities for unhindered use of the language to encourage them to go on automatic pilot by using their linguistic resources (ungrammatical as well as grammatical) without conscious control. As Krashen (1977) noted, overuse of monitoring needs to be guarded against. Nevertheless, monitoring is a useful strategy, and its encouragement has a place in the repertoire of grammar teaching activities.

Text Manipulation Activities

In a text manipulation activity, language is treated as an *object* to be practised. It has the following characteristics:

- There is a primary focus on a specific grammatical form or sometimes on two contrasting forms.
- There is no communicative purpose to the activity.
- The use of the target language is controlled so that learners need to make only very limited use of their own linguistic resources.
- The outcome of the activity is a predetermined linguistic display [i.e. the correct use of the target form(s)].

Typical examples of text manipulation activities are gap filling, sentence completion, substitution, transformation and matching. Such activities have a long history in grammar teaching. They are great survivors. My review of grammar practice books (Ellis 2002) showed that they are the dominant type of activity. Fortune's (1998) survey of six grammar practice books found that the two main types of practice were sentence completion and gap filling. Nitta and Gardner (2005) also found that what they called 'grammar exercises' figured in all but one of the nine books they investigated.

Text manipulation activities are claimed to provide a bridge between the explicit presentation of a grammatical structure and its use in free production activities. In other words, they help learners make the 'leap from form-focussed accuracy work to fluent, but acceptable, production' (Ur 1996: 83). Table 7.5 provides an example of this view of the role of practice. It is premised on skill acquisition theory. Applied to language learning, it proposes that the learning of a grammatical feature starts with declarative knowledge (i.e. an explicit representation of the target feature) and then evolves into procedural knowledge and finally into automatized knowledge that it is available for use without conscious processing. It is important to note, however, that this is not a matter of one type of knowledge turning into another but rather of 'one kind of knowledge playing a causal role in

TABLE 7.5 The Role of Practice in Second and Foreign Language Learning (Sheen 2004)

a) In classroom learning, it is essential for learners to understand the nature of form-meaning relationships.
b) In order for that understanding to become the foundation of productive oral-aural competence, it is essential to provide learners with frequent opportunities for controlled and monitored individual practice.
c) Though aural recognition may be achieved by means of teacher-fronted exercises, guided pair work is needed to provide sufficient oral production practice.
d) However, such exercises need necessarily to be subsequently supported by communicative activities that require the learners to use the forms learned and practised.

the development of the other' (DeKeyser 2010). DeKeyser emphasized that 'extensive practice is needed to proceduralize the form-meaning mapping for production and/or comprehension' (2010: 158).

However, according to Transfer Appropriate Processing (TAP) theory (Lightbown 2008), there is a direct relationship between the type of practice and the kind of learning that takes place. Thus text manipulation activities will be successful in engaging learners only in the controlled, conscious processing that such activities involve and are unlikely to prepare learners for participation in activities requiring spontaneous face-to-face communication. From this perspective, such activities will fail to build the 'bridge' that Ur and Sheen claim they do. There is in fact very little evidence to show that controlled practice activities are a step stone to the fluent use of grammar (see Ellis 2015).

Perhaps, though, even if one goes along with TAP, a case can still be made for including text manipulation activities in grammar teaching—albeit a more limited one than is commonly assumed. If preceded by activities directed at consciousness-as-understanding, they provide a means for learners to practice the application of their explicit knowledge in controlled language use. If they are used by themselves (i.e. without any prior explicit presentation), they serve an inductive consciousness-raising function that can lead to understanding. In other words, text manipulation activities create contexts for learners to develop, consolidate and apply their explicit knowledge of grammatical rules. Thus even if one questions the claim that they help the development of procedural knowledge, they may be justified as one way of assisting the formation and consolidation of declarative knowledge.[4]

Text Creation Grammar Activities

Text creation grammar activities go under various names—communicative grammar tasks, structured production tasks (Loschky and Bley-Vroman 1993) and focused tasks (Ellis 2003). My current preferred label is 'text creation activities' because this captures their essential feature—namely, that when performing them, learners need to draw on their own linguistic resources in order to achieve a communicative outcome. In this respect, they are like tasks in general. They require a primary focus on meaning rather than form, there is some kind of gap (i.e. an information, opinion or reasoning gap), and they are directed at achieving a communicative goal, not the display of correct language. However, they differ from general communicative tasks in that they have been designed to create a communicative context for either the receptive processing or the production of a predetermined grammatical structure. That is they are 'focused' rather than unfocused. They also differ from 'situational grammar exercises' in that the grammatical target is covert: learners are not explicitly informed of what grammatical structure they should use.

Text creation activities can be input based or output based. In an *input-based* activity, learners listen or read input that has been contrived to present learners with exemplars of the target structure. Shintani (2012), for example, designed a task she called Going to the Zoo to create a context where the learners (young, Japanese children with no prior knowledge of English) had to listen to commands that instructed them to take an animal (or animals) to the zoo by selecting the correct picture cards. Some of the cards referred to a single animal (e.g. 'Find the crocodile and take it to the zoo'), while others referred to more than one animal (e.g. 'Find the crocodiles and take them to the zoo'). In this way, the children had to distinguish singular from plural nouns and demonstrate that they had successfully done so by selecting the appropriate cards. One advantage of input-based text creation activities is that they forced processing of the target feature as learners cannot complete the task successfully without doing so.

Table 7.6 provides an example of a simple *output-based* text creation activity. This task has been designed to provide a context for the use of the singular and plural forms of the present simple tense to express general facts. That is it is expected that in order to describe the characteristics of the animals in the different groups, learners will produce sentences like, 'A human being moves around on legs' and 'All the animals in group 1 have legs'. One disadvantage of output-based tasks of this kind, however, is that it is always possible for learners to avoid using the target feature or to use it incorrectly. For example, while doing the Classifying Animals Task, the learners might say, 'They can move around on their legs' or '*A human being move on legs'. For this reason, corrective feedback plays a very important role in such tasks. Learners need evidence that they have failed to use the target structure or have used it incorrectly, and they also need to be pushed into using the target form. There is now an abundance of evidence (see, for example, Sheen and Ellis 2011) that when learners receive corrective feedback during the performance of a text creation activity, they become more accurate in the use of the target form in subsequent activities. The corrective feedback raises learners' consciousness of the target form in a context that requires its communicative use.[5]

TABLE 7.6 An Example of Text Creation Grammar Activity

Classifying Animals
We can classify animal species into groups according to their different characteristics. Work in pairs and answer these questions.

1. What are the characteristics that distinguish the following animals?
2. In each group, is there one animal that does not belong?

Group	Examples of Animals	Characteristics
1	Human being, dog, horse, frog	
2	Bird, fly, bat	
3	Fish, snake, lizard	

Lightbown (2000) was sceptical of the value of mechanical practice activities but argued that "[w]hen practice is defined as opportunities for meaningful language use (both receptive and productive) and for thoughtful, effortful practice of difficult linguistic features, then the role of practice is clearly beneficial and even essential" (443). Tasks such as the Classifying Animals Task create a context for the kind of practice that Lightbown is referring to. One of the principal differences in the two types of practice lies in the kind of learning they cater to. Text manipulation activities cater to intentional learning (i.e. learners know what it is they are supposed to be practising), whereas text creation activities cater to incidental learning (i.e. learners are not deliberately trying to practice a predetermined grammatical feature). The claim is that attention to form takes place naturally as learners perform a task that activates consciousness in the act of communicating and in so doing facilitates the development of grammatical knowledge that is deployable in communication.

Incidental acquisition, then, is not devoid of consciousness. Indeed, conscious attention to grammatical forms in both input and output is necessary for learning to take place. If learners are struggling to process a particular grammatical feature, they are likely to engage their conscious knowledge of that feature to help them. The purpose of text creation activities, therefore, is not implicit learning but to induce conscious attention to form (i.e. noticing) and even the application of existing explicit knowledge (i.e. understanding) in a context where the learners are primarily engaged in the effort to communicate. In so doing, in line with Task Appropriate Processing, learners are more likely to be able to transfer what they gain from performing a task to real-life communicative situations. The importance of consciousness in the performance of text creation activities cannot be ignored.

Conclusion

The underlying premise of this chapter is that grammar teaching needs to be viewed as a set of devices and techniques for raising learners' consciousness of grammatical forms and the meanings they realize. In claiming this, I might not be seen to be saying anything very different from the traditional view of what grammar teaching is understood to be. But I think I am. The traditional view of grammar teaching holds that by presenting and practising (mechanically and communicatively) a grammatical structure, teachers can intervene directly in interlanguage development by enabling learners to learn it so thoroughly that they are able to deploy it in their communicative language use (Ur 1996). I am suggesting a lesser goal, namely, that grammar teaching should aim at raising learners' consciousness in different ways but leave it to learners to make use of their explicit knowledge in their own way and in their own time.

To this end I have identified three different senses of consciousness in language learning—consciousness-as-noticing, consciousness-as-understanding and consciousness-as-control—and I have tried to show how these relate to a range of different instructional activities. I have argued that all these activities contribute to the conscious use of grammar and to the conscious learning of grammar in one way or another, and all therefore are of potential value. While it may be possible to propose theoretical grounds for believing that some types of consciousness-raising are more effective than others [and in some my other publications such as Ellis (1993) I have attempted to do just this], I have been more tentative here, believing it more important to distinguish how different instructional activities can contribute to different senses and uses of consciousness. Perhaps, though, it is possible to devise an approach to teaching grammar that incorporates all of these ways. See *Impact Grammar* by Ellis and Gaies (1998) for an example of how this might be done. I include a sample unit as an appendix to this chapter and invite readers to examine how the different activities (Listening to Comprehend, Listening to Notice, Understanding the Grammar Point, Checking and Trying It) map onto the different senses of consciousness discussed in this chapter. Missing from the unit, however, are mechanical practice exercises, which are perhaps the least useful means for raising consciousness although, as I have argued earlier, even these may have a role to play.

My claim that grammar teaching should have consciousness raising as its goal is based on current views about the nature of implicit knowledge (i.e. the kind of deployable knowledge needed for easy communication). Implicit knowledge constitutes a complex, adaptive system that is in continual flux. It takes the form of an elaborate neural network comprised of connections between elements that do not correspond to any of the categories or rules that figure in pedagogic or scientific descriptions of grammar and thus is fundamentally different from explicit knowledge. In Ellis (2015: 177), I described implicit knowledge in this way:

> Imagine a series of dots scattered over a page and a computer equipped with software for drawing lines between these dots. Over time the software programme generates a maze of lines. Some of them are faint, suggesting a low weight of connection. Others are heavier, suggesting more firmly established connections. Some dots will be connected to only a few other dots. Others will be connected to a large number of other dots—some with faint lines, others with stronger lines. As the software continues to run so the network of dots grows, gradually becoming more complex. New connections emerge but also some old ones fade and eventually disappear.

Implicit knowledge, therefore, does not consist of 'rules' or even 'features'. It is a maze of neural connections that develops gradually through exposure to input and through output and the feedback that this can elicit. It is organic. Rule-like behaviour (but not rules) emerges gradually as learners move from lexically based chunks to schematic patterns. So, if this is what implicit knowledge is like, it is difficult to see how a grammar lesson (or even a series of lessons) directed at some specific grammatical feature can result in implicit knowledge of that feature. What it can do is raise learners' consciousness of that feature, and over time this consciousness can prime the processes involved in the emergence of implicit knowledge. Perhaps, too, it can help learners to access their explicit knowledge more easily.

Consciousness plays an essential role in the development of implicit knowledge. As N. Ellis (2005) pointed out, 'conscious and unconscious processes are dynamically involved together in every cognitive task and in every learning episode' (340). Thus developing learners' consciousness of grammatical forms and giving them an opportunity to use their explicit knowledge of these forms when speaking and writing can facilitate the emergence of implicit knowledge. They assist the process of usage-based learning by helping learners to break down formulaic expressions such 'I don't know', 'I don't understand', 'I don't want'—the starting point of implicit knowledge—into their grammatical parts. But when learners do this, they do not learn rules but rather bootstrap their way to rule-like behaviour using their consciousness of forms and rules in the process.

I conclude with a brief account of a longitudinal case study of an adult learner of L2 German (Roehr-Brackin 2014) as illustrative of the role of grammar teaching in L2 learning. The learner received explicit instruction in various aspects of German grammar but was also exposed to substantial German input through listening activities, edited works of literature and magazine articles. Roehr-Brackin documented the usage-based trajectory of development that this learner manifested in expressions involving two German verbs (*gehen* and *fahren*). She also showed how explicit processes 'to some extent allowed the learner to side-step the expected developmental trajectory' (801) and illustrated how the learner fell back on explicit processes when he lacked the item-based constructions needed in fluent speech. In this case study, we see evidence of the role that conscious processes can play in both the learning and the use of the L2. For me, it illustrates a crucial point—namely that the interface between explicit and implicit processes rests in the hands of the learner, not in those of the teacher.

By recognizing that the goal of grammar teaching is consciousness raising, we acknowledge that ultimately it is the learner who has to handle the coordination of the explicit and implicit processes involved in building an L2 grammar.

Notes

1   Later, Schmidt (2001) modified his earlier position somewhat by asserting 'people learn about the things they attend to and do not learn *much* about the things they do not attend to' (30; italics added).

2   Another factor that is likely to affect noticing is whether the target feature is similar or dissimilar to an equivalent structure in the learner's first language. Tolentino and Tokowicz (2014) reported a study showing that text enhancement was more effective in the case of a similar than a dissimilar structure. In other words, the learner's L1 can block attention to the target form.

3   The explanation for why one-syllable and two-syllable dative verbs function differently is historical. One-syllable verbs are typically Anglo Saxon. The two-syllable dative words came into English from French and brought with them the French grammatical pattern for these words.

4   I have argued, however, that if the aim is simply to develop learners' explicit knowledge, a better way is the consciousness-raising task as this avoids the potentially damaging effect of controlled practice activities (see Ellis 1991).

5   Corrective feedback constitutes one way of doing Focus on Form, which 'overtly draws students' attention to linguistic elements as they arise incidentally in lessons whose over-riding focus is on meaning or communication' (Long 1991: 45–46).

References

Cunningham, S., & Moor, P. (2005). *Cutting edge intermediate.* Harlow, UK: Pearson Education.

DeKeyser, R. (2010). Practice for second language learning: Don't throw out the baby with the bathwater. *International Journal of English Studies, 10*, 155–165.

DeKeyser, R., & Prieto Botana, G. (2015). The effectiveness of processing instruction in L2 grammar acquisition: A narrative review. *Applied Linguistics, 36*(2), 290–305.

Eckerth, J. (2008). Task-based learner interaction: Investigating learning opportunities, learning processes, and learning outcomes. In J. Eckerth (Ed), *Task-based language learning and teaching: Theoretical, methodological, and pedagogical perspectives* (pp. 89–118). Frankfurt am Main: Peter Lang.

Ellis, N. (2005). At the interface: Dynamic interactions of explicit and implicit knowledge. *Studies in Second Language Acquisition, 27*, 305–352.

Ellis, R. (1991). Grammar teaching—practice or consciousness-raising. In R. Ellis (Ed.), *Second language acquisition and second language pedagogy* (pp. 232–241). Clevedon, UK: Multilingual Matters.

Ellis, R. (1993). Second language acquisition and the structural syllabus. *TESOL Quarterly, 27*, 91–113.

Ellis, R. (1995). Interpretation tasks for grammar teaching. *TESOL Quarterly, 89*, 88–105.

Ellis, R. (2002). Methodological options in grammar teaching materials. In E. Hinkel and S. Fotos (Eds.), *New perspectives on grammar teaching in second language classrooms* (pp. 155–179). Mahwah, NJ: Erlbaum.

Ellis, R. (2003). *Task-based language learning and teaching.* Oxford: Oxford University Press.

Ellis, R. (2005). Measuring implicit and explicit knowledge of a second language: A psychometric study. *Studies in Second Language Acquisition, 27*, 141–172.

Ellis, R. (2015). *Understanding second language acquisition* (2nd ed.). Oxford: Oxford University Press.

Ellis, R., & Gaies, S. (1998). *Impact grammar: Grammar through listening.* New York: Pearson Education.

Ferris, D. (2002). *Treatment of error in second language student writing.* Ann Arbor: University of Michigan Press.

Fortune, A. (1998). Survey review: Grammar practice books. *ELT Journal, 52*(1), 67–80.

Fotos, S. (1994). Integrating grammar instruction and communicative language use through grammar consciousness-raising tasks. *TESOL Quarterly, 28*(2), 323–351.

Fotos, S., & Ellis, R. (1991). Communicating about grammar: A task-based approach. *TESOL Quarterly, 25*(4), 605–628.

Kormos, J. (1999). Monitoring and self-repair in L2. *Language Learning, 49,* 303–342.

Krashen, S. (1977). Some issues relating to the monitor model. In H. Brown, C. Yorio, & R. Crymes (Eds.), *ON TESOL '77* (pp. 144–158). Washington, DC: TESOL.

Krashen, S. (1981). *Second language acquisition and second language learning.* Oxford: Pergamon.

Lantolf, J. (2007). Conceptual knowledge and instructed second language learning: A socio-cultural perspective. In S. Fotos & H. Nassaji (Eds.), *Form-focused instruction and teacher education: Studies in honour of Rod Ellis* (pp. 35–54). Oxford: Oxford University Press.

Lee, S., & Huang, H. (2008). Visual input enhancement and grammar learning. A meta-analytic review. *Studies in Second Language Acquisition, 30,* 307–331.

Leung, J., & Williams, J. (2011). The implicit learning of mappings between forms and contextually derived meanings. *Studies in Second language Acquisition, 33,* 33–35.

Lightbown, P. (1983). Exploring relationships between developmental and instructional sequences in L2 acquisition. In H. Seliger & M. Long (Eds.), *Classroom-oriented research in second language acquisition* (pp. 217–245). Rowley, MA: Newbury House.

Lightbown, P. (2000). Anniversary article: Classroom SLA research and language teaching. *Applied Linguistics, 21,* 431–462.

Lightbown, P. (2008). Transfer appropriate processing as a model for classroom second language acquisition. In Z. Han (Ed.), *Understanding second language process* (pp. 27–44). Clevedon, UK: Multilingual Matters.

Long, M. (1991). Focus on form: A design feature in language teaching methodology. In K. de Bot, R. Ginsberg, & C. Kramsch (Eds.), *Foreign language research in cross-cultural perspective* (pp. 119–132). Amsterdam: John Benjamins.

Loschky, L., & Bley-Vroman, R. (1993). Grammar and task-based methodology. In G. Crookes & S. Gass (Eds.), *Tasks and language learning: Integrating theory and practice* (pp. 123–167). Clevedon, UK: Multilingual Matters.

Lynch, T. (2001). Seeing what they meant: Transcribing as a route to noticing. *ELT Journal, 55,* 124–132.

Miller, G. (1962). *The science of mental life.* Gretna, LA: Pelican Books.

Mohamed, N. (2001). Teaching grammar through consciousness-raising tasks. Unpublished MA thesis, University of Auckland, Auckland.

Neguerela, E., and Lantolf, J. 2006. Concept-based instruction and the acquisition of L2 Spanish. In R. Salaberry & B. Lafford (Eds.), *The art of teaching Spanish: Second language acquisition from research to praxis* (pp. 79–102). Washington, DC: Georgetown University Press.

Nitta, R., & Gardner, S. (2005). Consciousness-raising and practice in ELT coursebooks. *ELT Journal, 59*(1), 3–13.

Roehr-Brackin, K. (2014). Explicit knowledge and processes from a usage-based perspective: The developmental trajectory of an instructed L2 learner. *Language Learning, 64,* 771–808.

Schmidt, R. (1994). Deconstructing consciousness in search of useful definitions for applied linguistics. *AILA Review, 11,* 11–26.

Schmidt, R. (2001). Attention. In P. Robinson (ed.). *Cognition and second language instruction* (pp. 3–32). Cambridge: Cambridge University Press.

Sheen, R. (2004). The role of practice in foreign and second language learning. Developing Teachers.Com. Available online at http://www.developingteachers.com/articles_tchtraining/pract5_ron.htm

Sheen, Y., & Ellis, R. (2011). Corrective feedback in L2 teaching. In E. Hinkel (Ed.), *Handbook of research in second language teaching and learning* (pp. 593–603). London: Routledge.

Shintani, N. (2012). Input-based tasks and the acquisition of vocabulary and grammar: A process-product study. *Language Teaching Research, 16*(2), 253–279.

Shook, D. 1999. What foreign language reading recalls reveal about the input-to-intake phenomenon. *Applied Language Learning, 10*, 39–76.

Soars, L., & Soars, J. (2003). *New headway: Intermediate students' book.* Oxford: Oxford University Press.

Swain, M. 1995. Three functions of output in second language learning. In G. Cook and B. Seidlhofer (Eds.), *Principle and practice in applied linguistics: Studies in Honour of H. G. Widdowson* (pp. 125–144). Oxford: Oxford University Press.

Tolentino, L., & Tokowicz, N. (2014). Cross-language similarity modulates the effectiveness of grammar instruction. *Language Learning, 64*, 279–309.

Ur, P. (1996). *A course in language teaching: Practice and theory.* Cambridge: Cambridge University Press.

VanPatten, B. (1990). Attending to form and content in the input. *Studies in Second Language Acquisition, 12*, 287–301.

VanPatten, B. (1996). *Input processing and grammar instruction in second language acquisition.* Norwood, NJ: Ablex.

Velmans, M. (1991). Is human information processing conscious? *Behavioral and Brain Sciences, 14*(4), 651–669.

Williams, J. (2005). Learning with awareness. *Studies in Second Language Acquisition, 27*, 269–304.

Vygotsky, L. 1986. *Thought and language* (newly revised and edited by A. Kozulin). Cambridge, MA: MIT Press.

APPENDIX

4

Holiday Postcards

Where do you like to go on holiday?
What do you like to do?

ERROR BOX

✗ Every day I am sitting by the pool.

✗ At the moment I drink a glass of wine.

LISTENING TO COMPREHEND

Brad and Gloria are on holiday. Listen to them read their postcards.

1. Where is Brad?
   a. at a jazz festival
   b. on an island
   c. in California

2. Where is Gloria?
   a. in Paris
   b. in London
   c. by the sea

WORD BOX
*nightlife
*jealous
*rush
*seafood

LISTENING TO NOTICE

Listen again. Fill in the blanks with a form of the verb in parentheses ( ).

This is the life! Every morning I _____ breakfast by the pool.
1 (have)
Then I _____ for a walk along
2 (go)
the beach or into town. In the afternoon I usually _____ a trip
3 (take)
somewhere on the island. In the
evening I _____ the nightlife.
4 (enjoy)
At the moment I _____ to some
5 (listen)
great jazz. Jealous? You should be!

Brad

Remember George Rush from
London? Well, surprise, surprise, he
_____ at the same hotel for a
6 (stay)
few days. We _____ a great
7 (have)
time. He _____ me all the best
8 (show)
places in Paris. Well, I must rush now.
We _____ out to this new
9 (go)
seafood restaurant right now. I
_____ you always.
10 (love)

Gloria

Brad
216
Los

UNDERSTANDING THE GRAMMAR POINT

1. Look at the postcards again.
   a. Circle all the verbs in the simple present tense. I (have)
   b. Underline all the verbs in the present continuous tense. I am listening.

2. Find these adverbials in the postcards.
   - every morning   • in the afternoon   • at the moment   • usually
   - for a few days   • in the evening   • always   • now

3. Write the adverbials in the correct column.

Simple Present	Present Continuous
every morning	
usually	

CHECKING

Can you correct
the errors in this
holiday postcard?

Dear Daniel,

    At the moment I am sitting in a little restaurant in Copacabana. It is late and
the sun ~~just begins~~ *is just beginning* to set. I am watch some teenagers. They playing volleyball on
the beach. A middle-aged man is jogging past my table. Every day I am coming to
the same restaurant. I am eating a light meal — just a salad or some fish — and
drinking a glass of wine. Sometimes I chat with the waiter. He is telling me about
his young boy and I tell him about you. Life is almost perfect, except, of course,
you are not here!

                Love always,
                Laura

LANGUAGE NOTE
Use some of the
adverbials (every
morning, always,
now) and the present
continuous or simple
present tenses.

TRYING IT

Imagine you are on holiday. Write a postcard to a friend.
Tell your friend what you are doing at the moment and what
you do every day. Try to make the person wish he or she was with you!

....
....
....

4

8

12 PRINCIPLES OF GRAMMAR INSTRUCTION[1]

Jack C. Richards and Randi Reppen

Introduction

Unlike other areas of language instruction, the pros and cons of grammar instruction are often hotly debated. While everyone agrees that the appropriate and precise use of grammar plays a major part in learners' success, how to achieve that is another matter. Cullen (2012: 258) contrasts two basic positions, one being "the view that the most effective form of instruction was no overt instruction: learners would acquire the grammar of the language implicitly through exposure to comprehensible input roughly tuned to their level and engagement in meaning-focused tasks", and the other the belief "that some kind of focus on form in the language classroom is necessary both to accelerate the process of grammar acquisition and raise ultimate levels of attainment".

Another dichotomy that is a challenge for grammar instruction is the distinction between grammatical knowledge and grammatical ability. Grammatical *knowledge* refers to knowledge of the rules that account for grammatically correct language. Its unit of focus is typically at the sentence level. In traditional approaches to language teaching, grammar is typically viewed as an independent component of language ability and assessed through discrete item tests that assess mastery of different grammatical items. Correct language use is achieved through a drill-and-practice methodology and through controlled speaking and writing exercises that are designed to prevent or minimize opportunities for errors. Practice of discrete grammar points in carefully controlled environments with the goal of producing grammatically correct sentences is viewed as the key to learning.

Grammatical *ability* refers to the use of grammar as a communicative resource in spoken and written discourse and requires a different pedagogical approach (Jones 2012). Its unit of focus is the context of use and the *text*. *Text* here is used to refer to structured and conventional sequences of language that are used in specific ways in different contexts. For example, in the course of a day, a person may use English for a variety of interactional and transactional purposes, both spoken and written, such as casual conversation, telephone calls, requests, reports, discussions, and so on. Each of these contexts of use involves language that conforms to norms of organization and content and that draw on appropriate grammar and vocabulary (Hewings and Hewings 2005). Grammatical ability involves using grammar as a resource to create appropriate different spoken and written texts depending on the specific context. These contexts might include studying in an English-medium university, working in a restaurant, working in an office, or socializing with neighbors in a housing complex.

As teachers, we know that students often develop a good understanding of grammatical *knowledge* through traditional teaching methods that focus on grammar as a somewhat isolated collection of rules—rules that exist independently of their use in the production of authentic written or spoken language. Students may have spent many hours practicing the rules for correct sentence formation but lack the ability to use grammar as a resource accurately and appropriately in communication beyond a sentence level. To enable learners to develop grammar as a communicative resource, it needs to be taught and assessed as a component of communicative ability and performance—particularly in relation to the productive skills of writing and speaking. In this chapter, we put forth 12 principles for grammar instruction that can help students move from *knowledge* of discrete grammar facts to the *ability* to use grammar appropriately and accurately in different contexts.

1. Identify the Grammatical Resources the Learners Need

The starting point in teaching grammar as an ability is an understanding of the tasks that learners will need to accomplish and the role of grammar in relation to those needs. This does not mean developing a list of grammar points that will be used as the basis for sentence-level practice but rather identifying the grammar demands of different kinds of spoken and written texts. For example, to what extent are the learners able to use appropriate grammar in expository or descriptive writing or in narratives and recounts? Table 8.1 shows one way to inventory and identify grammatical demands of different texts. This is followed by an example activity to raise awareness of verb use for a specific writing task.

Activity

Learners in many disciplines write reports that include survey results. To prepare for this task, learners can be given an article that includes discussion of the Methodology, Reporting, and Discussion of Results of a survey. Students can then identify the appropriate verbs and verb forms in the various sections. For instance, the

TABLE 8.1 Examples of Text Types and Grammatical Resources Needed

Text Type	Purpose	Structure	Major Language Features
Written: Informational report	To give factual information	Statements of facts Descriptions and explanations	Informational focus Presenting facts—present tense Packaging information—clausal embedding; noun–noun sequences Focusing on processes vs. people—passive voice Necessary vocabulary
Spoken: Conversation between friends	To share personal information and experiences	Interaction Shared time and space	Interpersonal focus Sharing information—personal pronouns; present tense; progressive aspect; questions & responses Past markers (*last week* etc.) Necessary vocabulary
Written: Opinion text	To put forth a particular point of view	Thesis Presenting evidence to persuade Arguments	Clauses for supporting evidence—purpose clauses; conditional clauses Causal subordination—*because, so* Necessary vocabulary

"natural" use of the passive voice in the Methods section in the following examples can be highlighted in a model text, then learners can be asked to draft a Methods section and compare their verbs to the example text.

Examples of Passive Voice from the Methods Section:

Participants were recruited on the basis of . . .
Survey respondents were selected from the general student population . . .
Survey questions were drafted after discussion with a focus group . . .
Surveys were distributed in the student cafeteria in order to maximize . . .

These two activities highlight how text types make use of particular grammatical resources. Identifying learners' grammatical needs in relation to texts that are being produced provides an authentic context for the presentation and practice of grammar. This promotes grammar ability, not just knowledge of the rules but also the ability to use rules and grammar knowledge to create accurate and appropriate texts.

2.   Teach Awareness of the Nature of Texts

While students are generally familiar with the role of grammar at the level of the sentence, exploring the role of grammar in the organization of texts involves looking at the ways in which language is used for particular purposes and how the social context for language use (school, work, colleagues, peers, friends, family) affects the choice of language (Paltridge 2006). The key feature of texts is the use of recognizable patterns of organization. For longer, written expository texts, the reader generally expects to see the text organized into paragraphs and, within paragraphs, to find main ideas and supporting details—features that contribute to the coherence of a text. However, a writer's use of the accepted organizational patterns of a text may vary, according to the intended audience. Hedge (2000: 323) points out that although a text describing a medical problem and its treatment might generally follow the pattern: *situation—problem—solution—conclusion*, a writer may vary this sequence of information for effect:

> The sequence of elements above would probably be considered normal, with conclusions coming last. However, a newspaper article on the topic might report on the treatment first, in order to raise curiosity, and then move on to explain the problem. In fact, there could be several possible sequences for the information.

There are several ways in which students can be introduced to the concept of text, to the ways in which texts work, and to how they reflect grammatical choices. For example:

a.   Have students read two texts with the same content and identify what makes one an effective text and the other not effective.
b.   Have students compare written and spoken texts on the same topic (e.g., a news event) to compare how they are organized and how the grammar of the texts differs.
c.   Have students listen to interactions such as requests made in different contexts (e.g., among friends vs. with a boss) and see how features such as modals and pronouns work together to create politeness.
d.   In more advanced academic contexts, give students examples or model texts of research articles and have them analyze how the text is put together within the different sections (e.g., methods, results) and to use the information to inform their writing. By studying the different "moves" or sections that make up a text (Swales 1990), students focus on questions. How does a text begin? Where is the main idea introduced? How is an idea developed? What verbs are typical of certain sections?

As a follow-up activity, the teacher can use authentic texts such as the following one, delete the verb forms, and have students complete them and compare in groups.

> To tourists who hail from more orderly, sanitized societies, Myanmar's street life can be charming. On the sidewalks of Yangon, radishes are shredded, corn is steamed, coconuts are hollowed out and stalks of sugar cane are crushed into juice. Vendors sell knickknacks. On one stretch of sidewalk,

they hawk teacups, used knives, Chinese-made plastic toys, two types of rat poison and a large pile of dusty, secondhand TV remote controls.

(Fuller 2013)

3. Develop Awareness of Differences Between Spoken and Written Language

An important feature of texts is the way they reflect differences between spoken and written grammar. One of the differences between written and spoken English is the use of clausal and nonclausal units (Biber et al. 1999). Conversation consists mostly of clausal units while in writing, particularly academic prose, nonclausal units, or phrases, are used to package information. Using the same texts from Activity b from Tip 2, students can compare the different grammar resources used in two texts that differ only in mode (i.e., spoken vs. written). Another activity option is for students to explore examples of spoken texts, such as the following example of a conversation between two friends in Japan who meet in a shopping mall (McAndrew 2007) and then turn the conversation into a written text (e.g., in the form of a blog to a friend or a recount) and compare the language (focusing on clausal vs. phrasal units) of the two texts.

A: Hi.

B: Oh hi, how's it going?

A: Good, good, fine.

B: Are you, er, doing some shopping?

A: Yeah, just a few things really, you know.

B: Yeah.

A: Yeah . . . actually, I've been looking for a present, for Hiroko, but it's difficult to . . . you know . . .

B: Yeah, umm, what kind of thing?

A: Oh, something like, umm, a present . . . something like, it's her birthday tomorrow actually. [laughs]

B: Tomorrow?

A: Yeah, tomorrow. So I've looked in Hamaya, like at the make-up and stuff, but it's not very exciting.

B: Tomorrow? How about Amu Plaza . . . they've got Tower Records and some kind of new shops.

A: Yeah. OK, great, Tower Records might be good. I might give that a go. I've got to go over to the station, anyway. So, anyway, good to see you, and thanks for the tip.

B: That's fine. Say "happy birthday" to Hiroko from me.

A: OK, I will. Bye.

B: Yeah, bye.

A: Bye.

Comparing examples of spoken and written texts can raise students' awareness of how spoken and written texts often make use of different grammatical resources.

4. Use Corpora to Explore Texts

Corpora provide a way in which teachers can help students learn grammar as it is actually used in spoken and written texts. The availability of online corpora that provide easily accessible data on authentic language usage, such as MICASE (micase. elicorpora.info), MICUSP (micusp.elicorpora.info), COCA (corpus.byu.edu/coca/), or Word and Phrase (www.wordandphrase.info), provides teachers and students with ready resources of discipline-specific writing or to highlight differences between spoken and written language. MICUSP (2009) is composed of over 800 papers (over 2 million words) with a grade of A written by upper-level college students across 16 different disciplines. The website is designed to allow for user-friendly searches of not only vocabulary but also across different types of papers (e.g., argumentative essays, research papers, reports), as well as organizational aspects of academic prose, including Methods sections, referring to sources, and problem solution patterns. An example of a classroom application use of MICUSP would be where students in an academic writing class explore which verbs are used to refer to figures or charts or what verb tenses are used in abstracts of academic articles.

Teachers can use COCA to prepare discovery activities that clearly demonstrate differences between spoken language and academic prose. An example of one activity of this type is to highlight the different types of verbs used in academic prose and conversation. Corpus research reveals that single-word verbs are generally preferred in academic prose over multiword verbs (e.g., tolerate vs. put up with; discover vs. find out). Novice writers, however, often use multiword verbs in their papers since these are more frequent in conversation and often more familiar to students. After reading student papers, a teacher can compile a list of multiword verbs that frequently appear in student papers and have students explore COCA to compare those with single-verb alternatives. Table 8.2 shows one way to have students record their results.

When drafting or revising academic writing, students can enter in multiword verbs that they plan to use and single-word verb equivalents (e.g., put up with tolerate; find out discover) to see which one is more suitable for their paper. This not only builds students' vocabulary but also helps reinforce differences between informal spoken and formal written texts.

Research from corpus studies enables teachers to identify information of this kind and to use it to inform both teaching and materials development (Reppen 2010). In this way, grammar can be taught in relation to different contexts of use and with different types of texts. Use of a corpus can help identify the vocabulary that is commonly used with different text types such as *procedural descriptions, informational texts*, and *persuasive texts*. Looking at corpus resources previously mentioned can help students become aware of the verbs that most frequently occur in

TABLE 8.2 An Example of a Table for Recording the Results of Searching COCA

	Written	*Spoken*
Find out	☑	☑ ☑ ☑ ☑
Discover	☑ ☑ ☑ ☑	☑ ☑
Look at	☑ ☑ ☑	☑ ☑ ☑ ☑ ☑
Examine	☑ ☑ ☑ ☑ ☑ ☑	☑
Put up with	☑	☑ ☑ ☑ ☑ ☑
Tolerate	☑ ☑ ☑ ☑ ☑	☑

the passive and which prepositions frequently go with certain passive forms, helping students master some of the more difficult aspects of English.

5. Use a Variety of Teaching Approaches

Learning grammar is a complex, multifaceted, and lengthy process, and no single pedagogical approach can claim priority in teaching (Ellis and Shintani 2014). Approaches to teaching grammar need to acknowledge that learners have different learning style preferences when it comes to learning grammar. Some students like explanations and are uncomfortable when they do not have a clear understanding of something. Others are more tolerant of ambiguity and do not feel the need for detailed explanations.

Therefore at times it may be appropriate to present grammar explicitly using a deductive or rule-driven approach (Thornbury 1999): the lesson may start with the teacher presenting information about the role a particular grammatical feature plays in texts and then examine one or more texts to see how the text reflects the grammatical feature. Thornbury (1999: 30) suggests a number of advantages of a deductive approach, including:

- It gets straight to the point, and can therefore be time-saving. Many rules—especially rules of form—can be more simply and quickly explained than elicited from examples. This will allow more time for practice and application.
- It respects the intelligence and maturity of many—especially adult—students, and acknowledges the role of cognitive processes in language learning.
- It confirms many students' expectations about classroom learning, particularly for those learners who have an analytical learning style.

A deductive approach can also be used within a problem-solving collaborative format. For example, to teach the differences between the use of the simple past and the present perfect, the class could be arranged into sets of pairs and given an information gap task. Half of the sets of pairs receives a summary of rules for the use of the simple past. The other half receives a summary of the use of the present perfect. Next, they all receive a partially completed text in which there are many instances involving a choice between simple past and present perfect. The students use their grammar summaries to complete those sentences where their rules apply. Following this, the pairs are regrouped so that pairs consist of one student who received rules of the past tense and one who received rules for the present perfect. They then examine the text again and share their ideas on how it can be completed, justifying their choices using the information from their summaries. Thornbury (1999: 43) describes the advantage of tasks of this kind:

> To complete the task (the grammar exercise) learners will need to share the information, which in turn will involve speaking English. They are learning about the language and getting communicative practice at the same time.

At other times, the teacher may prefer to use an inductive approach, providing examples of texts that include particular grammatical features and inviting the students to examine the grammatical features of texts. One way in which this can be achieved is through activities in which students compare two texts on the same topic or situation but that differ in their use of particular grammatical features. Students can consider differences that may reflect differences in *mode* (e.g., spoken or written), *purpose* (e.g., to persuade or to describe), or *genre* (e.g., newspaper report or an encyclopedia entry). For example, students might compare an extract from a travel guide that gives suggestions and advice on things to do and see in a city and compare this with a blog entry or an email message from a friend on the same topic. In comparing the two texts, they could consider how obligation is expressed in each text through choices related to modality. This could highlight the role of modal verbs as well as other means of expressing obligation and necessity.

In addition to different learning styles, grammar, like vocabulary, needs multiple exposures and practice. This repeated exposure needs to be engaging and meaningful, i.e., language practiced within its context of use rather than forced into an artificial context for the sake of practice.

6. Provide Opportunities for Guided Noticing

Second language acquisition research has drawn attention to the role of consciousness in language learning and in particular to the role of *noticing* (Schmidt 1990). Consciousness of features of the input can serve as a trigger that activates the first stage in the process of incorporating new linguistic features into one's language competence. The extent to which items are "noticed" may depend on the frequency of encounters, the perceptual saliency of items, instructional strategies that can focus the learner's attention, as well as the kind of task the learner is taking part in.

An example of a guided noticing activity is for the teacher to give out text extracts (e.g., magazine or newspaper articles) and to ask students to see how many examples they can find of a particular form or grammatical pattern. Students then examine these more closely to observe the functions they perform at both the sentence and text levels and to identify any patterns. For example, students could be given a text with count and noncount nouns, along with a list of some of the count and noncount nouns found in the text. Students then search the text to find those nouns and note which nouns have articles associated with them. However, this in itself is not usually sufficient and needs to be coupled with questions or tasks that prompt the students to reflect on or analyze the function or the pattern of the highlighted items in a text. By "guiding" the student in this way, this kind of activity raises awareness of the target forms and actively involves the student in the process of discovery.

In an ESL context, noticing activities can be taken outside the classroom. Students can act as "language detectives": they can be asked to observe and notice target forms in use in the "real world", such as by watching interviews and other speech events on the Internet or on television and documenting the use of particular grammatical features they have been asked to focus on. This can serve to reinforce vocabulary or particular forms, but it can also be used to help more advanced students become aware of how grammar works together at a textual level instead of focusing only on vocabulary or on sentence-level structures. Students can use a notebook or mobile device for recording examples and can bring these to class for further discussion or clarification.

7. Provide Opportunities for Meaningful Communicative Practice

It is important to keep in mind the distinction sometimes made among three different kinds of practice—mechanical, meaningful, and communicative. *Mechanical practice* refers to a controlled practice activity that students can successfully carry out without necessarily understanding the language they are using and in which the primary focus is on form. Examples are repetition drills and substitution drills designed to practice a particular form or an activity in which students have to change the tenses in a business letter from present to past tense. *Meaningful practice* refers to an activity where language control is still provided but where students are required to make meaningful choices when carrying out the practice. It involves a focus on both form and meaning. For example, using a model letter the teacher has provided in which particular grammatical features are highlighted, students might be asked to draft a letter of complaint to a company about a product they ordered. *Communicative practice* refers to activities where practice using language within a real communicative context is the focus, where real information is exchanged, and where the language used is not totally predictable. For example, students could write a letter to future students providing tips for academic success based on their recent class experiences.

Communicative practice implies practicing the use of language with a focus on form, meaning, and, most importantly, context. Jones and Lock (2011: 2) comment:

> Texts are always produced in some kind of context. As features of context change, texts change. Or, to look at it in another way, as texts change, the contexts they evoke also change. Because of this, it is rarely possible to give an adequate account of why a particular grammatical feature is used in a particular clause or sentence without referring to, or trying to reconstruct, some context, including both features of the text that it comes from (the context) and features of the situation in which the text was produced (the situational context).

Contextualized practice involves using grammar in the context of spoken or written communication. It also means ensuring that contexts for spoken or written practice are authentic and that the grammar of spoken or informal language is not practised in a formal written context just to provide additional practice. Meaningful practice also means that when overtly teaching a form, or focusing on accuracy, practice moves from controlled to open-ended. Once students can control the form, they then need opportunities to practice using it in a variety of ways and in tasks that move from sentence-level to complete texts.

Some forms, such as modals (e.g., *can, could, should*) are easy to learn when it comes to producing the correct form; however, using modals accurately is more difficult since they often serve pragmatic functions such as showing politeness. After students have mastered the appropriate forms through controlled and semi-controlled practice (e.g., tasks moving from a controlled gap-fill activity to more open-ended activities), students could be given practice that emphasizes the use of modals in different situations. They might be provided with scenarios of making requests to friends, strangers, or people who represent different power relationships (e.g., co-workers vs. supervisors or classmates vs. teachers). This activity could be done individually, following which students work in pairs to act out various scenarios for the class: classmates then vote on which scenario is being performed. If students vote on the "wrong" scenario, then a class discussion can be a valuable activity to raise awareness of what led the class to choose the incorrect scenario. Activities such as this provide students with real-world situations in the safe environment of the classroom and can build student confidence for interactions outside the classroom.

Communicative practice often involves collaboration on tasks, and this can be included at all levels of instruction. For example, in beginning-level classes, students can be given strips of texts (either sentences or paragraphs that have been cut apart) and then in pairs reconstruct the sentences and/or paragraphs. This task can raise awareness as to how texts, even at a sentence or paragraph level can be reordered to create different effects. At a more advanced level, the teacher can read a short passage very quickly, asking students to focus on the message and to take notes on the key points. Then students work in groups using their notes to create a summary text. This could include a group editing task tapping into expertise that students have creating a context for collaboration and the co-construction of texts. If some students are very good at synthesis, they could be responsible for combining information that others have gathered and presented in the form of notes from specific readings that other students have done on particular topics relevant to the task.

8. Provide Opportunities for Students to Produce Stretched Output

An important aspect of language learning is the complexity of the learner's language—in the case of grammar, the range of grammatical resources the learner is able to use. Skehan (1998) argues that ideally, fluency, accuracy, and complexity develop in harmony, but this is not always the case. In order for the learner's language to complexify, new linguistic forms have to be acquired and added to the learner's productive linguistic repertoire. This is referred to as *restructuring*. For restructuring to occur, two things seem to be required: (1) noticing features of language that the learner has not yet acquired (referred to as noticing the gap) previously referred to and (2) the use of tasks that require the learner to use new and more complex grammar that require the use of certain target language forms and that "stretch" the learner's language knowledge, requiring a "restructuring" of that knowledge. Activities that involve so-called stretched output are those that expand or "restructure" the learner's grammatical system through increased communicative demands and attention to linguistic form.

For example, a task may be completed orally, it may be recorded, or it may require writing. In each case, different opportunities for language awareness and production are involved. Swain (1999: 3) describes how tasks with a written product provide an opportunity for students to focus on form and to stretch their language resources.

> Students, working together in pairs, are each given a different set of numbered pictures that tell a story. Together the pair of students must jointly construct the story-line. After they have worked out what the story is, they write it down. In so doing, students encounter linguistic problems they need to solve to continue with the task. These problems include how best to say what they want to say; problems of lexical choice; which morphological endings to use; the best syntactic structures to use; and problems about the language needed to sequence the story correctly. These problems arise as the students try to "make meaning", that is, as they construct and write out the story, as they understand it. And as they encounter these linguistic

problems, they focus on linguistic form—the form that is needed to express the meaning in the way they want to convey it.

Jones and Lock (2011) recommend "elaborating" as a means of helping learners expand their grammatical resources. This refers to activities in which students add to and expand the information contained in a text and, in the process, need to use more sophisticated grammatical features. "Elaborating activities can help to dramatize for them the fact that learning grammar is not just about 'correctness' but that it is first and foremost about gaining control over resources for making communication more effective" (73). Jones and Lock (2011: 74) describe the general procedures used in elaborating as follows:

1. Present students with a simple text.
2. Create a situation in which questions are asked about the text in a way that students notice that additional information would make the text better and that this new information is typically associated with certain grammatical features.
3. Explore with students why certain kinds of additions in the text require certain grammatical features and others require different ones.
4. Have students practice by continuing to elaborate on the same text or elaborating on a similar text.

At the completion of a unit where students have been writing different types of texts on a particular topic (compare/contrast, argumentative, informative), give students several short texts on the same topic and ask them to respond to an essay question that draws on the texts and the students' experiences.

9. Make Links Between Grammar and Vocabulary

Although grammar and vocabulary are often presented separately, the boundary between them is not rigid. In fact, it is sometimes difficult to separate the two. The connections between grammar and vocabulary can be highlighted and developed in a number of ways. Advocates of the lexical approach suggest incorporating lexical phrases or chunks containing examples of grammar that will be acquired initially as vocabulary and later as grammar. For example, the modal *might* could be introduced in a chunk such as *It might take a while*, without focusing on its full range of modal meanings. Later, other phrases with *might* can be used such as *It might take a long time. It might take a couple of weeks. It might take even longer.* Similarly *the adjective +infinitive* construction might be introduced in a phrase such as *He isn't easy to talk to* and later extended to . . . *isn't easy to work with*, . . . *is easy to get along with*. In a lexical approach, the past perfect might occur first in chunks such as *worse/better than I'd expected, than I'd imagined, than I'd thought*, etc. Later it can be presented again but this time as grammar.

The use of corpora is another way of exploring links between grammar and vocabulary, as this teacher describes:

One way to utilize the Corpus of Contemporary American English (COCA) with advanced or upper-intermediate students is to help them discover the difference between hope and wish. Using the KWIC (key word in context) feature, students can see each word in a natural context. The parts of speech are color coded, so students can easily look for the words in their verb forms only. I provide some guiding questions before they begin in order to facilitate their understanding. I want them to see that *hope* is used when something is still possible and *wish* is used when something is no longer possible/likely, so my questions are designed to make that difference salient. Going further, students investigate which verb tenses occur with each word by answering more guiding questions. They find that *hope* often occurs with present tense discussing future possibility, whereas *wish* occurs with past tense, in reference to the present, or past perfect, in reference to the past. If students have studied conditionals, I try to help them make the connection that the meaning-tense connection follows the pattern of unreal conditionals, where past tense refers to the present and past perfect refers to the past.

In the next section, the activity presented, using student errors, also highlights the intimate relationship of vocabulary and grammar.

10. Use Student Errors to Inform Instruction

Students' grammar problems can be a useful source for teaching material. Students will likely make errors both at the sentence level as well as the text level, and teaching activities can be developed both around a collection of typical errors students have made in the past, as well as through addressing errors that arise in ongoing classroom work. Experienced teachers are often aware of certain challenging areas of grammar. However, novice teachers and even experienced teachers working with students from different language backgrounds can benefit from trying to identify patterns of errors found in student texts. These patterns of errors can then be used to inform instruction.

The following is an example of a sentence-level error where students were struggling with *result + preposition* and were using *result of* and *result in* interchangeably. The teacher noticed this error pattern and created an activity that led students through a guided noticing activity to help the student understand that *of* is used when *result* is a noun (The *result of* heavy rain is often flooding) and that *in* is used when *result* is a verb (Heavy rain can *result in* flooding). The teacher then developed a *result in/of* guided noticing activity (that also reinforces the relationship between vocabulary and grammar):

a. Fill in the blanks with either *in* or *of*. Check your answers with a classmate.

1. Failure to do so may result ____ an "F" for your final grade.
2. Five unexcused absences will result ____ a failure in this class.

3. You should become better writers as a result ____ this course.
4. The result ____ this exercise will be a carefully organized essay.
5. Excessive absences may result ____ a failing grade.

b. Look at the sentences and answer the following two questions:

1. What part of speech (noun or verb) is *result* when used with *in*? _____
2. What part of speech (noun or verb) is *result* when used with *of*? _____

The teacher then gave students a number of short texts based on extracts from students' writing that contained correct and incorrect uses of *result in/of* examples and asked students to work in pairs and correct the texts.

An example activity that draws on students' errors at the level of text is one that addresses problems with the active/passive distinction. This distinction can be understood only in the context of extended texts, since the correct voice depends on the context of the text and its communicative purpose and flow of information. Students can be given examples of texts containing clauses that could be completed in passive or active voice or that contain clauses with an incorrect voice, together with guiding questions prompting them to think about the context of the text and the information focus and to use this information to make the choice between active or passive. Using error patterns from student texts in this way is an efficient way to inform instruction.

11. Integrate Grammar with the Four Skills

Grammar does not exist in isolation as lists of rules for forming sentences but is an essential part of the structure of texts. It can be thought of as the "glue" that holds words and sentences together to create written and spoken texts and that serves as one of the ways we understand conversations or readings. Grammar is not an end in itself but a means to an end. With this in mind, it is essential that grammar is taught and practiced across all skills and in a manner that moves from part to whole or from sentences to entire texts. In our view, the appropriate place for grammar in the curriculum is as a component of skill-based courses in reading, writing, listening, or speaking or as part of an integrated approach that includes all skills such as content-based instruction and content and language integrated learning (CLIL), rather than as a stand-alone course on grammar. Much of what is often taught in traditional grammar courses focuses on sentence-based practice. This can be assigned for self-study using the resources that technology provides for practice activities, or it can be incorporated into a content lesson with a short mini lesson on the problematic form. Here are some ideas for incorporating grammar in skills-based classes and activities.

Grammar and Reading

Grammar can be included in a reading activity in several ways, several of which have been illustrated elsewhere in this chapter. For example, a reading text may contain "while-reading" tasks that may occur alongside the text to guide the reader through the text and through the reading process. Guiding or focusing questions can be used in this way and can be used to draw attention to grammatical choices made by the writer. The type of while-reading activity will depend upon the type of text. If the text is a narrative, students might number the sequence of events in the narrative on a list or chart and later write their own version of the narrative, using the information in the chart. Another example activity that combines reading and grammar is for students to use texts from a reading or a content class and locate the target grammar forms and then as pairs discuss the grammar choices.

Celce-Murcia (2002: 131) describes the use of authentic texts that are chosen to illustrate particular features of text grammar. These are used initially for reading comprehension, following which students explore the grammar of the texts in groups, guided by focus questions. The students then create their own written texts, using the grammatical features they have explored.

Grammar and Writing

Writing classes are often the most obvious place to link grammar as a resource used in the creation of texts. Hinkel (2002) uses oral interviews as a springboard to practising texts "that contain various time frames (and tense uses) within the conventions of English discourse" (195). Students are first assigned a topic and interview a number of people to collect information for use in a written information report. Feez and Joyce (1998: 28–31) illustrate how grammar and writing are integrated in a deductive and text-based approach.

Phase 1: Building the context

In this stage students are presented with a sample text (e.g. a newspaper editorial) and discuss the general cultural context in which the text type is used and the social purposes the text type achieves. They may compare the model text with other texts of the same type of with different text types.

Phase 2: Modeling and deconstructing the text

This stage focuses on exploration of the structural or organizational features and also the grammatical features of the model text. "Modeling and deconstruction are undertaken at both the whole text, clause and expression levels. It is at this stage that many traditional ESL language teaching activities come into their own" (1998: 29).

Phase 3: Joint construction of a similar text

Guided by the teacher, the students now begin to create a new text, one which reflects the grammatical and discourse features of the model text they have studied. The teacher gradually reduces his or her contribution to text construction, as the students move closer to being able to write their own text type independently. Activities at this stage include teacher questioning, discussing and editing class texts; small group construction of tests, dictogloss, self-assessment and peer assessment activities.

Phase 4: Independent construction of the text

In this stage, students work independently to write a text, drafting and revising a whole text.

Phase 5: Linking to related texts

Activities which link the text type to related texts include comparing the use of the text type across different fields, comparing spoken and written modes of the same text type, researching how a key language feature used in this text type is used in other text types.

Grammar and Speaking

In speaking classes, grammatical choices and features can be a focus at different stages of a lesson. For example, prior to a speaking activity focusing on casual conversation, students might be given a handout containing a transcript of a conversation and consider the use of discourse markers, personal pronouns, choice of tenses, and differences between spoken and written grammar as seen in contractions, ellipsis, and fillers. (See the transcript of a conversation in Tip 3.) Students then listen to some prerecorded conversations and listen for specific preselected features. Some of the conversations that students listen to should be more formal (e.g., containing fewer fillers and contractions) between strangers or a student with a teacher. In pairs, students can then discuss how the different contexts of conversation have a direct impact on the grammar of conversation. Students then practice speaking by role-playing different types of conversations.

Noticing activities can also be a useful feature of speaking activities. Students can observe examples of different oral activities on video or on the Internet and be given tasks that involve tracking the use of different features of grammar. They can then replicate some of the examples they observed in dialog development and role-plays.

Gap filling can also be used with conversation and other spoken texts, in which students are given examples of spoken texts from which key grammatical features or items have been deleted, and students complete them in pairs or groups.

Grammar and Listening

In a listening lesson, postlistening activities can be used that involve returning to the listening texts that served as the basis for comprehension activities and using them as the basis for language awareness (Field 2009; Richards 2005). For example, students can listen again to a recording or view a video in order to:

- Identify differences between what they hear and a printed version of the text.
- Complete a cloze version of the text.
- Complete parts of sentences taken from the text.
- Check off, from a list, forms that occurred in the text.

Restructuring activities are oral or written tasks that involve productive use of selected items from the listening text. Such activities could include:

- Written sentence completion tasks requiring use of grammar that occurred in the listening texts.
- Dialog practice based on dialogs that incorporate grammatical features from the text.
- Role plays in which students are required to use key language from the texts.

12. Use the Resources of the Internet and Technology

Both the Internet and technology or TLLT (technology for language learning and teaching) offer useful resources to help learners expand their grammatical resources. Technology and the Internet can bring many types of language use into the classrooms, allowing students to be exposed to and interact with a variety of spoken and written texts. At an advanced level, in content or ESP classes, students can use the Internet to find texts that are authentic examples of content-related texts. These can then be used in class activities to explore structures, such as the use of transitions, or to see how several features work together to create a particular type of text. For example, students can identify features that are used to signal opinions in persuasive texts or grammatical resources that are used to package information in scientific reports.

The Internet can be also used to provide a real audience for student writing. Students can submit movie or book reviews to online sites, expanding the audience beyond the classroom teacher. This can be a powerful motivator for students to produce accurate texts, since now the task is a real-world task and goes beyond simply writing a class assignment that only the teacher will read. In addition to the written texts, the audio available on the Internet is a rich resource for engaging, meaningful activities. Through the Internet, students can be exposed to variety of speakers and regional styles of English. In addition to being exposed to different speakers, students see how grammar in spoken language varies within different contexts of use. Students can listen and compare formal speeches and casual conversations (building on the activity from Tip 11) and see how the grammar used in these two spoken but different contexts of language use varies. A useful starting point for this activity is for students to notice or count the use of contractions and/

or different personal pronouns. In another activity, one student can read an online news article, while another student listens to a newscast on the same topic. Then the partners can compare how language varies in these two contexts of use. Raising student awareness of how grammar varies according to the context and function of language is a valuable tool that can help learners to become more autonomous and accurate language users.

Technology also offers a wide range of resources to support the learning of grammar (Erben et al. 2009). Software programs that focus on the role of grammar in spoken and written English have become increasingly sophisticated and have moved well beyond the error correction features of earlier programs. Modern programs provide interactivity with learners as they guide them through the processes of decision making, monitoring, and evaluation that are involved in the use of grammar. The use of technology-supported teaching for grammar instruction offers a number of benefits for teachers and students. It shifts the location of grammar-focused instruction from the classroom to the multimedia learning center, allowing the teacher to use valuable class time for other activities. It enables students to engage in form-focused learning online in their own time. It also provides a more stress-free environment to explore and practice grammar, one in which students can devote as much time to grammar as needed. Many teachers have experimented with digital games, webquests, and social networking sites to encourage a focus on the meaningful exchange of information, while asking students to pay attention to particular (formal) aspects of the language (e.g., forms of address on social networking sites, or requests for information in digital games). Software offers different forms of support for grammar instruction, allowing grammar to be taught both deductively and inductively. Specific suggestions include:

- *Diagnostic testing:* Computerized diagnostic tests can be used to assess learners' grammatical knowledge.
- *Monitoring students' performance:* Teachers can create a database constructed from learners' difficulties and use it in curriculum planning.
- *Integrating grammar with other skills:* Grammar can be seen as it is used in different skills and text types, such as narratives and conversation.
- *Comparing the grammar of spoken and written and language:* Learners can view clips of speakers using features of grammar in spoken and written language, or they can compare spoken and written versions of a text.
- *Using a concordancer:* Students can use concordancers to identify the rules behind the language they encounter. Students can also use concordancers to see the relationship between grammar and vocabulary.
- *Sentence and text awareness:* Activities can be used to develop awareness of the grammatical and discourse organization of texts. Paragraphs may be presented with jumbled sentences that students reorder, or a whole text may be presented with jumbled paragraphs. Some software allows the reader to create a visual presentation of how a text is organized or choose exercises that focus on such features as main ideas, topic sentences, and conclusions.

- *Editing and revising:* Commercial software is available to assist writers in editing their writing and identifying errors of grammar and sentence organization. Interactive writing and grammar software is also available on course book CD-ROMs and on the web. Students also can work collaboratively on writing assignments, either among themselves or with the teacher's guidance, using sites such as GoogleDocs or Dropbox, that allows students to create a text jointly. Some software can prompt students when they reach a block. Students can choose images and sound effects to accompany stories or texts that they write. Also students can post their written work on websites that serve this purpose, allowing them to compare their compositions with students around the world. Writing can thus become an interactive and collaborative activity, rather than a solitary one, giving students a greater motivation to write.
- *Peer and self-editing:* Students can use sites like Purdue University's OWL to find information and useful models, ranging from example texts to grammar advice. Another useful resource is Carnegie Mellon University's bibliography maker, BibMe (www.bibme.org), which allows users to choose different styles (APA, MLA etc.).
- *Additional resources:* For more recommendations of other useful sites, go to TeacherTrainingVideos (www.teachertrainingvideos.com/vids_for_students.html).

Conclusion

What we refer to as "grammar" refers to multidimensional aspects of language knowledge and ability. Central to the acquisition and effective use of grammar is a realization of how grammatical choices work together to create texts that reflect contexts of use and that accomplish different functions. Our pedagogy for teaching grammar seeks to develop learners' awareness of the nature of texts and the functions of grammar within them, as well as to expand the grammatical resources learners make use of when they engage in the production of spoken and written texts. The teaching of grammar begins with an identification of the kinds of texts learners need to master and awareness of their grammatical and discourse features. Both receptive and productive learning tasks are needed that provide opportunities for learners to explore how texts are organized and how they achieve their communicative effects. The use of corpora, the Internet, as well as a bank of both student-produced, as well as authentic texts, can be used as a resource for practice in creating, using, comparing, and evaluating different kinds of spoken and written texts. The principles and practices we have described here seek to suggest how a pedagogy for teaching grammar can move beyond discrete–item, sentence-level grammar and incorporate a focus on grammar as an essential communicative resource.

Note

1   This chapter draws on Richards & Reppen (2014) and can be downloaded from www. professorjackrichards.com. Several of the example activities used in this chapter have been provided by Sara Cotteriall.

References

Biber, D., Johansson, S., Leech, G., Conrad, S., & Finegan, E. (1999). *Longman grammar of spoken and written English*. Harlow, UK: Longman.

Celce-Murcia, M. (2002). Why it makes sense to teach grammar in context through discourse. In E. Hinkel & S. Fotos (Eds.), *New perspectives on grammar teaching in second language classrooms* (pp. 119–133). New York: Routledge.

Cullen, R. (2012). Grammar instruction. In A. Burns & J. C. Richards (Eds.), *The Cambridge guide to pedagogy and practice in second language teaching* (pp. 258–266). Cambridge: Cambridge University Press.

Ellis, R., & Shintani, N. (2014). *Exploring language pedagogy through second language acquisition research*. London: Routledge.

Erben, T., Ban, R., & Castañeda, M. (2009). *Teaching English language learners through technology*. New York: Routledge.

Feez, S., & Joyce, H. (1998). *Text-based syllabus design*. Sydney: National Centre for English Language Teaching and Research, Macquarie University.

Field, John. (2009). *Listening in the language classroom*. Cambridge: Cambridge University Press.

Fuller, T. (2013). As Myanmar modernizes, old trades are outpaced by new competitors. *New York Times*, November 20.

Hedge, T. (2000). *Teaching and learning in the language classroom*. Oxford: Oxford University Press.

Hewings, A., & Hewings, M. (2005). *Grammar and context*. London: Routledge.

Hinkel, E. (2002). Teaching grammar in writing classes: Tenses and cohesion. In E. Hinkel & S. Fotos (Eds.), *New perspectives on grammar teaching in second language classrooms* (pp. 181–197). New York: Routledge.

Jones, R. H., & Lock, G. (2011). *Functional grammar in the ESL classroom: Noticing, exploring and practicing*. New York: Palgrave Macmillan.

Jones, W. (2012). Assessing students' grammatical ability. In C. Coombe, P. Davidson, B. O'Sullivan, & S. Stoynoff (Eds.), *The Cambridge guide to second language assessment* (pp. 247–256). Cambridge: Cambridge University Press.

McAndrew, J. (2007). Responding to learners' language needs in an oral EFL class. In A. Burns & H. Joyce (Eds.), *Planning and teaching creatively within a required curriculum* (pp. 189–204). Washington, DC: TESOL.

MICUSP *(Michigan Corpus of Upper-level Student Papers)*. (2009). Ann Arbor: The Regents of the University of Michigan.

Paltridge, B. (2006). *Discourse Analysis: An introduction*. London: Continuum.

Reppen, R. (2010). *Using corpora in the language classroom*. Cambridge: Cambridge University Press.

Richards, J. C. (2005). Second thought on teaching listening. *RELC Journal*, *36*(1), 85–92.

Richards, J. C., & Reppen, R. (2014). Towards a pedagogy of grammar instruction. *RELC Journal*, *45*(1), 5–25.

Schmidt, R. (1990). The role of consciousness in second language learning. *Applied Linguistics*, *11*(2), 129–159.

Skehan, P. (1998). *A cognitive approach to language learning*. Oxford: Oxford University Press.

Swain, M. (1999). Integrating language and content teaching through collaborative tasks. In C. Ward & W. Renandya (Eds.), *Language teaching: New insights for the teacher*. Singapore: Regional Language Centre.

Swales, J. (1990). *Genre analysis: English for academic and research settings*. Cambridge: Cambridge University Press.

Thornbury, S. (1999). *How to teach grammar*. Harlow, UK: Pearson Education/Longman.

9

PRACTICAL GRAMMAR TEACHING

Grammar Constructions and Their Relatives

Eli Hinkel

Introduction: Constructions in Language Uses

In the past several decades, a few novel approaches to the analysis and teaching of English grammar constructions have been proposed. These are based on several theories that seek to account for how language structures are produced and understood. In cognitive linguistics, the coin *construction grammar* refers to a specific theoretical approach to grammar examination. This analytical and methodological innovation grew out of the inability of classical theories to account for linguistic formulas, idioms, and collocations (sequences of two or more words that are often used together in speech or writing, e.g., *fast food, take action, pouring rain, have a headache*) that dominate in language production and use (Croft and Cruse 2004).

In language research and textbooks, the term *construction* is usually associated with a linguistic form that has a particular grammar function and can be as short as a phrase or as long as a sentence (Hilpert 2014). In most traditional grammar theories, language users' grammatical knowledge is seen as a systematic organization of linguistic components, from which phrases or sentences are assembled. However, traditional grammars run into the problem of accounting for countless idioms (e.g., *to go Dutch, to blow up, to shut up, to lend itself to*) and collocations, which cannot be parsed (divided) into component parts and whose meaning cannot be predicted (Hinkel 2004, 2015).

Language research and analyses have long established that a great number of linguistic combinations simply sound "right" to proficient users of English and that collocations are very common in both speaking and writing (Wilkins 1972; Yorio 1989). More importantly, however, the combinations that do not occur frequently may sound unnatural and wrong, even when they are grammatically correct (e.g., *?to raise up a child, ?to speak speedily,* or *?a protracted song*).[1]

Studies of real-life language uses have shown that L2 (second language) learners almost universally underuse formulaic sequences and constructions, compared to first language (L1) users. Another important research finding is that a majority of L2 learners employ constructions that are not found in L1 discourse at very high rates. To put it another way, word combinations, phrases, and sentences that are grammatically correct but that are simply not "how people say it" strongly dominate in L2 production and thus mark L2 constructions as unidiomatic and unnatural (Shin and Nation 2008: 340).

Typically, phrases and collocations are learned by hearing them being used frequently enough by other speakers or by reading them in various written texts. Idiomatic constructions are usually encountered in everyday language and acquired in the process of communication, be it oral or written. Specifically, regular, frequent, and repeated word combinations are stored in linguistic short- and long-term memory and are processed cognitively as "whole units" (Arnon and Snider 2010; Stemberger and MacWhinney 1988).

In general terms, construction grammar brings together several models of grammar that rely on research in human cognition to show that the knowledge of a language is comprised of vast collections of form-and-function pairings. Here, the term *form* refers to a particular combination of words, and *function* to the meaning, content, or purpose of the combination in conventionalized language uses. In construction grammar, constructions are the main units of language in discourse but not incremental grammar and vocabulary elements that require rules to assemble them into phrases and sentences. A construction is a unit that connects grammatical structures and their meaning. Proficient users of the language by definition have the knowledge of grammar that allows them to link specific structures to express certain meanings.

This theoretical model is based on the findings of its precursor—studies in phraseology in the 1970s and 1980s. Constructions are considered to be part of a lexicon-grammar continuum. Unlike traditional grammars, the construction approach does not assume that a clear-cut division between lexicon and grammar exists. All grammar units from contextually bound words (e.g., *steady!, lovely, certainly!, whatnot*), to idioms and grammatical patterns are treated as constructions (Fillmore, Kay, and O'Connor 1988; Goldberg 1995, 2006; Kay, and Fillmore 1999).

Construction Grammar and Language Teaching

As has been noted, in language teaching and learning, construction grammar presents "a whole unit" approach to all kinds of conventionalized form-meaning combinations (Peters 1983; Wilkins 1972). In this light, the grammar of English is made up of various construction sets, e.g., quantifiers, prepositional phrases, and adverbs, which can be taught and learned as formulaic (and prefabricated) expressions (e.g., Nattinger and DeCarrico 1992; Wray 2000, 2002; Wray and Perkins 2000).

In their pioneering research in phraseology, Pawley and Syder (1983: 191) were among the first to take a close look at how highly proficient and fluent language users (e.g., native or near-native speakers) select phrases and constructions that are grammatical, natural, and idiomatic. According to these researchers, proficient language users thus demonstrate their "ability to produce fluent stretches of spontaneous connected discourse; there is a puzzle here in that human capacities for encoding novel speech in advance or while speaking appear to be severely limited, yet speakers commonly produce fluent multi-clause utterances which exceed these limits." Based on the findings of their studies, Pawley and Syder conclude that "fluent and idiomatic control of language rests to a considerable extent on knowledge of a body of 'sentence stems' which are 'institutionalized' or 'lexicalized'" (more on this later in the chapter). Sentence stems are units of language as long as a clause in which grammatical form and meaning are largely fixed. The fixed elements, in fact, represent culturally or pragmatically recognized expressions, concepts, or formulae.

Investigative reports on the uses of recurrent and frequent language constructions emerged in the 1990s and 2000s. In this body of research, such constructions are variously called collocations, fixed phrases/strings, lexicalized sentence stems, chunks, formulaic language, formulaic sequences, or prefabricated (or prefab) constructions (Cowie 1988, 1992; Coxhead 2008; N. Ellis 1996, 2011; Hilpert 2014; Howarth 1996, 1998; Schmitt 2004; Wray 2002, 2004; Wray and Perkins 2000). The main reason for the increased attention to these language units has to do primarily with the proliferation of electronic language corpora that have allowed for identifying and quantifying recurrent combinations of words and phrases that occur in real language production.

At present, researchers agree that, mentally and in language comprehension (listening and reading) and production (speaking and writing), prefabricated constructions behave more similarly to individual words than structures that need to be assembled based on rules. According to some estimates, the number of such constructions in English is in the hundreds of thousands. Thus, it seems that learning to use L2 idiomatically is requisite for L2 learners who aspire to attaining proficiency and fluency that can enable them to achieve their educational, professional, vocational, social, and personal goals.

Although there is probably no single encompassing definition of construction grammar or formulaic language, prefabricated constructions and formulaic sequences include:

- Frequently recurring constructions (e.g., *Some people are never happy; what's this all about; according to the author . . .;* or *it remains unclear. . .*).
- Collocations (e.g., *to open an account; to give/receive advice; to deposit cash/checks; to do one's best; to keep in mind;* or *a good/bad mood*).
- Idioms, as well as phrasal verbs (e.g., *bring up/about/down/along/around; basket case; problem child/children; back to the drawing board; burn the midnight oil; piece of cake;* or *easy as pie*).

- Turns of phrase (such as metaphors) (e.g., *how hard can it be?; to start all over again; to be on the right track/to move in the right direction; to point someone in a new/the right/a different direction*).
- Conversational routines (e.g.,

  -Hi, how are you? -Great, and you? -Awesome!;
  -Thank you/I am sorry. -No problem;
  -What's up? -Nothing much. What's going on with you?).

- Set phrases (in which components are fixed in a certain *order*) (e.g., *one's best/a whole lot of/with all [someone's] effort; get it together; need(s) to get [someone's] act together/priorities straight/straighten(ed) out/up/[someone's] head in the game*).
- Proverbs (e.g., *two wrongs don't make a right; the squeaky wheel gets the grease; better late than never; no man is an island*).

Wray (2002: 9) provides one of the most thorough and careful definitions of a formulaic sequence: "a sequence, continuous or discontinuous, of words or other elements, which is, or appears to be, prefabricated: that is, stored and retrieved whole from memory at the time of use, rather than being subject to generation or analysis by the language grammar." It is important to note that this definition is only one of many, and various alternatives have been adopted by other researchers.

The purpose of this chapter is not to attempt to condense the vast knowledge and practice materials on, with, or about construction grammar and formulaic language. Nor does this chapter aspire to being a concise construction grammar manual. The goal of this chapter is to provide efficient tools and a few shortcuts for teachers and learners by means of presenting and illustrating uses of constructions in speaking and writing. These research-based and time-tested techniques for using constructions and formulaic expressions in the teaching of productive skills can greatly assist learners in developing facility with grammar and vocabulary expeditiously.

Key Advantages

In light of the fact that language instruction almost always takes place under great time and curricular constraints for many teachers and learners, it seems essential to maximize language gains, develop fluency, and make learning as efficient as possible. There are seven key advantages for teaching and learning formulaic sequences and prefabs:

- Formulaic sequences and grammar constructions can provide learners access to expressions in, for example, conversational interactions or academic writing, that may not yet be available to them in creative production (Nattinger and DeCarrico 1992).

- Conventionalized expressions and constructions are usually easy to remember because they are deployed in specific and appropriate social contexts.
- Using language chunks in teaching and learning to speak and write in L2 is likely to be one of the few available expedient routes to relative L2 accuracy and fluency that leads to repeated uses and subsequent automatization (Hinkel 2004, 2005, 2011, 2015).
- A tremendous advantage of construction grammar lies in expedited learning, reduced workload, and developing fluency. For example, high-frequency academic constructions, collocations, and expressions can be learned as whole units, instead of just their elements that have to be further combined during the process of speaking and writing (Hinkel 2011, 2013).
- Differences and similarities between constructions allow learners to create new formulaic sequences in various combinations or to modify those that are already "stored away."
- For L2 speakers and writers, common grammar problem areas, say, with articles, verb tenses or prepositional phrases can also be relatively easily avoided when these are dealt with as whole constructions.
- In language teaching, a very efficient perspective is to look at grammar and vocabulary as a continuum of constructions, from highly systematic and regular (e.g., third person singular verbs or subject-verb agreement) to much more fixed constructions, such as collocations or idioms (e.g., *change is in the air* or *this evidence sheds a great deal of light on . . .*).

The construction grammar approach to language teaching can be employed with language elements of all shapes and sizes, from tiny bits, such as word prefixes and suffixes, to phrases to whole sentences or even to sets of sentences, including the perennial areas of learning difficulty, such as metaphors and idioms.

L2 Speaking and Interaction: Construction Grammar and Formulaic Expressions

Learning to understand and produce spoken language means being able to understand how language components combine and interact to produce meaning and discourse (Nattinger and DeCarrico 1992). L2 learners need to become skilled users of words, sentences, and language elements to build their spoken discourse repertoire in order to participate in conversations as they progress.

Participating in conversations requires engaging in a range of complex cognitive and linguistic tasks. In social settings, the uses of language convey personal views and attitudes, as well as social values and relationships, in addition to the overt and easily recognized assumed purpose of exchanging information and "transacting" content (Coulthard 1985: 123). Conversations are jointly constructed as they unfold, with participants adjusting, modifying, altering, and tweaking what they are saying—or going to say—depending on the social situation and flow. In the course of a conversation, participants' speech has to remain reasonably cohesive, coherent, fluent, socially appropriate, culturally suitable, as well as grammatically, lexically, and phonetically intelligible. In other words, conversing takes a little work.

A vast body of research on the pragmatics of interaction that saw the light of day in the 1980s and 1990s has demonstrated convincingly that conversational language and discourse are highly conventionalized, routinized, and formulaic. Some studies have found, for example, that in casual conversations, most exchanges are prefabricated and extremely stereotyped (Brown and Levinson 1987; Coulmas 1981; Levinson 1983). For example, in his investigation of spoken and conversational interactions among adults, Bygate (1988) identified an astounding array of grammatical and pragmatic uses of formulas. These were employed in an extraordinary range of functional contexts and for a practically unlimited variety of pragmatic purposes. According to the author, speakers' choices of formulaic expressions are continually adjusted to suite specific discourse and social contexts.

Based on extensive analyses of social interactions in general, many analysts have definitively concluded that it is not just conversational expressions and responses to them that are highly conventionalized, but also, by their very nature, social interactions "employ a number of standardized and stereotyped procedures" that mark and characterize them (Nattinger and DeCarrico 1992: 114) (more on this later in the chapter).

Teaching the grammar-vocabulary constructions and formulaic expressions needed in conversation provides a number of important benefits for both teachers and learners.

1.   Most casual social encounters are brief and highly structured. Typically, they consist of a handful of interactional patterns that can be easily expressed by means of formulaic sequences and prefabs. For example, greetings, conversational openers, topic nominations, closings, and partings are relatively simple and highly conventionalized.
2.   Deploying conversational prefabs and routinized expressions can make learners appear to be more fluent than they actually are (thus potentially improving their motivation for engaging in social interaction).
3.   In social interactions, pragmatically appropriate conversational constructions and formulaic expressions are not particularly numerous. They are efficient, effective, easy to use, and a priori accurate (if used without alterations).
4.   Research has established that formulaic expressions often become a basis for a later development of creative language uses and communicative competence. L2 learners often internalize constructions and formulaic chunks and then later break them down for analysis and variations to expand their range (R. Ellis 1984).

It has been determined that much language acquisition among both L1 and L2 adults consists of the acquisition of formulas and memorized sequences. In the short term, repetition and rehearsal promote the development of long-term sequence representation and eventual language acquisition (N. Ellis 1996). Teaching and learning spoken and conversational formulaic sequences, similar to learning other types of L2 constructions, requires frequent opportunities for repeated practice, practice, and more practice. This is especially true with regard to those phrases and combinations that present areas of difficulty for learners (e.g., *make*-collocations and *get*-passives, as in *get married/it done*). It is also important to make sure that constructions are learned correctly at the outset. If they are not, accurate and productive variations of formulaic expressions may not be easy to construct. Through instruction, to increase learners' repertoires, many conversational formulas and routines can be added over time.

An extensive list of conversational, interactional, and/or relatively formal (semi-academic) formulaic constructions and ubiquitous spoken prefabs can be found in Appendix A to this chapter. "*Enjoy*," as they say in routinized North-American restaurant English prefabs.

L2 Academic Writing: Construction Grammar and Formulas

Currently, a great deal is known about essential grammar constructions for L2 academic writing, such as adverb phrases (e.g., *in this case. . ., according to . . ., for this purpose. . .*) or impersonal *it*-constructions (e.g., *it is essential/clear/has been established*). Similarly, much is known about how to teach various grammar elements and components, and grammar teaching materials for both teachers and students are published every year. In applying construction grammar to teaching L1 and L2 academic writing alike, research has shown that making use of formulaic expressions and learning "long chunks" of text, such as *the central issue/concern* or *according to XXXX (2015)* and their variations, is far more efficient and effective than assembling written text from text (Graff and Birkenstein 2015).

As Wilkins (1972: 102) comments, learning an L2 through vocabulary and grammatical units (chunks), instead of through discrete words or word elements, means one can often "cover in half the time what is . . . expected from a whole year's of language learning." Many adults can recite L1 or L2 poems or texts that they learned several decades earlier, and there is little reason to doubt that L2 learners are quite capable of similar feats in their L2 production.

Like spoken interactions, academic written discourse is highly and rigidly structured. The typical university essay that seems to dominate in higher education in English-speaking countries (and probably far beyond) is written to express an opinion, support a position, develop an argument, or present a research project. The stereotypical structure of the university essay, as well as most other types of academic writing, consists of relatively well defined "discourse moves" (Swales 1990). These include:

- Opening/introduction (also called the statement of a problem, or topic priming).
  - ○ Topic nomination/thesis statement (as well as the statement of purpose).
  - ○ [Optional] statement of rhetorical organization.
- Body (a series of overtly marked rhetorical steps to develop the position/ argument).
- Closing/conclusion (restatement, summary, and closing/conclusion).

These discourse moves are marked by formulaic expressions and grammar constructions that are specific to each category (see a complete list in Appendix B to this chapter). For example, openings/introductions can be identified by such statements as *For a long time xxx, it has been the case that yyy*; or *One of the most controversial/important/interesting issues/problems is yyy*. Thesis statements are also fairly easy to identify by their formulaic and prescribed forms: e.g., *The purpose of this essay/paper is to xxx*, or *This paper discusses/examines/investigates xxx*. In research, many such conventional and highly marked phrases are called institutionalized because they occur more frequently in certain types of discourse than in others (Howarth 1998; Pawley and Syder 1983; Wray and Perkins 2000).

In the production of written academic prose, using conventionalized formulas and prefab constructions is not a language skill that is innate in L1 users and writers. Nor is academic writing a universal ability that most (or even many) L1 writers come by in the course of their daily life. Typically, learning to write academic texts comes about in the process of schooling and education. Both L1 and L2 academic writers have to acquire an extensive range of language skills, such as grammar, vocabulary, and idea organization (Cowie 1988, 1998; Ferris 2003, 2004). It is widely recognized in language research and pedagogy that developing academic writing abilities takes many years—sometimes longer than a decade (Hinkel 2002, 2003, 2009, 2011). A truly enormous amount of evidence has shown that L2 academic writers have a great deal of difficulty becoming proficient users of formulaic sequences, without which formal written prose probably cannot be produced.

As most teachers know from experience, even advanced L2 learners continue to make grammar and vocabulary errors in their writing. Generally speaking, inaccuracies in written prose can be more damaging and costly than, for instance, those in L2 oral production (James 1998; Rifkin and Roberts 1995). An important advantage of using formulaic expressions in academic writing is that learned prefabricated constructions are likely to be more grammatically and lexically accurate than those that have to be constructed based on a myriad of rules.

The following example demonstrates how many morphemes (tiny and medium-sized pieces of language) need to be put together in an introductory sentence string.

It is becom*ing* increas*ing-ly* difficult/challeng*ing to* ignore/decide ... *[to—* infinitive / *if-* or *whether–*adverb phrase or clause]. . .

In this example, due to the grammatical and lexical complexity of the phrase and sentence elements, L2 academic writers can potentially make errors with impersonal constructions, tenses and verb forms, adverbial derivations, active/passive forms of adjectives, infinitives, and the like. All these error-prone grammar elements can be avoided when these and other similarly complex constructions are taught and learned as formulaic expressions.

To some extent, the uses of specific language features may depend on the discipline and context in which spoken or written text is produced. Rather predictably, business case studies, historical narratives, or descriptions of experiments in psychology may contain a higher number of past tense verbs than a paper that discusses generally applicable observations. For example, most introductory textbooks in philosophy, sociology, economics, or biology include high rates of present tense verbs.

Despite some amount of variation that can be noted in the grammar and vocabulary features of texts across disciplines and academic subgenres, many researchers have identified what some call recurring second language attributes in academic register and text that do not appear in L1 writing (Ferris and Roberts 2001; Nation and Webb 2011), e.g., incorrect verb tenses, verb forms, or noun endings. Other studies of L2 written text production have also uncovered a range of vocabulary and grammar features that require focused instruction and concerted effort from both teachers and learners (Nation 2009, 2013; Widdowson 2003). All these can be taught and learned in conjunction with the phrases and sentence stems (see Appendix B) where they tend to occur.

For a vast majority of L2 learners, the task of becoming proficient users of L2 academic vocabulary may not be attainable within the time commonly considered reasonable for the completion of their preparatory studies. A more feasible and attainable goal of increasing the vocabulary range in students' L2 writing is to work with prefabricated expressions—and lexical substitutions within them—that learners can use for building written texts in most academic tasks. For example, around a dozen reporting verbs can be employed to mark paraphrases, and they can be learned with relative ease while working on a writing assignment: e.g., *the author says, states, indicates, comments, notes, observes, believes, points out, emphasizes, advocates, reports, concludes, underscores, mentions, finds,* not to mention phrases with similar textual functions, such as *according to the author, as the author states/indicates, in the author's view/opinion/understanding,* or *as noted/stated/ mentioned.*

A Final Note

Teaching formulaic expressions and constructions can be profitable for learners at any level of proficiency. For beginners, a small number of fixed or minimally variable expressions could be a good place to start. As the learner progresses, the constructions that mark conversational sequences are likely to be handy and easy to learn. In writing instruction, learning grammar constructions can take place in the context of early writing practice, say, when constructing formulaic essay openings with variants and substitutions, e.g., *Many authors/books/articles state/say/that . . . .*

As has been mentioned, in spoken or written discourse, formulaic expressions characterize discourse junctures and moves, and function as discourse organizers. A very effective teaching technique is to introduce learners to discourse openers first to help them understand how to begin a casual conversation or a piece of formal academic writing. A similar technique can be used with discourse closings.

To work with a few opening constructions, learners can practise conversational greetings, attention getters, or lead sentences in writing (see Appendixes A and B). Then, for instance, the practice can move on to formulaic topic nominations and progress further along the discourse structure. Practising conversational and written topic nominators can be highly efficient for learners who need to see the connections between openers, topic contents, and closings.

The greatest benefit of construction grammar is that it allows language teachers to work with more efficient pathways in practical language teaching. It is well known today that grammar constructions are a key component of natural language comprehension and production. Pedagogically speaking, a great deal of exposure to and practice with naturally occurring formulaic sequences in speaking and writing would be to learners' best advantage, as it is likely to promote language analysis and acquisition. As with all language teaching and learning, using diverse grammar construction types can also lead to learners' developing systematic variations within construction and thus increase their linguistic repertoire. Above all, however, it seems very important for teachers to be aware of and become familiar with formulaic sequences that find their way into practically all language uses.

Currently, a relatively large number of spoken and written constructions have been collected, catalogued, and systematized. Two short sets of formulaic constructions are presented in Appendixes A and B. This might be as good a place to start as any.

Sample Activities and Suggestions for Teaching

1. *Identifying formulaic expressions and prefabs in level-appropriate authentic texts.* Locate four or five (short) newspaper articles (easily found on online) and hand them out to the students. In small groups or as a whole class, learners are asked to note and make a list of formulaic expressions and prefabs. These expressions are counted to figure out their overall number relative to the

number of words in the texts. How common do formulaic expressions and prefabs appear to be? [A side question: Do you think that it is possible for learners to notice and recognize prefabs in texts: why or why not?] In English as a foreign language settings, the same activity can be repeated in learners' first language(s).

2. *Responding to formulaic expressions with appropriate formulaic expressions.* Create a worksheet of appropriate responses to formulaic conversational expressions in English. Learners are asked to match questions or statements to situational appropriate responses. For example:

Hi! How's everything going?	*Thank you! I study very hard.*
I missed the class yesterday. Could I borrow your class notes?	*I think, but I am not sure, that it's **on**[2] zzz (day) **at** xxx (time).*
When is the xxx? (day and time)	*Sure! I am afraid, though, that they are a little bit messy.*
Where is the yyy?/How far is xxx? (location)	
Your English/Spanish/French is great!	*I am sorry, but I don't know. Maybe, yyy could tell you?*
	Great/good/fine. How about you?

Discussion Questions

1. What do the terms *conversational formulae* and *conventionalized uses* mean when it comes to various expressions, phrases, or chunks of sentences? Do textual conventions exist in speaking and written genres other than the academic? Can you think of a few examples?
2. How do school-age learners develop the skills necessary to write formal school prose, such as book reports or small essays/compositions, in their first language, say, in English? When does learning to speak or write in formal academic language learning begin for L2 users who might be of any age, from elementary school learners to adults? How long might it take an L2 learner to learn to produce formal prose?

Essential Readings

Graff, G., & Birkenstein, C. (2014). *They say, I say: Moves that matter in academic writing* (3rd ed.). London: Norton.

Hinkel, E. (2004). *Teaching academic ESL writing: Practical techniques in vocabulary and grammar.* New York: Routledge.

Hinkel, E. (2015). *Effective curriculum for teaching L2 writing: Principles and techniques.* New York: Routledge.

Nattinger, J., & DeCarrico, J. (1992). *Lexical phrases and language teaching.* Oxford: Oxford University Press.

Wray, A. (2000). Formulaic sequences in second language teaching: Principle and practice. *Applied Linguistics, 21*(4), 463–489.

Notes

1 In linguistics, * (an asterisk) marks constructions that are grammatically incorrect, and ? (a question mark) marks something that is questionable but not obviously right or wrong.
2 The preposition *on* is used with days and dates and *at* with time points.

References

Arnon, I., & Snider, N. (2010). More than words: Frequency effects for multi-word phrases. *Journal of Memory and Language*, *62*, 67–82.

Brown, P., & Levinson, S. (1987). *Politeness*. Cambridge: Cambridge University Press.

Bygate, M. (1988). Units of oral expression and language learning in small group interaction. *Applied Linguistics*, *9*, 59–82.

Coulmas, F. (Ed.). (1981). *Conversational routines*. The Hague: Mouton.

Coulthard, M. (1985). *An introduction to discourse analysis* (2nd ed.). London: Longman.

Cowie, A. P. (1988). Stable and creative aspects of vocabulary use. In R. Carter & M. McCarthy (Eds.), *Vocabulary and language teaching* (pp. 126–137). Harlow, UK: Longman.

Cowie, A. P. (1992). Multiword lexical units and communicative language teaching. In P. Arnaud & H. Bejoint (Eds.), *Vocabulary and applied linguistics* (pp. 1–12). London: Macmillan.

Cowie, A. P. (Ed.). (1998). *Phraseology: Theory, analysis, and applications*. Oxford: Oxford University Press.

Coxhead, A. (2008). Phraseology and English for academic purposes. In F. Meunier & S. Granger (Eds.), *Phraseology in language learning and teaching* (pp. 149–161). Amsterdam: John Benjamins.

Croft, W., & Cruse, A. (2004). *Cognitive linguistics*. Cambridge: Cambridge University Press.

Ellis, N. (1996). Sequencing in SLA: Phonological memory, chunking, and points of order. *Studies in Second Language Acquisition*, *18*, 91–126.

Ellis, N. (2011). The emergence of language as a complex adaptive system. In J. Simpson (Ed.), *The Routledge handbook of applied linguistics* (pp. 654–667). London: Routledge.

Ellis, R. (1984). *Classroom second language development*. Oxford: Pergamon.

Ferris, D. (2003). *Response to student writing: Implications for second language students*. New York: Routledge.

Ferris, D. (2004). The grammar correction debate in L2 writing: Where are we, and where do we go from here? (and what do we do in the meantime. . .?). *Journal of Second Language Writing*, *13*(1), 49–62.

Ferris, D., & Roberts, B. (2001). Error feedback in L2 writing classes: How explicit does it need to be? *Journal of Second Language Writing*, *10*, 161–184.

Fillmore, C., Kay, P., & O'Connor, M. (1988). Regularity and idiomaticity in grammatical constructions: The case of let alone. *Language*, *64*, 501–538.

Graff, G., & Birkenstein, C. (2015). *They say, I say: Moves that matter in academic writing* (3rd ed.). London: Norton.

Goldberg, A. (1995). *Constructions: A Construction grammar approach to argument structure*. Chicago: University of Chicago Press.

Goldberg, A. (2006). *Constructions at work: The nature of generalizations in language*. Oxford: Oxford University Press.

Hilpert, M. (2014). *Construction grammar and its application to English*. Edinburgh: Edinburgh University Press.

Hinkel, E. (2002). *Second language writers' text*. Mahwah, NJ: Erlbaum.

Hinkel, E. (2003). Simplicity without elegance: Features of sentences in L2 and L1 academic texts. *TESOL Quarterly, 37*, 275–301.

Hinkel, E. (2004). *Teaching academic ESL writing: Practical techniques in vocabulary and grammar*. Mahwah, NJ: Erlbaum.

Hinkel, E. (2005). Analyses of L2 text and what can be learned from them. In E. Hinkel (Ed.), *Handbook of research in second language teaching and learning* (pp. 615–628). Mahwah, NJ: Erlbaum.

Hinkel, E. (2009). The effect of essay prompts and topics on the uses of modal verbs in L1 and L2 academic writing. *Journal of Pragmatics, 41*(4), 667–683.

Hinkel, E. (2011). What research on second language writing tells us and what it doesn't. In E. Hinkel (Ed.), *Handbook of research in second language teaching and learning* (Vol. 2, pp. 523–538). New York: Routledge.

Hinkel, E. (2013). Research findings on teaching grammar for academic writing. *English Teaching, 68*(4), 3–21.

Hinkel, E. (2015). *Effective curriculum for teaching L2 writing: Principles and techniques*. New York: Routledge.

Howarth, P. (1996). *Phraseology in English academic writing: Some implications for language learning and dictionary making*. Tübingen, Germany: Max Niemeyer.

Howarth, P. (1998). Phraseology and second language proficiency. *Applied Linguistics, 19*(1), 24–44.

James, C. (1998). *Errors in language learning and use*. London: Longman.

Kay, P., & Fillmore, C. (1999). Grammatical constructions and linguistic generalizations: The "What's X doing Y?" construction. *Language, 75*, 1–33.

Levinson, S. (1983). *Pragmatics*. Cambridge: Cambridge University Press.

Nation, I.S.P. (2009). *Teaching ESL/EFL reading and writing*. New York: Routledge.

Nation, I.S.P. (2013). *Learning vocabulary in another language* (2nd ed.). Cambridge: Cambridge University Press.

Nation, I.S.P., & Webb, S. (2011). Content-based instruction and vocabulary learning. In E. Hinkel (Ed.), *Handbook of research in second language teaching and learning* (Vol. 2, pp. 631–644). New York: Routledge.

Nattinger, J., & DeCarrico, J. (1992). *Lexical phrases and language teaching*. Oxford: Oxford University Press.

Pawley, A. & Syder, F. (1983). Two puzzles for linguistic theory: Nativelike selection and nativelike fluency. In J. Richards & R. Schmidt (Ed.), *Language and communication* (pp. 191–225). London: Longman.

Peters, A. (1983). *The units of language acquisition*. Cambridge: Cambridge University Press.

Rifkin, B., & Roberts, F. (1995). Error gravity: A critical review of research design. *Language Learning, 45*, 511–537.

Schmitt, N. (2004). *Formulaic sequences: Acquisition, processing and use*. Amsterdam: John Benjamins.

Shin, D., & Nation, P. (2008). Beyond single words: The most frequent collocations in spoken English. *English Language Teaching Journal, 62*(4), 339–348.

Stemberger, J., & MacWhinney, B. (1988). Are inflected forms stored in the lexicon? In M. Hammond & M. Noonan (Eds.), *Theoretical morphology: Approaches in modern linguistics* (pp. 101–116). New York: Academic Press.

Swales, J. (1990). *Genre analysis*. Cambridge: Cambridge University Press.

Swales, J., & Feak, C. (2012). *Academic writing for graduate students* (3rd ed.). Ann Arbor: University of Michigan Press.

Widdowson, H. (2003). *Defining issues in English language teaching.* Oxford: Oxford University Press.

Wilkins, D. (1972). *Linguistics in language teaching.* London: Edward Arnold.

Wray, A. (2000). Formulaic sequences in second language teaching: Principle and practice. *Applied Linguistics, 21*(4), 463–489.

Wray, A. (2002). *Formulaic language and the lexicon.* Cambridge: Cambridge University Press.

Wray, A. (2004). 'Here's one I prepared earlier': Formulaic language learning on television. In N. Schmitt (Ed.), *Formulaic sequences* (pp. 249–268). Amsterdam: John Benjamins.

Wray, A., & Perkins, M. (2000). The functions of formulaic language: An integrated model. *Language and Communication, 20*, 1–28.

Yorio, C. (1989). Idiomaticity as an indicator of second language proficiency. In K. Hyltenstam & L. Obler (Eds.), *Bilingualism across the lifespan* (pp. 55–72). Cambridge: Cambridge University Press.

APPENDIX A

Constructions, Formulaic Sequences, and Sentence Stems for Speaking, Presenting, and Participating in Meetings

When engaging in spoken interactions, each participant has a great deal to attend to, in addition to the grammar and vocabulary in their speech. For instance, there are such matters as sound, word, and sentence parsing, timing, pacing, articulation, stress, intonation, volume, pitch, facial expressions, and body language.

For L2 learners and users, the cognitive load (the total amount of mental effort, including the working memory, required to perform a task) and the amount of attention that are needed simply to converse can be occasionally overwhelming. Having a stock of grammatically accurate and socially suitable constructions can greatly ease the task, project a degree of fluency, and simplify the job of discourse structuring.

All of the following sentence stems and formulaic expressions can be used in teaching and learning a range of grammar constructions and vocabulary that frequently occur in spoken communication, formal and informal alike.

Getting Attention, Greetings, and Responses

Hey/hi/hello/Long time, no see
Good morning/afternoon/evening
How are you?/How are you doing?/What's going on/happening?/How's everything going?
Excuse me/Pardon me . . .

Responding to Attention Getters/Greetings

Hey/hi/hello, Good/Great/Fine/(and you?)

Nominating and Shifting Topics

What's xxx? Where's xxx?
Do you know/remember yyy? Have you heard about zzz?
. . .say . . .
By the way/As a matter of fact/OK, all right (so far) . . .
Not to change the topic/This is a bit of the subject/topic . . .
Oh, that reminds me of xxx/brings yyy to mind . . .
I'd like to suggest/mention/say something about xxx . . .
Speaking of. . .
This reminds me . . ./Oh, before I forget, . . .

Preclosings

Well, that's about it/I guess that's all of it/That's about it.
I should go/I gotta go/run/do/fly.
(it's been) nice/great/ talking to you/meeting you/chatting with you.
I shouldn't keep you/should let you go.
It's been fun/good to talk/catch up/to see you.
Thanks/Thank you (very much/a lot) (for xxx)/Much appreciated
I've enjoyed talking to you/seeing you (again).
OK, then/well/yeah/so far, so good.
Nice meeting you/talking to you/seeing you.
There you go/Here you are.

Closings and Partings

Bye/bye for now/ goodbye, see yah/see you later/see you around/well, so long/'till
*   later/Stay well*
So long/Toodle-oo
Have a nice day/rest of your day/afternoon/evening/time

Asking for an Opinion or Reaction

What's your opinion of . . .
What's your position on . . .
What do you think of. . .
I was wondering where you stood on . . .
Could I ask for / I'd like to hear your reaction to /your views on . . .

Giving Opinions

Strong Opinions

I really/honestly/strongly/firmly believe/feel/(think) that . . .
I'm completely/strongly/firmly/greatly convinced that . . .

There's no doubt/question (in my mind) that . . .
Without a doubt/question . . .
It's really/quite/very clear that . . .
I'm (absolutely) sure/certain/positive that . . .
It is my belief that

Personal Opinions

I personally believe/think/feel that . . .
Not everyone will agree with me, but . . .
To my mind/In my personal experience . . .
From my point of view, . . .
Well, personally, . . ./ In my case, . . .

Adding Reasons

And besides/also/in addition . . .
What's more/And another thing . . .
Not to mention that fact that/the situation with
Plus, the fact that, /Not only that, but . . .

Neutral and Tentative Opinions

I think that /It is possible to think of it as . . .
In my opinion/As I see it/As far as I'm concerned. . .
From my point of view/perspective/, / In my view, / From where I stand
It seems to me that. . ./I would say that. . .
As far as I am able to judge . . .
I think it would be fair to say that . . .

Agreements

Strong Agreements

I completely/totally/really/entirely agree that / with
I am of exactly/completely the same opinion

Neutral and Partial Agreements

I agree.
I think you're right.
I agree in principle, but. . .
I would tend to agree with you on that. . .
By and large, I would agree, but . . .
Although I agree on the whole/with most of what you say/have said . . .

Disagreements

Strong Disagreements

I completely/totally/entirely disagree with you.
I don't agree at all.
You are mistaken.
What you are saying/proposing/suggesting is not (possible/feasible/suitable). . . .

Softening Strong Disagreements

Frankly,. . ./To be honest . . .
To put it bluntly,/be quite frank,. . .
I am afraid/sorry . . ./ don't see how . . .
I doubt (that) . . .
With respect, . . .
This raises the problem of . . .
Possibly, but . . .
What I am worried about is/bothers me is . . .

Neutral Disagreements

I don't completely agree with you on that . . ./I really can't agree with you on
  that. . ./I can't say that I share your view . . .
I can't help feeling/thinking that . . .
I'm not totally convinced by your argument/that/what you said.
I can't help feeling that. . .

Softening Neutral Disagreements

I'm sorry, . . .
I'm afraid. . .
I agree up to a point/to a certain extent, but. . .
To a certain extent I agree with you, but. . .
You have a point there, but. . .
I can see/take your point of view, but (surely/have you considered). . .

Interrupting

May/Could I interrupt you for a moment/second?
Sorry to interrupt, but. . .// Sorry, but. . .
Excuse me for interrupting, but . . .
I don't want to interrupt, but. . .
If I could just interrupt you for a moment, I'd like to. . .
Can I add here that . . .//Can I add something/ask a question?

May I ask something/a question?
I'd like to say something (if I may). . .

Taking the Floor

May/Could I come in at this point?
But the (real) question is . . ./ I am sure you can see . . .
Could I (just) say something here (about). . .?
If I could just come in here/say a word about . . .
If no one objects, I'd like to say a few words about . . .

Commenting

Excuse me, but I'd just like to point out that. . .
Excuse me, but I think/believe (that) it's relevant/important/useful to add that . . .
I wonder if I could comment on/say something about the last/earlier point.
I wonder if I could comment on/add something here (on/about). . .
Before we go any further, may I point out/comment on/ note that . . .

Coming Back to a Point

As I was saying. . ./To return to . . .
To return/to come back/coming back to what I was saying. . .
I may just go back to the point I was making/what I was saying,. . .

Preventing and Preempting an Interruption

If I might/could just finish. . .
Perhaps I could return to this point later (on).
With your permission, I'd like to/rather finish what I was saying. . .
If you'd allow me to continue/finish/say, . . .
If you'd be so kind as to let/permit me (to) finish, . . .
Very briefly, . . ./I'd just like to . . .
There are two/several points I would like to make.

Correcting Yourself and Conversational Repair

The term *conversational repair* refers to dealing with problems in speaking, hearing, or understanding.

Sorry, what's the word I'm looking for?
Let me rephrase/restate this what I (just) said.
Let me put it in another way.
What I am saying is/trying to say is . . .

Sorry, I should just mention one thing.
Don't misunderstand me, . . .
Sorry, let me rephrase that.
If I said that, I didn't mean/intend to/have in mind that . . .
Sorry, what I meant is/was (this)/what I mean is . . .
So, just to give you the main points here.

Presenting and Making an Argument

Beginning an Argument

I would like to begin by. . ./to say a few words . . ./to comment on . . .
There are three points I'd like to make.
I would like to mention briefly that. . .
I would like to make a few remarks concerning. . .

Sequencing an Argument

To begin with. . ./First of all . . . /To get started . . .
Firstly,. . . Secondly, . . . Thirdly,. . . Finally, . . .
At the outset (beginning). . .

Introducing a New Point

The next issue/question I would like to focus on is. . .
Turning to. . ./(Now) I'd like to turn (briefly) to/address/focus on . . .
I would like to introduce a new point/matter/consideration . . .
Another matter/topic . . .

Adding a Point

In addition, . . ./I might add that. . .
Not only . . ., but also. . .
Furthermore, . . ./Moreover, . . .
And another thing/point/factor/consideration . . .
Just a small point, . . .
Perhaps, I should mention/add/note/say . . .
Oh, I almost forgot . . .

Giving an Example

Let me give an example (of). . .
To illustrate this point, let us consider. . .
I'd like to mention/bring your attention to xxx, as an example
A case in point is. . .
By way of illustration. . ./To illustrate, simply (take a) look at . . .
An example/a few examples include(s)

Balancing Points

> *On the one hand xxx, but on the other hand, yyy*
> *In spite of zzz, I still think aaa/Despite (the fact that) bbb, I . . .*
> *Although . . ., we/I should (also) think about/remember that . . .*

Generalizing

> *On the whole, . . ./Overall, . . .*
> *In general, . . ./Generally speaking, . . ./To generalize . . .*
> *By and large, . . .*
> *All in all, . . ./All things considered, . . .*

Stating Preferences

> *I'd rather xxx than yyy.*
> *What I'd prefer. . ./My preference would be. . . /Preferrably*
> *I prefer xxx to yyy*
> *The main advantage of xxx is (that) . . .*

Concluding

> *Let me conclude by saying . . .*
> *I'd like to conclude by stating that . . .*
> *In conclusion, I would like to reiterate that . . .*
> *Allow me to conclude by stating/saying/reiterating that . . .*

Asking Questions

Introductory Words and Phrases

> *Actually, . . ./Well, . . .*
> *Frankly, . . ./To be honest, . . .*
> *As a matter of fact, . . ./In fact, . . .*
> *Okay (then). . ./Alright . . .*
> *As a point of departure, I'd like to . . .*

Asking General Questions

> *Would you mind. . .? / Would you mind if I asked. . .?*
> *I was wondering if you. . .?/I wonder if you could. . .?*
> *May I ask. . .?*

Asking for Further Information

> *Could you be a little more precise?*
> *I'm sorry, but could you explain in a little more detail/Could you give us some details*
> *about . . .?*

Could you expand on that? /Would you please elaborate on that?
I wonder if you could explain that/elaborate on that . . ./ Would it be possible to . . .?

Stalling for Time

That's a very interesting question.
That's a difficult question to answer.
I'm glad you asked that question.
You've brought up/raised a good/important/excellent point here.
It is not hard to see / You will appreciate how important this point is.

Saying Nothing

Well, it's (rather/maybe) difficult to say. . .
I'm afraid I don't have enough information (right now) to answer that.
I'd need/will need to think about xxx/learn more about xxx /look into xxx further/
in greater detail

Further Questioning/Looking for Clarification

It depends / I'm not quite sure what you mean by. . .
I'm afraid I don't quite follow. . .
I don't think it's quite as simple as that. . .

Asking for Clarification

Clarifying When Communication Is Not Heard

Sorry, I missed that. Could you say that again, please?
Sorry, I didn't catch/get that. Could you repeat it/that, please?
Would you mind repeating xxx, please?
Sorry, I couldn't quite hear/hear well.

Clarifying When Communication Is Not Understood

Sorry, I don't quite follow you. Could you just run through that again, please?
Sorry, I don't quite see what you mean. Could you just explain that, please?

Clarifying After the Point Has Been Made

When you were saying/talking about/describing (to us)/dealing with/summing up/
showing us/telling us. . .
You quoted/commented on/made the point that/(may have) said that/spoke on/
about/referred to. . .
Could you tell us /say a bit more about/explain to us what you meant by that/be a
little more specific/run us through that again.

Other Clarification Sequences

What exactly did you mean by. . .?
Could we go back to what you were saying about. . .?
How did you arrive at the figure of. . .?
I think I misunderstood you. Did you say. . .?
You spoke about. . . . Could you explain that in more detail?
Going back to the question of. . . . Can you be more specific?
You didn't mention. . . . Why not?
If I understood you correctly, ... Is that right?
I'm not sure I fully understood. . . . Can you run through/go back to that again, please?
There's one thing I'm not clear about: . . . . Could you go over that again, please?

Getting Information on the Phone

I am calling about/to ask/find out/hear about/in regard to/in connection with . . .
I'd like to ask (about)/find out. . .
Could you tell me . . .?
I wonder if you could tell me/help me . . .
I'd like to talk to somebody about . . . / if someone could help me with . . .

APPENDIX B

Constructions, Formulaic Sequences, and Sentence Stems for Academic Writing

The teaching of grammar constructions and sentence stems can co-occur with supplemental instruction on grammar, vocabulary, and common academic colloca-tions. Using stock sentence stems in academic writing is probably one of the most efficient ways of expanding L2 writers' repertoire of form-meaning combinations and prefabs. Formulaic expressions can be particularly useful when they include variations on their discrete elements (as shown in Appendix A). Commonly occurring sentences, clauses, and phrases can be found in many languages, and these constructions dominate in formal writing.

All of the following sentence stems[1] can be used in teaching and learning a range of grammar constructions, vocabulary, and discourse patterns prevalent in academic and formal prose.

Openings/Introductions

The central issue in xxx is yyy.
The development of xxx is a typical/common problem in xxx.
Xxx and yyy are of particular interest and complexity.
For a long time xxx, it has been the case that yyy.
Most accounts/reports/publications claim/state/maintain that xxx.
According to Smith/recent (media) articles/reports/studies, xxx is/seems to be yyy.
One of the most controversial/important/interesting issues/problems/xxx (recently/in recent literature/media reports) is yyy.
In recent discussions/debates/reports of xxx, a controversial/complex/intertwined issue has been whether xxx. On the one hand, some argue that xxx. On the other hand,

however, others argue that yyy. (modified from Graff and Birkenstein 2015)
It is becoming increasingly difficult/challenging to ignore zzz.
*Xxxx plays an important/significant/prominent role in the maintenance/support/
    dissemination of zzz.*
*In the new global/changing/evolving aaa, bbb has become a central/most important/
    pivotal/persistent issue for ccc.*
Xxx is an increasingly important area/field in ccc.
Xxx and yyy have been an object of research since the 1920s/1960s/1990s
Bbb is a major/vital/central area of interest within the field of zzz.
The issue of xxx has received notable/considerable critical/favorable attention.
Xxx is a classic problem in zzz.
Yyy has been studied by many researchers using/employing/utilizing vvv.

Negative Openings with Countable Nouns

Few reports	*have discussed/examined zzz.*
Few discussions	*have addressed/noted/examined*
Few articles	*have focused on/noted*
Few studies	*have investigated/dealt with*

Thesis/Topic Statements

The purpose of this essay/paper/analysis/overview is to xxx,
    e.g., take a look at/examine/discuss yyy.
The main emphasis/focus/goal/purpose of the/this essay/paper/project is to xxx,
    e.g., is to analyze/provide an overview/discussion of xxx.

This paper describes and analyzes . . . xxx.
This paper discusses/examines/investigates xxx.
This paper claims/shows that xxx is/is not yyy.
This essay/paper addresses/examines/
                is designed to/
                    analyzes/provides an overview of/takes a look at xxx.
My aim in this paper is to . . .
In this paper, I/we report on/discuss . . .
I intend/will demonstrate/show/explain/illustrate that xxx
My (basic/main/most important) argument/claim is largely/essentially that xxx
The idea/notion/concept/thought/proposition that xxx is yyy is a
    striking/provocative/thoughtful/promising/thought-provoking one, and this is what
    I support/subscribe to/advocate.

Secondary Purpose

The primary aim/purpose of this paper is xxx. In addition, it examines/discusses . . . yyy
Additionally, yyy is discussed/examined.

A secondary aim of this paper is to yyy.
Another reason/point/issue addressed/discussed in this paper is yyy.

Rhetorical Mode/Discourse Organization Statement

This paper (will) compare(s)/describe/illustrate xxx first
   by analyzing/comparing/demonstrating yyy (that yyy is zzz),
   then by yyying zzz, and finally by yyying aaa).
This paper first analyzes/discusses xxx,
   followed by an examination/illustration/overview of yyy and zzz.
The differences/similarities between xxx and yyy are
   important/pronounced/striking/unmistakable,
                                     and they merit/warrant/deserve/call for a
            close/careful/thoughtful/thorough/rigorous
               examination/analysis/scrutiny.
While some differences between aaaaa and bbbbb are
   clear/evident/noticeable/pronounced/unmistakable,
            the similarities are (also) evident/striking/prominent/noticeable/relevant.
The main points/questions/issues addressed/discussed in this essay/paper are: aaa, bbb,
   and ccc.
This paper begins by ddd. It will then/later go on /move on to xxx.
The first/second/third section of this essay/paper will examine/take a look at/discuss vvv.

Introducing Review of Literature and Evidence from Readings

In recent discussions of xxx,
The issue of zzz is important: [stated reasons]
In recent publications, the topic/issue of xxx has received considerable/prominent
   attention.
Recently researchers/investigators/scholars have examined the effects of ccc on ddd.
In the past two/three/four decades/twenty/thirty years, a number of researchers/authors
   have sought/attempted to identify/determine. . . .
Previous/earlier/studies/investigations have reported/noted/determined that. . . .
A considerable/substantial/notable amount of literature has been published on vvv.
   These studies/reports/investigations have found that . . . .
Surveys/studies/investigations such as that conducted by YYY (2015)
   showed/demonstrated that . . . .
Recent evidence/findings suggest(s) that . . . .
Several attempts have been made to . . . .
A large body of literature on xxx has been published/made public on zzz.
A number of researchers/investigators have reported that . . . .
Studies of ccc show/demonstrate/emphasize the importance of bbb in/for xxx.

Other Types of Sentence Stems for Essay Development

Assertion

It can be claimed/said/assumed that xxx.
It seems certain/likely/doubtful that xxx.
I/we maintain/claim that xxx.

Agreement with the Author/Source

As XXX perceptively/insightfully states/
    correctly notes/
    rightly observes/
    appropriately points out,   *xxx is/seems to be yyy* (adjective/noun)

I/we rather/somewhat/strongly agree with/support (the idea that) xxx
XXX provides/lends support to YYY's argument/claim/conclusion that zzz

Disagreement with the Author/Source

I/we rather/somewhat/strongly disagree with XXX/that yyy.
As XXX states (somewhat) unclearly/erroneously,
XXX does not support YYY's argument/claim/conclusion about zzz/that zzz
Although XXX contends that yyy, I/we believe that zzz
However, it remains unclear whether . . .
It would (thus) be of interest to learn more about yyy/how . . .
Xxx is mistaken because he/she overlooks/neglects to account for aaa.
I disagree with XXX's view that aaa because, as recent research has shown that. . . .

Comparison

Both xxx and yyy are (quite) similar in that zzz
Xxx is like/resembles yyy
Both xxx and yyy are/seem to be zzz (adjective/noun)
Xxx and yyy have/share some aspects of zzz.
Xxx is similar to/not unlike yyy (with respect to zzz).

Contrast

Xxx is (quite) different from yyy (in regard to zzz).
Xxx is not the case with yyy/the same as yyy.
Xxx does not resemble yyy (in regard to zzz).
Xxx contrasts with yyy (with regard to zzz).
Xxx is unlike yyy in that/with respect to zzz.

Recommendations

Let me recommend/suggest that xxx be/have/do yyy.
What I want/would like to recommend/suggest is that xxx.
One suggestion is/may be that xxx (do yyy).

Citing Sources/Supporting Arguments, Claims, Conclusions, and Generalizations

As proof/evidence/an example (for this), (let me cite/quote xxx)
According to xxx,
As XXX says/claims,

XXX provides evidence/support for yyy / that yyy
XXX demonstrates that yyy
   shows evidence for yyy / that yyy
Xxx is an illustration/example of yyy.

Citing Sources/Referring to External Sources of Knowledge

It is/has been (often) asserted/believed/noted that xxx   *(YYY, 2003)*
It is believed that xxx   *(YYY, 1999)*
It is often asserted that xxx
It has been noted that xxx

Classification

Xxx can/may be divided/classified into yyy (and zzz).
Xxx and yyy are categories/divisions of zzz.
There are xxx categories/types/classes of yyy.

Giving Examples

A well-known/prominent/notable/memorable/classic/useful/important
                              example of vvv is xxx/can be found in YYY (2015).

Generalization

Overall,
In general,
On the whole,
Generally speaking,
In most cases,
One can generalize that xxx

For the most part,
With the exception of xxx,
With one exception,

Summarizing

Reporting Verbs and Noun Clause Chunks for Summaries (*author first*)

The author goes on to say/state/show that xxx
The author further argues/explains/shows that
The article further states that
(Smith) also states/maintains/argues/asserts that
(Smith) also believes/concludes/feels that
In the second half of the article/report, (Johnson) presents xxx to show/explain that

Sentence Stems and Noun Clause Chunks for Summaries (essay/paper first)

The article/report concludes that
This essay/paper has examined/reviews/given an account of vvv.
                                    the reasons/causes for ccc.
This essay/paper/project has argued/made it clear that vvv is the best/worst bbb
    to aaa.
This assignment/essay/paper has explained the central/crucial/vital importance of
    ddd in aaa.
This assignment has investigated . . . .
The present investigation has compared three different yyys in terms of zzz.
This essay/paper has examined the role of ccc in/for ddd.

Closing Statement

In sum/conclusion,
To sum up/conclude,
To tie this (all) together,

Note

1 Based on and Graff and Birkenstein (2014), Hinkel (2015), Nattinger and DeCarrico (1992), and Swales and Feak (2012).

PART III

Grammar for Productive Skills

SPEAKING AND WRITING

10

TEACHING GRAMMAR AT THE ADVANCED LEVEL

Michael J. McCarthy

Introduction

Defining what the advanced level is may seem, on the face of it, to be a pretty straightforward affair. Ideally, this would include a considerable expansion of vocabulary to take in lower-frequency words and expressions beyond the core 2,000–3,000 words deemed to be essential for the upper-intermediate-level learner. One would also expect a refinement of phonological skills to bring the learner to a sophisticated level of articulation and intelligibility and the achievement of a level of fluency in speaking and writing that can proceed with an increased level of automaticity and ease of production. Over and above this, a knowledge and awareness of pragmatic and cultural appropriateness and a confident control of complex and lower-frequency grammatical configurations might be expected. Such descriptions of levels of achievement are found in the documentation of proficiency-labelling systems such as the Common European Framework of Reference (CEFR); see, for example, the descriptors for the advanced C1 and C2 levels in Council of Europe (2001).

The core, or highest-frequency, vocabulary, consisting of 2,000–3,000 word families (see Schmitt and Schmitt 2014 for a discussion of the variability in this figure), once acquired, gives access to around 80% of all the words in typical non-specialist texts that learners are likely to encounter. Beyond the core lies what Schmitt and Schmitt (2014) call the midfrequency vocabulary of around a further 5,000 or more items required to enable independent reading at a 98% comprehension level, which we can safely label as the zone in which learners move from an intermediate level to the advanced level. Richards (2008: 21) sees the 5,000- to 6,000-word frequency band as the most useful area in which to assist learners to make the move to the advanced level. The move not only involves a larger vocabulary but also, quite clearly, a move towards independence, as reflected in the CEFR's label for the B-level learner: "Independent user" (Council of Europe 2001: 23–24). But in the area of vocabulary learning, at least, the advanced level seems to be a relatively clearly demarcated territory. The CEFR C1 and C2 levels of the *English Vocabulary Profile*, a free online resource offering descriptive listings of typical learner productive vocabulary knowledge at different CEFR levels, adds substantial empirical evidence to underpin the characteristic international profile of the advanced level learner (Capel 2010, 2013).

Richards (2008) identifies five key areas that need to be dealt with to take learners across the advanced threshold: (1) the potential gap between receptive and productive knowledge, (2) fluency developing at the expense of complexity, (3) a limited vocabulary, (4) a lack of naturalness in production, and (5) persistent errors that may have become fossilised. Dealing with all of these matters is beyond the scope of this chapter; however, the issue of fossilized errors is one that will be returned to, and naturalness in the use of grammar will be a recurring theme, based on illustrations from written and spoken corpus data.

What, then, of grammar at the advanced level, specifically? Schleppegrell (2006) presents grammatical criteria for the successful completion of a high-level writing task that include a control of nominal structures, features of modality, connectors for organizing the text, and so on. This is grammar at the discourse level, and there seems to be a general consensus that grammatical ability beyond the sentence level should be part of the advanced-level repertoire (see also Hinkel 2002), an area we will return to. The creation of the *English Grammar Profile*, a parallel resource to the learner corpus–informed *English Vocabulary Profile*, has reached completion at the time of writing. It will, it is hoped, once online and available, offer a similar level of empirical underpinning in terms of what we can expect a typical CEFR C1- or C2-level learner to be able to use from the repertoire of English grammatical items and patterns (O'Keeffe and Mark in press), as the Vocabulary Profile does for the learner's lexicon. The *English Grammar Profile* will considerably enhance the resources available to grammar teachers and materials writers at the advanced level by listing those items and structures and their meanings (including discoursal and pragmatic aspects) that a typical C1/C2 learner can be expected to know.

In the meantime, we exist in a situation where the general, global consensus that drives the elementary level of grammar teaching becomes somewhat dissipated at the higher levels. Elementary course books and materials, broadly speaking, share common ground in their grammatical syllabuses. Basic ways of talking about present, past and future time, high-frequency items such as determiners, modal and auxiliary verbs and simple prepositions are felt to be essential and can be found in just about all currently popular published elementary- and lower-intermediate-level materials. However, I have elsewhere exemplified from current globally popular advanced-level course books a lack of consensus with regard to what grammar should be included at the higher levels (McCarthy 2015), citing features such as aspects of the usage of the subjunctive and cleft sentences, which may be present in one course but not the other and vice versa. This is understandable because, to a certain extent, materials always have to be selective; the problem is that it is not always clear what the criteria for selection are. The lack of consensus raises the challenge of whether a systematic and coherent grammar syllabus at the advanced level is a realistic (or even desirable) aim or whether we should just be content with a varied menu of low-frequency, complex and (perceived to be) difficult items and structures (for a critique of the notion of difficulty, see Ellis 2002).

Corpora and Grammar

Language corpora have changed our perceptions of grammar in a number of ways. The impact of corpora on language teaching was first felt in the area of learners' dictionaries (e.g., COBUILD 1987), which were soon followed by comprehensive reference grammars informed by both written and spoken data (e.g., Biber et al. 1999; Carter and McCarthy 2006) and corpus-informed reference-with-practice grammars for students (e.g., Carter, McCarthy, Mark, and O'Keeffe 2011a, 2011b). Perhaps the major defining feature of these works was their focus on the differences between written and spoken grammar and sensitivity to register and pragmatic appropriateness, along with a descriptive respect for the forms that speakers and writers actually use, as opposed to proscriptions derived from intuition, written conventions and so-called educated norms.

All of these traits pose significant challenges for grammar pedagogy at the higher levels, in the sense that, at the elementary level, there is naturally a focus on basic forms and their most generalisable meanings, with little time or need to devote pedagogical energies to register differentiation, pragmatic factors or public controversies over standards of correctness. That is not to say that corpora have nothing to contribute to elementary-level grammar teaching; the grammar lessons in McCarthy, McCarten, and Sandiford (2005, 2006) are fully corpus informed at all levels of the course. But it is true that it is at the advanced level that corpora can make, and have made, the greatest contribution to the quest to construct empirically sourced, coherent, and relevant grammatical syllabuses where issues such as register, natural usage and pragmatic meaning can be fully and usefully explored. It is to such syllabuses and to the teaching approaches that they may require that we now turn.

Towards the Advanced Grammar Syllabus

The title of this section might suggest that there is one golden goal as regards grammar at the advanced level. This, of course, is not true. There will be as many advanced-level grammar syllabuses as there are types of advanced-level learners and different local conditions. However, one characteristic of advanced-level English language learners that will be familiar to anyone with experience of teaching at that level is that learners often have more directed, vocational, professional or academic motivations to continue to learn, rather than pursuing an open-ended 'general' English. Specialized needs will involve careful analysis of the types of discourse these more goal-directed learners will be involved in (Celce-Murcia 1991). This means that syllabuses will be maximally useful when the grammar is directed towards the more specialized needs, for example features of the grammar that are notably frequent or have specialized pragmatic functions in business English (McCarthy and Handford 2004; McCarthy, McCarten, Clark, and Clark 2009; Handford 2010). Conversely, features of the grammar that are of low frequency or rare in specialized contexts can be safely downgraded in importance (see Hinkel 2013 for discussion and examples).

Nonetheless, the many possible differences in detail among syllabuses can be subsumed under a set of criteria that, arguably, are valid for any advanced-level teaching situation. What will vary are the realizations, texts and contexts through which the grammar is taught. Some general criteria for advanced grammatical syllabuses will be set out later in the chapter and are derived from the analysis of corpora, both native-user and learner corpora. As discussed above in relation to pragmatic features, the examination of grammar in the raw data of corpora leads us squarely into the realm of senders and receivers (speakers, writers, listeners, readers) and, by the same token, discoursal and pragmatic meaning and function. From a pedagogical point of view, the evidence of corpora also makes us sit up and take note that we may be missing important things about grammar in our existing syllabuses and methodologies.

General Principles

In this section I present a selection of notions from the literature that support the overall view of grammar teaching espoused in this chapter and that I see as being of particular relevance to the advanced level.

1. Grammar teaching is as much about understanding what grammar is and how it functions as it is about getting learners to use it correctly and appropriately (Ellis 2002). This will involve discussion *about* grammar, not just learning grammar.
2. Language awareness and the ability to induce rules and meanings is an important aspect of advanced-level grammatical competence. At this level, autonomy and the independent user come to the fore and displace the spoon-fed learner who receives and perceives grammatical rules merely as an abstract system.
3. Grammatical competence is an essential element of communicative competence; they are not divorceable entities. Grammar is a resource for communication (Canale and Swain 1980; Celce-Murcia 1991).
4. Grammatical choice has implications beyond the level of the sentence. Grammar contributes to the creation of discourse, in terms of textual cohesion and

the macro organization of texts (McCarthy 1991: chapter 2; Hinkel 2002; O'Keeffe, McCarthy, and Carter 2007: chapter 6).

5. Spoken grammar has particular characteristics that distinguish it from written grammar, especially the grammar of everyday conversation (Rühlemann 2006; Carter and McCarthy 2015; Clancy and McCarthy 2015).

6. The distinction between grammar and lexis breaks down when confronted with the evidence of corpora; much of language production is chunked, consisting of recurring strings and multiword items that are not fruitfully analyzable but are simply acquired and used as holistic items (Sinclair 1991; Sinclair 2004; O'Keeffe, McCarthy, and Carter 2007: chapter 3; Martinez and Schmitt 2012). An important aspect of this blurring of the distinction between grammar and lexis is the evidence from corpora that particular grammatical patterns are often strongly associated with groups of lexical items such that it becomes more useful to think of lexico-grammar rather than just 'grammar' (Hunston and Francis 2000).

7. Specialized usage such as the grammar of academic or business language can be complex and demanding, with meanings and functions that go beyond the general, everyday meanings of items and features and rightly belong to more advanced levels of proficiency (Biber, Conrad, Reppen, Byrd, and Helt 2002; 2002; Hinkel 2002).

It now remains to see how these principles can be operationalized in categories of a syllabus fit for purpose for advanced learners. From here on, the chapter will be organized under a series of pedagogically oriented headings, each one exemplified with grammatical items and structures based on corpus evidence and discussion of pedagogical implications. Each section reflects and echoes, in one way or another, aspects of the seven principles just outlined.

Pedagogical Principles for an Advanced-Level Grammar Syllabus

Frequency and Usefulness

The quickest and most painless way to assess frequency is to use corpora. In this chapter the examples are drawn from both British and North American English corpus data. The British English examples are taken from the 100-million-word British National Corpus (BNC) and the North American data from the 450-million-word Corpus of Contemporary American English (Davies 2008–; hereafter COCA). Additionally, some non-native user learner examples are drawn from the Cambridge, Limerick and Shannon (CLAS) Corpus (Healy and Onderdonk Horan 2012).

Corpora enable us to measure the relative frequency with which both items (e.g. articles, prepositions) and patterns (e.g. pronoun + auxiliary + *not* + lexical verb, as in *She will not agree*) occur in the grammatical configuration of the corpus texts. Beyond the massively high frequency of basic everyday items, such as pronouns, articles, modal verbs, etc., and structures, such as present and past simple tense forms, lie items, structures and patterns (e.g. particular recurrences of lexical items and grammatical configurations) that may be of striking frequency but that are often neglected in teaching materials. Equally, we find corpora items that are of low frequency but that, paradoxically, seem to be important items in the 'flip-test', when teachers and curriculum bosses skim quickly through course materials at conferences and publishers' sales pitches to check if their favoured items and features are present.

At the same time, the criterion of usefulness should not be ignored. Some mid- to low-frequency grammatical features may be of little relevance to learners aiming principally at achieving conversational fluency (e.g. certain types of coordination of adjectival modifiers of nouns, for example, *a frightening **yet** poignant story*), but the same items may be immensely useful to students of academic English, especially in cases where such items have been shown by research to be positive discriminators in the achievement of high examination grades, as discussed in below in the section entitled 'Accentuating the Positive'.

The Case of the Subjunctive

Hinkel (2013) rightly points to the English subjunctive as a low-frequency and, for many learners, a low-usefulness structure. This may indeed be the case, especially the negative form, as exemplified in the following Extract 2. The subjunctive is formed with the base form of the verb, with no inflexional-*s* for third person singular and no auxiliary *do* in the negative.

Extract 1

*Shirlee demands that he **go** to the last game of the season.* (COCA)

Extract 2

*[H]e insisted that he **not be** introduced by name.* (BNC)

Extracts 1 and 2 show the typical [verb + *that* + subject + (*not*) + verb in base form] pattern often found in advanced-level course materials, a structure that can usually be avoided by making the subjunctive verb a finite, indicative verb inflecting in the normal way or else using [*should* + (*not*) + verb in base form]. However, in terms of usefulness, the subjunctive in fact has a wider range of usage when observed in corpora, albeit still of relatively low frequency, than most teaching materials suggest. As well as the verb + subjunctive pattern, adjective and noun forms related to the typical verbs that trigger the subjunctive [e.g. *insist (insistent/ insistence), demand (demand), require (requirement)*, etc., a family of verbs having to do with desirability and necessity] can also trigger the subjunctive, especially in formal contexts:

Extract 3

[S]*tories were told about her generosity and kindness, her* **insistence** *that all people* **be** *treated with dignity.* (COCA)

Extract 4

I believe therefore that our music is to be recognized by its melodies, and that it is highly **important** *that they* **be** *distinctive.* (BNC)

The adjective + subjunctive form (sampled with the adjectives *important*, *crucial* and *essential*) is more than 30 times more frequent in the written academic texts of the BNC than in the fictional texts. As I have reported elsewhere (McCarthy 2015), 100-line random samples of instances of the nouns *insistence* and *requirement* in the COCA corpus show 38% and 63%, respectively, having a subjunctive clause following the noun. The subjunctive in postmodifying clauses in noun phrases also offers the opportunity for practice in the manipulation of a phrase-class (noun phrases and the packaging of information through the process of nominalization—see the section on noun phrases and nominalization), which has been shown to be a significant feature of academic writing (Hinkel 1997, 2002; Biber and Gray 2010).

For academic and professional contexts, grouping together verbs, nouns and adjectives plus the subjunctive form becomes a viable teaching point with sufficient corpus-informed material to create substantial and meaningful activities, activities that may enhance student writing. The point here is that (low) frequency of a particular structure alone is not a sufficient criterion for excluding it; its frequency may be greater in more specialized domains, and/or the pedagogical relevance and usefulness of the structure may be greater because of its occurrence in a wider range of patterns than is commonly perceived to be the case. As in all cases, careful corpus searches should be the bedrock of decisions to include or exclude matter when the syllabus is being created.

Another form that has a wider range of usage than that typically presented in course materials is the [*will* + *have* + -*ed*] form of verb or [*will* + *have* + *been* + -*ing*] form of verb, as in *By the end of the year I* **will have finished** *my course*, mostly referred to as future perfect (simple and continuous). Again, corpus evidence shows a notably frequent, wider range of meaning for this form, principally that of projecting an assumption about the present or past, as in Extract 5.

Extract 5

I'm sure Kathy **will have found** *your letter very reassuring.* (BNC)

Learners at the CEFR B2 level, crossing that threshold into the advanced, C-level, may or may not have already encountered the *will* + *have* form presented in its future perfect contexts. If they have not, then presenting both the future projection function and the statement of assumptions function once again stands a chance of making the material more substantial and relevant and useful for learners. If they have already met and practised the future perfect meaning, then the statement of assumptions meaning offers a new meaning and function for a known form, making the cognitive burden less complex. New meanings for old forms takes us nicely into the next section, which deals with just that principle of advanced-level syllabus design.

Known Forms, New Meanings

By the time learners reach the threshold to the advanced level (B2 level in terms of the CEFR), they have amassed a considerable repertoire of grammatical items and structures. Realistically, most of these grammatical features will have been presented, practised and produced in (what are perceived to be) their most common meanings and contexts, after which attention moves on to new features. One useful service the advanced-level syllabus can offer is to revisit those features and, based on corpus evidence, explore the several meanings that most everyday grammatical items have, i.e. what O'Keeffe and Mark (in press) call their "grammatical polysemy", a conscious parallel to the notion of polysemy in vocabulary.

An example of this phenomenon reiterates the point about more specialized meanings that attach to particular registers such as academic or professional language. Most learners will have encountered the modal verb *may* in its meanings of possibility (*I may be late tomorrow*) or permission (*May I leave early today?*). Over and above these basic, everyday meanings, academic, technical and professional language has a very commonly occurring 'factive' use (i.e. referring to what is factually the case) of *may*, as in Extract 6.

Extract 6

*Examples of such a development **may** be found in many works of literature, especially in Joseph Conrad.* (COCA)

This is also a case where the principle of lexico-grammar comes usefully into play. The factive use of *may* combines frequently with verbs of observation such as *seen, found, observed, noted.* This kind of pattern grammar (Hunston and Francis 2000) is ideally suited to the advanced-level syllabus. Another strong lexico-grammatical pattern with *may* in academic texts is its use when authors propose explanations or interpretations of phenomena, with verbs such as *explained, understood, interpreted, viewed, compared, thought, described.*

Thus the familiar item *may* takes on a new role as the carrier of a variety of functions, both within and without specialized contexts and a regularity in lexico-grammatical patterning that can be positively exploited in pedagogy. Revisiting the item in this way offers an opportunity for revision of the 'old' meanings as well as expansion into new territory. However, the additional meanings and functions of everyday items are not always amenable to intuition, and robust corpus data is needed to verify attested usage. In corpora, we can observe regular and pedagogically exploitable correlations between many grammatical structures and their associated lexical items: a grammatical feature can offer more than being seen in the abstract as a generative 'slot' to be filled but rather as being the preferred configuration for particular lexical contexts (Sinclair 2004: 164–176).

Known Meanings, New Forms

The meanings and functions of grammatical items and structures are typically taught through their most frequent realizations. For example, modal meanings and functions such as possibility and necessity are first presented through the high-frequency modal verbs (*will, could, might,* etc.), albeit research has suggested for some considerable time that modal meanings pervade all the word classes (Hermerén 1978; Stubbs 1986; Holmes 1988). Modal adverbs conveying meanings related to possibility such as *definitely, possibly, probably, maybe, perhaps* are of high frequency, especially in speaking, and one fruitful area of comparison between spoken and written grammar for the advanced level is the flexibility of word order for these adverbs. Extracts 7 and 8 show end-positioning in the clause, which, for these same adverbs, is rare in formal writing but common in informal speech.

Extract 7

[Context: speaker is describing a roughly drawn graph.]
*I mean this isn't anything like to scale but it's going to be something like this **perhaps**.* (BNC)

Extract 8

[A rescue helicopter pilot is talking about his work.]
*Well, I rescued a lot of people, and some people don't even thank me because they are in hurry to go home and meet their family, **maybe**.* (COCA)

Another function that can be revisited is the expression of habituality or typicality, most commonly taught initially via the simple present tense form. Extracts 9 and 10 show habitual actions expressed in two ways—the present simple form and with *will*.

Extract 9

*[W]hat he often **does** is because he lives in this area, he'll often **cut** through this way to go over to Wellington into Crowthorne and walk all the way round.* (BNC)

Extract 10

*Mosquitoes also **prefer** some perfumes and certain parts of the body, such as the face and hands. But they **will** usually **attack** whatever body part is not covered.* (COCA)

Such contexts make for interesting exploration and discussion of usage at the advanced level and can be used fruitfully for noticing and language awareness activities, as well as fostering more natural patterns of use.

Taking meanings and functions that learners are familiar with and have already practised through basic or high-frequency forms and reintroducing them via new or different forms provides variety in the syllabus and the feeling that growth and progress are continually being achieved in the study of grammar.

Speaking and Writing

A great deal of research has been carried out over the last two or three decades into the characteristics of everyday, spoken grammar (see Carter and McCarthy 2015 for a survey). Spoken grammar, especially the grammar of conversation, displays items and patterns not found or only rarely found in writing. By the same token, certain patterns in writing are rare in conversation. Enabling learners to explore these differences and to exercise appropriate choices in written and spoken contexts should be a feature of the advanced-level syllabus. Even if learners have been exposed to spoken grammar outside of the classroom, it is often the case that the materials used in class do not offer that "opportunity of use" that Buttery and Caines (2012) refer to, let alone adequate exposure to the grammar of speaking.

Sometimes the spoken/written difference is one of frequency, where an item may be disproportionately frequent in one register or the other. For example, the linking adverb *nonetheless* is 17 times more frequent in the written segment of the BNC than in the spoken segment, the adverb *consequently* is 23 times more frequent in the academic writing segment of the COCA corpus than in the spoken segment and the adverb *scarcely* is hundreds of times more frequent in the BNC written data than in the spoken data. On the other hand, as we saw in Extracts 7 and 8, the flexibility of word order for certain adverbs seems to be much greater in the spoken language than in writing.

As well as individual items, patterns of usage too can vary greatly in their distribution as between spoken and written data. Certain verb phrase structures, for example, certain types of subordination and sentence-initial nonfinite passive clauses, as in Extracts 11 and 12, are rare in conversational grammar.

Extract 11

Surrounded by gardens, the resort takes you back to the sixties by way of low-slung couches and charmingly dated routines like afternoon tea accompanied by live piano music. (COCA)

Extract 12

Encouraged by local school teachers who recognised his outstanding intellect, he resumed his education at Ayr Academy and went on to Glasgow University. (BNC)

The lexico-grammatical evidence shows a preference for verbs such as *organize, design, inspire, lead, publish, surround,* and *influence* occurring in the preceding pattern.

Similarly, placing the negative nonfinite-*ing* in an initial position is rare in conversation but often found in formal writing.

Extract 13

Not wanting to take any risks, they brought forward the dates for the 1992 tournament to September. (BNC)

For more examples of nonfinite clause types, see Carter, McCarthy, Mark, and O'Keeffe (2011a: 119–120).

Aside from the question of frequency, speaking, even among highly educated native users, often displays patterns of usage that would be considered incorrect in formal writing but generally go unnoticed in the real-time flow of face-to-face talk. An example is the use of *there's* with a plural complement, as in Extracts 14–16.

Extract 14

I've got a sister that's in a care home, and she's going to be affected. **There's a lot more areas** *that are going to be affected with that.* (COCA)

Extract 15

So we talk about all those people visiting Liberty Island. **There's only two people** *who actually live here full-time.* (COCA)

Extract 16

Now some of the archaeologists dig, some look at old buildings like this, but **there's lots of other jobs** *that archaeologists do.* (BNC)

Another example is the steady demise of the determiner *fewer* in favour of *less* used with both uncountable and plural nouns.

Extract 17

*It's just that what happens is we, we've got less, sometimes we have **less pizzas** than we've got people.* (BNC)

Extract 18

*Healthier bodies mean **less pharmaceuticals**.* (COCA)

The point about such apparently infelicitous usages ('apparently' only in regard to the conventions of writing) is that learners will hear them frequently outside of the classroom if they are exposed to English use, whether in face-to-face talk or in listening to media broadcasts, films, Internet podcasts, videos etc. Whether any particular teachers or group of learners wish to adopt such forms in their speaking is a matter of choice, though that choice may be severely restricted by the demands of formal examination contexts. Whatever the case, exposure to such forms, noticing them and discussing them as part of language awareness activities is a good example of what an advanced-level grammar syllabus can offer. In the two examples regarding *there's* and *fewer*, no new items are involved, simply a new perspective on already acquired ones.

Grammar at the Discourse Level

The strongest argument for approaching grammar at the discourse level is simply that sentences rarely occur in isolation; grammar exists to create texts, spoken and written. Grammar at the discourse level means leaving behind the sentence as the enclosed container of grammatical choices and examining the kinds of grammatical patterns we find across sentences and paragraphs in writing or within and across turns in speaking, the rhetorical structure of texts, the preferences that attach to textual genres such as academic articles and so on. At the advanced level, the grammatical choices that present themselves during the writing of a sentence are best examined in the light of the text in which that sentence is to be located.

At the elementary level of proficiency, most learners struggle with the creation of good, accurate sentences, and the cognitive demands of making supra-sentential choices are probably more than most elementary learners can meet. However, at the advanced level, beyond-sentence grammatical choices can be explored. Hinkel (2002) presents examples of unnatural sequences of tense choices in student writing at the advanced level, focusing on text-level contextual or discoursal frames that conventionally employ particular tense-aspect choices.

In an earlier paper (McCarthy 1994), I explored the choice between the personal pronoun *it* and the demonstrative pronouns *this* and *that* in the context of anaphoric (backward) reference in texts. Extracts 19–21 illustrate these choices.

Extract 19

[W]hy not put on an evening for young people? ***It's*** *hard work but very rewarding.* (BNC)

Extract 20

When dealing with an independent trainer, you need to make sure he or she obtained liability insurance personally. ***This*** *protects both you and the trainer in case you are injured during a workout, according to fitness experts.* (COCA)

Extract 21

I sat in my cell expecting to be called out for execution at any moment. I remember feeling really happy when I was told I had at least six or seven years to live. ***That*** *makes me angry now.* (BNC)

By exercising the choices of pronoun form, writers and speakers can simply signal a continuation of a topic (using *it*), they can highlight a topic and raise its importance in the mind of the receiver (using *this*) or they can distance a topic in some way using *that*, perhaps by attributing the topic to someone else or by rejecting it emotionally and psychologically. These choices operate across sentence boundaries and are true examples of grammar at the discourse level. The usual contrast of *this/these* vs. *that/those* in one paradigm (the demonstratives) and *he* vs. *she* vs. *it* vs. *they* in another (the personal pronouns) is insufficient to explain actual choices in texts. In a discourse paradigm, the pronoun *it* has to be removed from the context of *he* and *she* and paired instead with *this* and *that* in a new, discourse-level paradigm, which requires a new angle on teaching and a different level of grammatical noticing and awareness.

Another example of teaching a grammatical feature in a discourse context is *wh*-cleft sen*tences*, as in sentences such as ***What you need to do*** *is update your software*, or ***Where we went wrong*** *was to sow the seeds too early in the year.* These constructions could be presented and practised as sentences out of context, yet one can rarely imagine them occurring without being attached to some other sentence(s). The study carried out into clefts of this kind by Jones and Jones (1985) suggested that such sentences, when embedded in paragraphs, were often a more reliable guide to the main message of the paragraph than so-called 'topic sentences' (paragraph-initial sentences). Extract 22, from a longer paragraph, shows just this kind of focus on the writer's main argument.

Extract 22

The main penalty of recession is unemployment, and ***what we need is more jobs, not more consumption.*** *We already have too much consumption, particularly of things damaging to health and the environment.* (BNC)

For discussion of further grammar-as-discourse examples, see Hughes and McCarthy (1998); they define discourse grammar as "grammar that is only fully explicable with reference to contextual features and speakers'/writers' moment-by-moment creation of interaction". The advanced-level syllabus is the perfect opportunity to introduce notions of discourse grammar, both in terms of form-function correlates and language awareness.

Persistent and Fossilized Error

Very few learners survive to the advanced level without some element of persistent or fossilized error in their use of the target language. This may not be a problem for individual learners, and the extent to which a high level of accuracy is the goal will vary from person to person and from one situation to another. For some advanced-level learners, fluency may be the main goal and a smattering of grammatical infelicities may not matter. For others, the goal may be to maximize both accuracy and fluency, and certainly in assessment and examination contexts, accuracy is often a criterion of success.

Errors in grammatical usage are present in learner corpus data at all levels, and one area of persistent error seems to be noun countability. Extracts 23 and 24 come from the CLAS corpus, which consists of data collected in a college of hotel management in Ireland, where students, both native users and non-native users of English, train to work in the hospitality industry. In both extracts, non-native-speaking advanced-level students are presenting, and errors of countability occur. The context for the extracts is simulations of website design within the hospitality sector.

Extract 23

*Um well first we looked at the **informations** that all the websites contained and uh we learned that some of the websites had more **informations** than the other websites.* (CLAS; C1-level student)

Extract 24

*Therefore it is very important to provide high technology, high technological **softwares**.* (CLAS; C1-level student)

While many teachers will be familiar with the errors in both extracts, what to do about such errors at the advanced level requires a well thought-out approach. Returning to a grammatical feature that learners may well feel they have covered many times or at much lower levels can be demotivating. However, returning to a problematic feature with a mixture of known items and new ones that are within the same domain to explore them in new contexts might provide better motivation. So, in the case of countability, uncountable nouns the learners are not familiar with can be combined with ones that they are already familiar with to generate discussions about the nature of countability and to increase language awareness. Equally, at the advanced level, exercises such as enabling uncountable nouns to be counted by the use of collocating nouns can be created (e.g. *two pieces of furniture, several software applications, a stroke of luck, a piece of advice, a spell of fine weather* etc.).

One important aspect of error is that mentioned by O'Keeffe and Mark (in press). They noted, in their research into grammatical development, that errors in a grammatical category sometimes increased rather than decreased as their investigations moved up the CEFR levels. Increased error could be explained by the growth in the range of uses of a given feature. In the case of countability errors, as more uncountable nouns are learnt, countability errors might show a higher statistical occurrence in a corpus, or, in other cases, the grammatical polysemy of an item or structure may generate errors as the contexts of use widen. Evidence of error at the advanced levels enables us to decide whether the errors are due to fossilized items (e.g. the persistence of errors such as *informations* and *furnitures*, nouns that were probably learnt at much lower levels) or, if also evidenced in new or more recently acquired higher-level uncountable items (e.g. *radiation, tuition, congestion*), due to an underlying problem with the understanding of the notion of countability.

Enhancing Academic and Professional Style

Accentuating the Positive

Recent research into student writing for the English Profile project (for information on the project, see http://www.englishprofile.org/) suggests that certain types of grammatical complexity contribute to academic success. For example, Alexopoulou, Yannakoudakis, and Salamoura (2013) point to the use of a modal verb plus an adverb (e.g. *would obviously, could always, should certainly*) in successful examination essays in the Cambridge Learner Corpus. It seems that such features operate as discriminating factors in achieving good grades, though there is no implication that examiners/raters are purposefully looking for such features, and their positive reaction may well be unconscious. McCarthy, McCarten, and Sandiford (2012: 70) include the modal verb plus adverb pattern in their higher-level materials. Another such feature that Alexopoulou and colleagues (2013) mention is -*ing*-clauses as postmodifiers in noun phrases, as in Extracts 25 and 26.

Extract 25

*Most people **applying to drama school** will be seeking to enrol on the full-time diploma course, . . .* (BNC)

Extract 26

[B]eneath the pine trees there were shadows of children **standing around a bonfire**. (COCA)

It is precisely such features that are often ignored or only paid scant attention in syllabuses and pedagogy, but there are good arguments for taking note of research that highlights the presence and importance of particular items or patterns in successful learner texts and for raising their profile in the syllabus, materials and classroom activities so that all learners can have the opportunity of practice and use in grammar that has been shown to be highly valued.

Noun Phrases and Nominalization

We have already claimed when dealing with the subjunctive, that practising the subjunctive after nouns such as *insistence, requirement* etc. is beneficial not only because it broadens the scope of an otherwise narrow-range structure but also because it provides a focus on the complex noun phrase.

A related aspect of the noun phrase, which we also mentioned in the discussion of the subjunctive, is nominalization, the process whereby elements in the clause that are typically realized by verb phrases, adjective phrases or adverbials are realized as noun phrases (e.g. **The prisoners of war were handed over** *at a frontier post* becomes **The handover of the prisoners of war** *took place at a frontier post*). Halliday (1994) pointed out the important role of nominalization in scientific writing, and the presence of complex noun phrases in academic writing in general has been clearly demonstrated, particularly in the ways that noun phrases package information (Hinkel 1997, 2002; Biber and Gray 2010). Liu (2011) discusses complex noun phrases as an example of a structure that learners might work with as they move towards the advanced level. This would seem to be a wise counsel, and nominalization is a process that can be practised in the classroom in exercises requiring the transfer of other clause elements to the subject and object noun phrase slots (for a practical example, see McCarthy, McCarten, and Sandiford 2012: 50).

Conclusion

In this chapter I have argued for a careful consideration of what would constitute the general principles of an advanced-level grammar syllabus. The first requirement in forging such a syllabus is to understand what learning a language at higher levels involves. Clearly it is more than just an accumulation of more and more new grammatical items and structures. Most learners at the advanced level have some motivation other than learning general English, motivations typically associated with academic, professional and vocational contexts. The advanced-level syllabus will therefore gauge the usefulness of any given item or structure in terms of the contexts of the learners. To know what those items and structures might be requires robust corpus evidence, especially since some grammatical features may appear marginal or of little interest until we see them in their contexts of use. The English subjunctive, for example, is of low frequency but occurs in a wider range of patterns than the typical indicative verb + subjunctive object clause often found in textbooks. Based on evidence of its wider use involving noun- and adjective-based patterns, the subjunctive may provide enough substantial material to merit attention in more formal academic and professional contexts. Exploring such patterns also allows a shift of emphasis away from abstract grammar rules to a more concrete, useful exploration of the lexico-grammatical patterns that grammatical features naturally occur in. I have also argued that known grammatical features should be revisited in light of their grammatical polysemy and their several meanings and functions explored. The corollary of this is to expand known, familiar meanings and functions (e.g. habitual actions) into different formal realizations, once again based on corpus evidence.

However, where corpus evidence probably provides the most enlightening insights is in the areas of grammar at the discourse level, the differences between spoken and written registers and the style enhancements that seem to act as positive discriminators in academic success. With the evidence of good corpus data, the advanced level need not be a mishmash of disparate items held together only be some vague notion of 'difficulty' but can be a coherent vehicle for progress to a level of proficiency where expression in the target language becomes sophisticated and complex but, above all, becomes natural and useful in the contexts in which advanced level learners, or learners on the threshold of the advanced level, typically find themselves.

References

Alexopoulou, T., Yannakoudakis, H., & Salamoura, A. (2013). Classifying intermediate learner English: A data driven approach to learner corpora. In S. Granger, G. Gilquin, & F. Meunier (Eds.), *Twenty years of learner corpus research: Looking back, moving ahead* (pp. 11–23). Louvain-la-Neuve: Presses Universitaires de Louvain.

Biber, D., Conrad, S., Reppen, R., Byrd, P., & Helt, M. (2002). Speaking and writing in the university: A multidimensional comparison. *TESOL Quarterly, 36*(1), 9–48.

Biber, D., & Gray, B. (2010). Challenging stereotypes about academic writing: Complexity, elaboration, explicitness. *Journal of English for Academic Purposes, 9*, 2–20.

Biber, D., Johansson, S., Leech, G., Conrad, S., & Finegan, E. (1999). *Longman grammar of spoken and written English*. London: Pearson/Longman.

Buttery, P., & Caines, A. (2012). Normalising frequency counts to account for 'opportunity of use' in learner corpora. In Y. Tono, Y. Kawaguchi, & M. Minegishi (Eds.), *Developmental and crosslinguistic perspectives in learner corpus research* (pp. 187–204). Amsterdam: John Benjamins.

Canale, M., & Swain, M. (1980). Theoretical bases of communicative approaches to second language teaching and testing. *Applied Linguistics, 1*(1), 1–47.

Capel, A. (2010). A1–B2 vocabulary: Insights and issues arising from the English Profile Wordlists project. *English Profile Journal*, 1. Available online at http://journals. cambridge.org/action/displayJournal?jid=EPJ

Capel, A. (2013). Completing the *English Vocabulary Profile*: C1 and C2 vocabulary. *English Profile Journal*, 3. Available online at http://journals.cambridge.org/action/ displayJournal?jid=EPJ

Carter, R. A., & McCarthy, M. J. (2006). *Cambridge grammar of English*. Cambridge: Cambridge University Press.

Carter, R. A., & McCarthy, M. J. (2015). Spoken grammar: Where are we and where are we going? *Applied Linguistics*, 1–21. First published online January 30, 2015. doi:10.1093/ applin/amu080

Carter, R., McCarthy, M. J., Mark, G., & O'Keeffe, A. (2011a). *English grammar today. Reference book*. Cambridge: Cambridge University Press.

Carter, R., McCarthy, M. J., Mark, G., & O'Keeffe, A. (2011b). *English grammar today. Workbook*. Cambridge: Cambridge University Press.

Celce-Murcia, M. (1991). Grammar pedagogy in second and foreign language teaching. *TESOL Quarterly*, *25*(3), 459–480.

Clancy, B., & McCarthy, M. J. (2015). Co-constructed turn-taking. In K. Aijmer & C. Rühlemann (Eds.), *Corpus pragmatics: A handbook* (pp. 430–453). Cambridge: Cambridge University Press.

COBUILD. (1987). *Collins COBUILD English language dictionary*. London: Collins.

Council of Europe. (2001). *Common European framework of reference for languages: Learning, teaching, assessment*. Cambridge: Cambridge University Press.

Davies, M. (2008–). *The Corpus of Contemporary American English: 450 million words, 1990-present*. Available online at http://corpus.byu.edu/coca/

Ellis, R. (2002). The place of grammar instruction in the second/foreign language curriculum. In E. Hinkel & S. Fotos (Eds.), *New perspectives on grammar teaching in second language classrooms* (pp. 17–34). Mahwah, NJ: Erlbaum.

Halliday, M. A. K. (1994). The construction of knowledge and value in the grammar of scientific discourse, with reference to Charles Darwin's *The Origin of Species*. In M. Coulthard (Ed.), *Advances in written text analysis* (pp. 136–156). London: Routledge.

Handford, M. (2010). *The language of business meetings*. Cambridge: Cambridge University Press.

Healy, M., & Onderdonk Horan, K. (2012). Looking at language in hotel management education. In F. Farr & M. Moriarty (Eds.), *Language, learning and teaching: Irish research perspectives* (pp. 141–165). Berlin: Peter Lang.

Hermerén, L. (1978). *On modality in English*. Lund: CWK Gleerup.

Hinkel, E. (1997). Indirectness in L1 and L2 academic writing. *Journal of Pragmatics*, *27*(3), 360–386.

Hinkel, E. (2002). Teaching grammar in writing classes: Tenses and cohesion. In E. Hinkel & S. Fotos (Eds.), *New perspectives on grammar teaching in second language classrooms* (pp. 181–198). Mahwah, NJ: Erlbaum.

Hinkel, E. (2013). Research findings on teaching grammar for academic writing. *English Teaching*, *6 8*(4), 3–21.

Holmes, J. (1988). Doubt and certainty in ESL textbooks. *Applied Linguistics*, *9*(1), 21–44.

Hughes, R., & McCarthy, M. J. (1998). From sentence to discourse: Discourse grammar and English Language Teaching. *TESOL Quarterly*, *32*(2), 263–287.

Hunston, S., & Francis, G. (2000). *Pattern grammar: A corpus-driven approach to the lexical grammar of English*. Amsterdam: John Benjamins.

Jones, L. B., & L. K. Jones. 1985. Discourse functions of five English sentence types. *Word*, *36*(1), 1–21.

Liu, X. (2011). A corpus-based evaluation of syntactic complexity measures as indices of college-level ESL writers' language development. *TESOL Quarterly*, *45*(1), 36–62.

Martinez, R., & Schmitt, N. (2012). A phrasal expressions list. *Applied Linguistics*, *33*(3), 299–320.

McCarthy, M. J. (1991). *Discourse analysis for language teachers*. Cambridge: Cambridge University Press.

McCarthy, M. J. (1994). *It, this* and *that*. In M. Coulthard (Ed.), *Advances in written text analysis* (pp. 266–275). London: Routledge.

McCarthy, M. J. (2015). The role of corpus research in the design of advanced level grammar instruction. In M. A. Christison, D. Christian, P. Duff, & N. Spada (Eds.), *Teaching and learning English grammar: Research findings and future directions* (pp. 87–102). New York: Routledge.

McCarthy, M. J., & Handford, M. (2004). 'Invisible to us': A preliminary corpus-based study of spoken business English. In U. Connor & T. Upton (Eds.), *Discourse in the professions. Perspectives from corpus linguistics* (pp. 167–201). Amsterdam: John Benjamins.

McCarthy, M. J., McCarten, J., Clark, D., & Clark, R. (2009). *Grammar for business*. Cambridge: Cambridge University Press.

McCarthy, M. J., McCarten, J., & Sandiford, H. (2005). *Touchstone. Student's Books 1 & 2*. Cambridge: Cambridge University Press.

McCarthy, M. J., McCarten, J., & Sandiford, H. (2006). *Touchstone. Student's Books 3 & 4*. Cambridge: Cambridge University Press.

McCarthy, M. J., McCarten, J., & Sandiford, H. (2012). *Viewpoint. Student Book 1*. Cambridge: Cambridge University Press.

O'Keeffe, A., & Mark, G. (in press). The English Grammar Profile—describing a criteria-based empirical methodology for calibrating learner grammar competencies using the Cambridge Learner Corpus. *International Journal of Corpus Linguistics*, *20*(4).

O'Keeffe, A., McCarthy, M. J., & Carter, R. A. (2007). *From corpus to classroom*. Cambridge: Cambridge University Press.

Richards, J. C. (2008) *Moving beyond the plateau: From intermediate to advanced levels in language learning*. Cambridge: Cambridge University Press.

Rühlemann, C. 2006. Coming to terms with conversational grammar. *International Journal of Corpus Linguistics*, *11*(4), 385–409.

Schleppegrell, M. (2006). The linguistic features of advanced language use: The grammar of exposition. In H. Byrnes (Ed.), *Advanced language learning: The contribution of Halliday and Vygotsky* (pp. 134–146). London and New York: Continuum.

Schmitt, N., & Schmitt, D. (2014). A reassessment of frequency and vocabulary size in L2 vocabulary teaching. *Language Teaching*, *47*(4), 484–503.

Sinclair, J. McH. (1991). *Corpus, concordance, collocation*. Oxford University Press.

Sinclair, J. McH. (2004). *Trust the text. Language, corpus and discourse*. London: Routledge.

Stubbs, M. (1986). 'A matter of prolonged fieldwork'; notes towards a modal grammar of English. *Applied Linguistics*, *7*(1), 1–25.

11

PROMOTING GRAMMAR AND LANGUAGE DEVELOPMENT IN THE WRITING CLASS

Why, What, How, and When

Dana R. Ferris

No one would dispute that all writing involves language. Every sentence or even part of a sentence we write requires choices—about what words we will use, what the structure of the phrases and the sentence will be, how we will order and emphasize information within that sentence, and how we will connect ideas within and across different sentences and parts of the text.

With this truth in mind, it is perhaps surprising that the notion of grammar instruction and language development in the context of a writing class is highly controversial within applied linguistics and especially composition studies. Because of the uncertain (or even dispreferred) status of grammar in the writing class, writing instructors often do not receive adequate (or any) training in English grammar, linguistics, and/or pedagogical grammar. In turn, grammar in the writing class is often addressed haphazardly or neglected entirely. This is more than a missed opportunity for student writers. It is counterproductive to their development as writers and productive users of English as a second/other language.

This chapter takes the position that language development and grammar instruction in particular *should* and *can* be effectively accomplished within a second language (L2) writing class (or a mixed writing class that includes English learners). Because of the controversy already noted, we begin by discussing the *why* of developing grammar knowledge within the context of writing instruction. We then move to the *what*: With all of the competing concerns of writing instruction (content, process, rhetoric, etc.), how can a teacher choose from the many elements of English language on which to focus? We will spend the most time and space on the crucial question of *how* instructors can successfully provide language instruction to student writers, and we will tie it all together with a consideration of *when*, within a crowded writing class syllabus, a teacher might incorporate language-focused work. The goal of this chapter is that teachers will walk away with a range of tools and options that could be applied to a wide variety of pedagogical contexts.

Language Development: Why?

As already noted, it borders on absurd to argue that attention to language is unimportant in the endeavor of writing. It would seem especially salient for L2 writers, who have the double burden not only of making the same linguistic choices that every writer must make but also of sorting through their knowledge of two (or more) languages to make those choices. There are at least three distinct reasons why teachers of L2 writers should think carefully about how to promote their students' ongoing second language development in the particular context of writing instruction.

First, L2 writers make *errors*, which I have defined elsewhere as "morphological, syntactic, and lexical forms which deviate from rules of the target language, violating the expectations of literate adult native speakers" (Ferris 2011: 3). Errors are not the same as *accent* or *style*, meaning idiomatic expression that doesn't necessarily violate a rule of English grammar but that also doesn't sound quite like something a native speaker would write. Consider this sentence from the conclusion of a Chinese international student's first essay in her writing class at a U.S. university: "I hope this class could teach us how to rewrite our essays with **wonderful** words, sentences, and *paragraph*." The use of "wonderful" in this sentence is a good example of *accent*—not incorrect and indeed rather charming but also not likely something a native speaker would write. In contrast, the singular form of *paragraph* is clearly an error in this context; in a list with other plural nouns, it should have also been marked for plural here. Errors are also not to be confused with *mistakes*, which happen to all of us when we are tired, rushed, inattentive, or applying poor proofreading strategies. Errors suggest rather that the writer/learner is not entirely clear on the application of the rule or the correct structure for that sentence.

Some readers might counter that all writers—not only L2 writers—make errors, and this is certainly true. However, research suggests that L2 student writers make *more* errors and *different* errors than do native English-speaking peers (Bitchener and Ferris 2012; Ferris 2006; Hinkel 2002; Hyland 2002; Lunsford and Lunsford 2008; Silva 1993). Other research, known in the literature as *error gravity* studies, has investigated readers' reactions to written error in university and workplace settings, finding that some real-world readers (i.e., not writing/language teachers) are highly critical of errors, and some are less tolerant of errors that mark the writer as a second language learner (Beason 2001; Hairston 1981; Janopolous 1992; Santos 1988; Vann, Meyer, and Lorenz 1984). In short, not only do L2 writers make errors that are different from and often more frequent than those of their peers, but the errors also may stigmatize them (Hendrickson 1980; Shaughnessy 1977). The errors exist, and they often (not always) do matter.

A second, related point is that students are unlikely to be able to remediate such errors without expert intervention in the form of feedback and instruction. Two distinct lines of research support this generalization. First, 1980s-era thinking on L2 writing, derived largely from trends towards process-oriented instruction in L1 composition, suggested that L2 writers would improve their language use naturally through continued exposure to language and writing practice with minimal formal instruction or error correction (see, e.g., Krashen 1984; Zamel 1982). However, others argued that L2 learners were likely to "fossilize" (get stuck and fail to progress) if they were not given feedback about ways in which their language production (both speech and writing) deviated from the norms of the target language (see, e.g., Long and Robinson 1998; Russell and Spada 2006; Schmidt 1995). A second line of research on written corrective feedback (CF) in L2 writing has demonstrated repeatedly that students who receive CF are more likely to make short- and long-term progress in their control of targeted language features than students who receive no feedback (see Bitchener and Ferris 2012, for a review of the research on this point). In short, many/most L2 writers need expert instruction and feedback if they are to make progress in language control in their writing.

Third, beyond errors, L2 writers tend to write more simply than do their native speaker peers, demonstrating less variety and complexity in their texts (Hyland 2002; Silva 1993), and this relatively immature writing style can cause their writing to be judged of lower overall quality than perhaps is deserved (Hamp-Lyons 1991, 2003). Whether L2 writers' simpler style suggests a desire to avoid errors for which they may be punished (see Schachter 1974) or merely reflects their relatively less developed linguistic repertoires, they clearly need to continue developing and applying a more sophisticated range of lexical and syntactic features to their writing, especially for academic and professional purposes. Thus, beyond helping learners to find and remediate actual errors in their texts, writing instructors should help their students to analyze authentic language and consider how best to apply it for different genres and audiences.

Before moving on from this question of why we should help L2 writers to gain more control of the language of their texts, it is worth considering the reasons why scholars and some teachers would argue against doing so. These arguments tend to be both philosophical and practical. Second language acquisition scholars have questioned the notion of "error," arguing that "error" should more properly be considered a natural developmental stage in the process of language acquisition, similar to what young children display as they acquire their first languages. However, as noted, adult L2 learners (adolescents and beyond) tend not to move through those developmental stages in the same way that children do (if they move through them at all), and often such learners do not have the luxury of time to wait to "naturally" acquire enough language to prevent errors in their L2 writing or speech.

In composition studies, objections to grammar instruction and/or attention to written errors have focused on two issues: a belief that other aspects of writing ("higher-order concerns" such as ideas, development, organization, and process) are more important than language control (see, e.g., Brannon and Knoblauch 1982; Sommers 1982) and a concern that trying to enforce so-called Standard English on students is imperialistic and culturally insensitive in a world where many different varieties of English are being employed (see the recent collection edited by Horner, Lu, and Matsuda 2010, for many different perspectives on this point). Both points are valid, as far as they go: The other elements of writing *are* important, and a writing class must never become solely or primarily a course in English grammar. Further, there are many different regional/ ethnic varieties of English that are valid and valuable in their own contexts; these should never be disparaged or treated as "less than" by teachers or even by student writers themselves. Rather than being bullied by a pedagogical focus on language, however, students will be empowered if they have knowledge of and control over a broad range of language structures so that they can make appropriate choices for the specific rhetorical situation in which they are writing and/or speaking.

Finally, it is fair to mention that sometimes "philosophical" opposition to grammar teaching or error feedback in writing classes masks teachers' own insecurities over their lack of training and experience in how best to provide such instruction or feedback—or, frankly, their lack of interest in focusing on aspects of writing that they find tedious or less engaging than other topics they could explore with students. If lack of interest is the issue, teachers probably need to think more carefully about their students' needs. However, if lack of competence/knowledge is really the problem, there are practical ways for writing teachers to obtain such training and experience (see Bitchener and Ferris 2012 and Ferris 2011, for suggestions along these lines).

Language Development: What

Even teachers who are fully convinced that L2 writers need language instruction and feedback are sometimes overwhelmed by the sheer volume of choices they must make. Yes, L2 writers should expand their productive vocabulary, but English has an enormous lexicon. Where should teachers and their students begin? Of course, students need more knowledge of English grammar, but there are so many topics to cover; how do teachers approach this issue while not neglecting other equally important aspects of writing? What about other elements of writing style that vary across genres and registers, such as punctuation, mechanical choices (capitalization, bolding, italics, etc.), and formatting? Teachers need, if not a road map through this maze of options, at least some principles from which to start. Three principles that may be helpful are: (1) consider specific student needs, (2) exploit the language used in authentic texts, and (3) prepare students for the specific language structures elicited by particular writing tasks. We will discuss each of these in turn.

Investigating Student Needs

Every writing class is different. L2 students come with varying knowledge bases that depend upon their L1 background (and its similarity to or distance from English), their L2 proficiency levels, and their educational pathways (i.e., whether they have encountered formal English grammar instruction in their previous exposure to English). Teachers should not simply open a grammar textbook or writing handbook and teach through it. They must discover what that particular group of students knows and what they need most at that point in their development as L2 learners and writers.

Teachers should conduct two distinct types of needs analysis with regard to grammar for L2 writers. First, they should collect and analyze an early writing sample to assess strengths, weaknesses, and patterns of error for individual students and for the whole class. Instructors can do this analysis themselves, but it can be very time-consuming. For many classes, the procedure shown in Table 11.1 should work nearly as well.

Error analysis should also be ongoing, as teachers should hope and expect that their students will show progress with some patterns of error as the term goes on. Instructors can also conduct an analysis of common class errors every time they grade or respond to a particular set of student papers, turning patterns and student

TABLE 11.1 Suggested Procedures for Preliminary Error Analysis (adapted from Ferris and Hedgcock 2014: 314–315 and Ferris 2014: xviii–xix)

1. Preselect particular errors on which to focus (e.g., verbs, plurals, articles, word choice, punctuation, etc.). Pick enough error types to get a good picture of student needs but not so many that the task will be overwhelming for you or the students.

2. Go through the writing samples and mark (highlight, circle, or underline) all instances of errors in the categories you have chosen.

3. Return the papers to the students in class, and briefly go over a brief explanation of the error categories you marked, with examples of each type.

4. Ask the students to go through their texts, numbering each marked error and trying to categorize it. They can ask classmates or the teacher for help if they're confused about a particular error(s). Have them record their findings in an error chart you create for the activity.

5. Ask them to identify, below the chart, three patterns of errors they noticed most frequently when they were completing the exercise.

6. Collect the exercise, spot-check the students' work for accuracy, and record the information (make a spreadsheet or take copies of the exercise) for individual students and compile findings for the whole class. Now you have a fairly good sense of what the class as a whole might benefit from in terms of in-class instruction and of what individualized feedback each student might need.

7. Share the whole-class findings with the students so that they understand why you will focus more on certain issues than others for in-class work.

examples into a quick and contextualized mini lesson based on the students' own recent work.

Another useful tool for needs analysis is students' own self-reported areas of strength and weakness, as well as their preferences and views regarding error feedback and their awareness of their own existing self-editing strategies. Questionnaires such as those shown in Ferris and Roberts (2001: 181–183) or in Ferris (2014: xiii–xvi) can be very informative for teachers and enlightening to students themselves, if they have never looked at their own language knowledge so analytically before. These two types of data—error analysis of an early writing sample and self-reports of grammar knowledge—not only can help teachers to focus their efforts most successfully but also can facilitate student cooperation, if they feel that instructors' grammar instruction and feedback choices are rooted in thoughtful consideration of how their time would be best spent.

Exploiting Language in Assigned Readings

Most writing classes include some sort of reading component, or at least they should—students need content to write about, and they benefit from authentic models for both rhetorical and linguistic analysis. However, teachers will often stop at having students consider only the content (main ideas and details) of assigned texts, and this is a missed opportunity. Once students have read the text with comprehension and critically analyzed it, the teacher can then lead the class a step further and have them consider the language choices made by the author. Depending upon the text and the teacher's goals for the lesson, the class might focus on vocabulary (e.g., adjectives or modal auxiliaries) used to convey a specific emotion or argument, on ways in which punctuation and sentence structure communicate with a target audience, or they might simply examine target linguistic structures (e.g., verb tense usage or article vs. zero-article noun phrases) in authentic written prose. Such language lessons have the benefit of being authentic (based on real texts the students have already engaged with) and naturally integrated with other course content. Stand-alone grammar lessons in writing courses often are less engaging because they are not connected to anything else the class is doing, but if language analysis activities are instead directly tied to course readings, they will have added face validity for students. Table 11.2 shows language samples from one authentic text (Reilly 2012) and points out different elements of the language used and how it deviated from formal academic conventions while clearly conveying the author's message. Such analysis could be applied to any class text a teacher is using with students.

Anticipating Structures Elicited by Writing Tasks

A third suggestion for narrowing the universe of English structures on which to focus comes from considering the actual writing tasks students are being asked to accomplish. For example, if students are being asked to write papers that include

TABLE 11.2 Sample Language Analysis Activity Based on Authentic Text (from Reilly (2012))

What a [fool, tool, stooge, sap] I was

Jealous egghead, I thought.

What'd they do instead? **Alerted nobody. Called nobody**.

I hope Penn State loses civil suits until the walls of the accounting office cave in. **I hope** that Spanier, Schultz and Curley go to prison for perjury. **I hope** the NCAA gives Penn State the death penalty it most richly deserves.

What Students Could Consider

• How Reilly's repeated use of the same sentence frame ("What a _____ I was") helps to express his overall meaning.
• Why Reilly turned the sentence "Jealous egghead, I thought" around, instead of the more conventional "I thought he was a jealous egghead."
• Why Reilly flouted typical writing rules about avoiding contractions and sentence fragments.
• Why Reilly repeated "I hope . . ." several times in a row. (Isn't sentence variety supposed to be a virtue?)

---

material from other sources, it makes sense to provide instruction on paraphrase, summary, and quotation—both what those techniques accomplish in a text as well as the syntax and punctuation choices associated with them. Similarly, in some disciplines, ideas written by other authors are conveyed in the "literary present" tense ("As Shakespeare **says** in *Romeo and Juliet*. . ."), while in others, such as the social sciences, the work of other authors is described using the past tense ("Krashen **noted** in his landmark 1982 book that. . ."). Narrative writing, which can be relevant in various genres or disciplines (e.g., describing an interview or a field study, summarizing the plot of a novel in a literature class, writing up a case study in business or a lab report), requires an understanding of how verb tenses shift when telling a story (especially between simple present and simple past, with other tenses coming into play as well). Scientific writing often requires the skillful use of the passive voice, while writing for the humanities conversely requires minimizing it (instead writing other types of long, syntactically complex constructions to show intellectual sophistication).

With these distinctions in mind, teachers of L2 writers should examine their own writing prompts/assignments to assess what language structures (syntactic and lexical) students might need to write effectively and to consider, as part of the prewriting and drafting process, facilitating mini lessons on those points so that students are comfortable with the tools they will need for their specific rhetorical purposes. This type of analysis should also be applied to writing prompts used for assessment (i.e., in-class essay examinations or timed writing for placement or diagnostic purposes). If the wording or content of a particular writing task will elicit structures over which students do not have adequate control at their stage of

L2 development, this may put them at an unfair or unnecessary disadvantage. One example from my own experience was a midterm examination prompt given to students in a low-intermediate L2 writing class about arranged marriages: "Imagine that you are the parent of a grown son or daughter . . . ." The teachers and administrators in the program didn't realize until they read the responses that this wording required students to use hypothetical conditional structures: "If my son wanted to choose his own bride, I would . . ."—and almost none of them were able to do so, leading to an excess of verb tense/form errors in the essays. In such instances, teachers may want to either reconsider the prompt and/or take the challenges presented by the prompt into account when assessing written examinations. (In our program, we decided to throw the examination out and have students write to a different prompt that did not present such syntactic challenges for them.)

To summarize this section, teachers who want to help students proactively develop better knowledge of the English language and improved control over language choices in their own writing have many options to consider as to what linguistic topics they might cover in their classes. The three principles discussed here—targeting student needs for a specific class, examining language used in assigned course readings, and anticipating structures required to successfully complete a particular writing task—provide teachers with some contextualized ways to make choices for their own particular teaching situation.

Language Development: How

Having considered the *why* and the *what* of language development for L2 writers, we now turn to arguably the most important (and difficult) question: the *how*. Both L1 and L2 composition research is replete with examples of how *not* to address grammar instruction or error feedback for student writers (for reviews, see Bitchener and Ferris 2012; Connors and Lunsford 1988; Frodesen and Holten 2003; Lunsford and Lunsford 2008). For easy reference here, Table 11.3 provides an overview of what doesn't work and why.

TABLE 11.3 Ineffective Language Development Strategies

What (Usually) Doesn't Work	Why It Doesn't Work
Decontextualized grammar lessons by the teacher on random topics	Not enough connection to students' own writing
Decontextualized grammar presentations by the students on random topics	Not well integrated with other class activities
Unfocused peer editing activities	Students don't know what to look for
Unstructured "outsourcing" or "self-study"	Self-study materials may be too hard or not relevant enough (or too artificial)

As already noted, in-class grammar instruction that is unconnected to other reading and writing that students are doing may have limited effects: "The return on grammar instruction is often disappointing. Teachers find that even when a grammatical feature has been covered and practiced, students may not use it accurately in their own writing" (Frodesen and Holten 2003: 142). Thus, stand-alone grammar lessons—for example, inserted into the first or last 20 minutes of a writing class meeting—may not have their desired effects. Though student-led presentations have the advantage of variety and being more engaging, at least for the student leader(s) of the day, they share the same disadvantage as teacher-led grammar lessons of being decontextualized from other writing class concerns. Further, since designing grammar mini lessons is challenging even for trained teachers, student-led lessons present the additional risk of erroneous or incomplete instruction for the rest of the class.

The latter two items in Table 11.3 refer to overgeneralized peer or self-study activities that, while they provide students with more agency and responsibility, may fail to give students enough guidance for the exercises to accomplish their desired objectives. Peer editing activities can be very useful to help students learn what to look for in their own writing, but they need to be carefully structured to be effective. Table 11.4 provides two examples of well focused peer editing activities. The first follows a teacher-delivered mini lesson on verb tense shifts in a narrative. The second is a more general peer editing activity for the penultimate draft of a student paper.

TABLE 11.4 Sample Peer Editing Activities

Example 1

Peer Editing Exercise as a Mini Lesson Application

Instructions: *Exchange papers with a partner. Mark (circle, underline, or highlight) each example you find of **present tense, past tense, or present perfect tense** (ignore other verb tenses and forms for now). Then complete the following chart. If you find any errors in verb tense, do not correct them, but you can discuss them with your partner in a few minutes.*

Verb	Tense	Why This Tense Is Used Here (Discussed in Mini Lesson)

Source: Adapted from Ferris (2011, figure 5.4: 135).

Example 2

Peer Editing of Almost Final Paper Draft

Instructions: *Exchange papers with another member of your writing group.*

1. Read the paper carefully for any problems with:

   - Missing or "extra" words.
   - Typos or spelling errors.
   - Word/phrase choice that is incorrect (or not exactly correct).
   - Errors with commas.
   - Errors with apostrophes.
   - Errors with citations (APA format, punctuation).
   - Grammar errors such as subject-verb agreement, run-on sentences or comma splices, verb tense/form errors.

2. **Do not** "rewrite" words, phrases, or sentences simply to improve "style." Focus on actual errors.

3. If you find errors, mark them as follows:*

   ➢ Use ~~strikethrough~~ for unnecessary words or word endings.
   ➢ Use yellow highlight for unnecessary punctuation.
   ➢ Use a red font to insert a word or word ending or punctuation that is missing.
   ➢ Use "Comments" to add any comments in the margins about word choice or grammar.

---

*These instructions assume that students are using computers for the peer editing task, but they can be adapted for pen-and-paper activities as well.

Similarly, while it can be useful to provide students with a list of self-study resources for grammar, vocabulary, or mechanics (websites, handbooks, etc.), instructors need to review those resources themselves, just as they would a textbook they might adopt for a class (see Ferris and Hedgcock 2014 for concrete approaches about how to do this). Simply handing students a book or giving them a link(s) without ensuring that such resources are easy to navigate, well designed, and appropriate for students' proficiency levels and needs may result in more frustration than assistance for them.

Having discussed some pitfalls or common errors to avoid in facilitating language development for L2 writers, we now turn to more successful approaches. These can be divided into three general categories: instruction through in-class mini lessons, self-directed language study, and corrective feedback.

Language Mini Lessons

Mini lessons on salient language points can be an appropriate way to integrate grammar, vocabulary, mechanics, or strategy instruction into a writing class without putting such language concerns out of balance with other writing course priorities. As their name implies, mini lessons should be *brief and narrowly focused*, not taking up too much class time and not trying to cover too much in one chunk of instruction (for more complex structures, a series of connected mini lessons may work well). The teacher may also want to build in homework either before or after the mini lesson so that additional analysis or practice can occur without taking over the entire in-class lesson.

Topics for Mini Lessons. Nearly any language-related topic can be addressed in the mini lesson format—vocabulary, self-editing strategies, punctuation, or grammar (see Ferris 2014 for examples). The teacher should consider the suggestions in the previous section of this chapter (the "what" of language development in the writing class) to identify possible mini lesson topics for a particular class. These mini lessons can also include the "common errors" lesson referred to in the previous section (for an example used in a writing class, see Ferris and Hedgcock 2014, appendix 9: 350–351).

Format of Mini Lessons. I recommend the following elements for class mini lessons, usually but not necessarily in this order:

- **Discovery**: Analysis activities to elicit students' prior knowledge about the structure or focus to be discussed in the mini lesson.
- **Explanation**: Brief, clearly focused instruction on the structure/rules/topic under consideration, with on-point and straightforward examples.
- **Practice**: Opportunities to practice the rules/strategies described in the mini lesson with language samples (e.g., sentences or paragraphs, with or without errors) and/or with texts that students find themselves (e.g., a newspaper article online if they have computer access).
- **Application**: Focused activities that require students to apply the concepts presented in the mini lesson to their own writing—either a paper they are currently working on or one they wrote recently.

While most grammar/language textbooks and websites routinely include explanation/instruction and practice activities, the discovery and application sections of a mini lesson may be less common. Arguably, the application section is the most important and indispensable part of the mini lesson, as there is ample evidence that students' inability to apply grammar knowledge to their own writing, not lack of knowledge itself, is a primary problem for L2 writers. Appendix A to this chapter shows a sample mini lesson (on verb tense shifts in narratives) as a simple example of how the different parts of a mini lesson can work together.

Self-Directed Language Study

I have noted that unfocused referrals to self-study materials can be an ineffective approach to language development for L2 writers. However, in combination with other approaches, some self-directed language study can be useful, motivating, and empowering for student writers. Self-study has two major advantages over whole-class instruction: (1) Students can choose to work on topics/issues that they are interested in and/or have problems with, which reflects the reality that in any given class, students will not all have the same needs. (2) Students can work at their own pace, choosing to move on quickly if they feel comfortable with a topic or structure or slowing down to investigate it more deeply if they are confused. Self-study activities can include individual study of specific grammar/mechanics topics (e.g., sentence boundaries, verb tenses, apostrophes, etc.), self-directed vocabulary learning (vocabulary journals, collocations journals), or analysis of stylistic choices made by other authors in assigned or self-selected reading texts. They can be assigned for homework and/or extra credit and can be graded on timely, good faith completion. To be most successful, self-study activities should include the following components:

- Initial diagnostic activities in which the student and/or the teacher can assess possible topics/issues for the student to work on during the course (a diagnostic error analysis and/or grammar knowledge questionnaire, as described in the "what" section).
- Clear structure for the assignment, including models (e.g., of a vocabulary journal entry or a style analysis entry).
- Recommended resources (what the student might use for grammar self-study, what the student might read for vocabulary learning or style analysis).
- Regular checkpoints to avoid procrastination or loss of focus (reasonable due dates, in-class sharing of questions or insights from self-study).
- Reflection, especially at the end of the project, about what the student has gained from self-study and what they might continue working on in the future.

Appendix B to this chapter shows one example of a language self-study project assigned in a first-year composition course (a mixed class including both L1 and L2 English writers). This could be adapted as needed/desired for a variety of class contexts.

Corrective Feedback

Providing instruction and self-study opportunities does not remove the need for L2 writers to receive focused corrective feedback (CF) on errors they make, particularly if they are persistent, patterned errors and/or if the errors interfere with overall comprehensibility of the message (see Bitchener and Ferris 2012; Ferris 2011; Hendrickson 1980). Written CF has been an extremely controversial topic in L2 writing, and space does not permit a thorough discussion of it here, so I will simply summarize the following suggestions or principles from existing research on CF (for a more elaborated version of this list with additional citations, see also Ferris and Hedgcock 2014: 283):

- Existing research suggests that CF, if provided effectively, can help student writers to both revise existing texts and carry over to new texts.
- Focused CF (on selected patterns of error) is more effective than unfocused CF (on anything that happens to catch a teacher, tutor, or peer editor's eye).
- Indirect CF (in which the teacher/editor points out errors but does not correct them) may be more effective in the long run for writing development than direct CF (in which the editor makes the correction), but there may be legitimate roles for direct CF as well (more efficient, more informative for idiomatic errors such as preposition usage).
- Some sort of explanation of error patterns (error codes, rule reminders in the margins, summary comments in an end note) is probably more helpful than simply circling or highlighting an error without an explanation.
- Some categories of error are more responsive to written CF than others; for more complex errors, a one-on-one conference may be needed.
- Students should be required/directed to apply, analyze, and reflect on CF they have received so that the feedback isn't wasted or ignored.

These guidelines for effective CF apply whether the feedback provider is the teacher, a tutor or consultant in a writing center, or a peer editor (see the preceding discussion about more/less effective approaches to in-class peer editing workshops). The point here is that CF can and should be part of an overall approach to language development in an L2 writing class, but it should neither be the only approach (because students can benefit from focused instruction and from self-study) nor abandoned entirely (because students can benefit from targeted feedback on their own work).

"Dynamic" Written CF. One specific application of CF combines the goals of self-study and CF in an integrated approach. This approach, developed by faculty members at Brigham Young University, includes the following components:

1. Students regularly produce a short timed-writing sample (5–10 minutes each time), based on an accessible prompt.
2. The teacher marks it immediately (before next class) using a list of preestablished error codes.
3. Students correct the marked errors (in the next class or for homework) and chart their error patterns. (The teacher may require several revisions/resubmissions as needed.)
4. The process is repeated regularly throughout the course.

This approach is *dynamic* because it shifts from student to student and over time. It also has the advantage of being *frequent and manageable* for both instructor and students, providing more consistent feedback and revision opportunities on shorter pieces of texts. It also promotes mindfulness in students (because they are directed to focus regularly on specific language issues and to chart their progress) that can carry over to longer writing projects and promote language acquisition. Preliminary research (see Evans, Hartshorn, McCollum, and Wolfersberger 2010; Hartshorn, Evans, Merrill, Sudweeks, Strong-Krause, and Anderson 2010) suggests that students benefit from this approach, and anecdotal reports from teachers and students at BYU and at my own institution (which adopted it program-wide in 2013) attest to its popularity with many/most students in L2 writing classes.

To summarize this section, instructors wishing to provide integrated opportunities for language development in their writing classes should consider a combination of approaches, from language mini lessons that address the needs of the whole class, to guided self study opportunities, to well designed CF given to students about their own writing. This combination provides students with the right mix of teacher expertise, specific feedback on areas in their own writing on which they need to focus, and autonomy for/responsibility over their own learning.

Language Development: When

In this chapter so far, we have looked at the *why*, *how*, and *what* of language development in L2 writing classes. We close this discussion by briefly examining the challenging question of *when* such activities should take place. Writing class syllabi can be among the most difficult to construct because as students move through the stages of the writing process—drafting, receiving feedback, revising, and editing—the timing of the different stages can be complex, and teachers need adequate time to provide quality feedback. With this in mind—together with the apparently competing goals of a writing course (content, process, rhetoric)—how can teachers integrate language development in ways that are authentic and that complement other writing activities without distracting too much time and energy away from them?

While every writing class is different, there are at least four distinct points within normal writing class cycles where a focus on language fits naturally:

1. When a new writing assignment is being presented and discussed (to present possible vocabulary and grammar structures that may be salient for the task and genre).
2. When the class is discussing assigned readings (to "exploit" the language features of the text, as discussed in the "what" section).
3. When students are in the final stages of editing a paper (a mini lesson on a key language point followed by a peer editing activity and self-editing exercises).
4. When the instructor has finished grading or responding to a class set of papers and delivers a "common errors" mini lesson based upon patterns observed in the students' texts.

In addition to these naturally recurring points in the life cycle of a writing course, the teacher may also want to build in an early class activity in which students' individual and collective needs are diagnosed (as discussed), as well as an end-of-course activity in which students reflect on the various language development activities they have completed and talk about where they have made progress and where they still need to focus attention in the future. An early mini lesson (in conjunction with the first major paper) on strategies for proofreading and self-editing writing may be appropriate for most classes, as well.

Because the instructor may not know until the class begins exactly what mini lessons and workshops might be most needed for a particular group of students, it might be beneficial to simply note "Language Focus TBD [to be determined]" at strategic points (as previously outlined) on the syllabus, explaining to the students at the course outset that topics for grammar and language instruction will be decided based upon demonstrated class needs. Students will likely appreciate this thoughtful, contextualized approach, as opposed to the typical march through the handbook/grammar book (whether or not the topics all relate to their current needs) that they may have experienced.

Conclusion

Language development in the writing class is challenging for teachers to envision and implement, which explains why, too often, such instruction is either delivered haphazardly or ignored altogether. I hope that the opening section of this chapter has provided some clear arguments for why it is important that teachers effectively integrate language development with other course goals for L2 writers—and that the subsequent sections have provided some practical guidance as to how to proceed in doing so. Teachers who follow the suggestions in this chapter may be pleasantly surprised to find that their students respond positively to thoughtfully selected, well integrated language focus activities and that they themselves feel more satisfied about their efforts in instruction and feedback. Language is an inevitable and inextricable part of writing; to neglect it in instruction is to deliver only part of a writing class.

Discussion Questions

1. Before reading this chapter, did you believe that "bottom-up instruction" (on grammar and vocabulary) was a necessary and important component of an L2 writing class or that it was an inappropriate focus for a writing class? Has your thinking changed or been strengthened after reading this chapter?
2. In the "what" section of this chapter, it is suggested that teachers "exploit" the language of assigned readings, anticipate the language elicited by different writing tasks, and use these analyses to plan targeted, contextualized language lessons for their students. Practice this principle by examining a sample

reading (e.g., from an L2 textbook or from a current newspaper article) and listing interesting features of how language is used that could potentially be discussed with a class of students. Also, if you can obtain one or more authentic writing assignments/prompts, try to imagine what kinds of language (reporting verbs, passive voice, use of quotations, key vocabulary, etc.) might be required to respond effectively to that writing task. If you are reading this book in a methods class, discuss your findings with your classmates and instructor.

3. Another suggestion was to analyze student papers written at the beginning of a writing class to get a sense for individual and class error patterns. Obtain a set of 5–10 L2 student papers written to the same prompt in the same class. Follow the suggestions for error analysis provided in/Table 11.1, and create a list of 3–5 error patterns that seem to be consistent across the set of papers. If these were your students, on what language features would you focus (for instruction and/or feedback) in this class? How might you approach the issues you noted, considering the various suggestions in this chapter (e.g., through mini lessons, self-study, feedback, or some combination)?

4. Considering your findings in questions 2 and/or 3, pick a topic for a possible class mini lesson for a writing class—based upon student needs (as seen in the error analysis) or on the language features modeled in a reading text or required by a writing class. What ideas do you have for designing a mini lesson on this topic?

5. Beyond mini lessons, the chapter also suggests that the teacher should utilize language self-study activities and provide corrective feedback (written, oral, and in peer/self-editing workshops). What is your reaction to these suggestions? What do you like about them? What are your concerns, as a prospective or current teacher of L2 writers?

Essential Readings

Connors, R. (2003). Grammar in American college composition: An historical overview. In L. Ede & A. A. Lunsford (Eds.), *Selected essays of Robert J. Connors* (pp. 117–138). Boston: Bedford/St. Martin's.

Ferris, D. (2011). *Treatment of error in second language student writing* (2nd ed.). Ann Arbor: University of Michigan Press.

Hartshorn, J. K., Evans, N. E., Merrill, P. F., Sudweeks, R. R., Strong-Krause, D., & Anderson, N. J. (2010). The effects of dynamic corrective feedback on ESL writing accuracy. *TESOL Quarterly, 44*, 84–109.

MacDonald, S. P. (2007). The erasure of language. *College Composition and Communication, 58*, 585–625.

Matsuda, P. K. (2012). Let's face it: Language issues and the writing program administrator. *WPA: Writing Program Administration, 36*(1), 141–163.

Zimmerman, C. B. (2008). *Word knowledge: A vocabulary teacher's handbook.* Oxford: Oxford University Press.

References

Beason, L. (2001). Ethos and error: How business people react to errors. *College Composition and Communication, 53*, 33–64.

Bitchener, J., & Ferris, D. (2012). *Written corrective feedback in second language acquisition and writing.* New York: Routledge.

Brannon, L., & Knoblauch, C. H. (1982). On students' rights to their own texts: A model of teacher response. *College Composition and Communication, 33*, 157–166.

Connors, R., & Lunsford, A. A. (1988). Frequency of formal errors in current college writing, or Ma and Pa Kettle do research. *College Composition and Communication, 39*, 395–409.

Evans, N., Hartshorn, J., McCollum, R., & Wolfersberger, M. (2010). Contextualizing corrective feedback in second language writing pedagogy. *Language Teaching Research, 14*, 445–464.

Ferris, D. R. (2006). Does error feedback help student writers? New evidence on the short- and long-term effects of written error correction. In K. Hyland & F. Hyland (Eds.), *Feedback in second language writing: Contexts and issues* (pp. 81–104). Cambridge: Cambridge University Press.

Ferris, D. R. (2011). *Treatment of error in second language student writing* (2nd ed.). Ann Arbor: University of Michigan Press.

Ferris, D. R. (2014). *Language power: Tutorials for writers.* Boston: Bedford St. Martin's.

Ferris, D. R., & Hedgcock, J. S. (2014). *Teaching L2 composition: Purpose, process, and practice* (3rd ed.). New York: Routledge.

Ferris, D. R., & Roberts, B. J. (2001). Error feedback in L2 writing classes: How explicit does it need to be? *Journal of Second Language Writing, 10*, 161–184.

Frodesen, J., & Holten, C. (2003). Grammar and the ESL writing class. In B. Kroll (Ed.), *Exploring the dynamics of second language writing* (pp. 141–161). Cambridge: Cambridge University Press.

Hairston, M. (1981). Not all errors are created equal: Nonacademic readers in the professions respond to lapses in usage. *College English, 43*, 794–806.

Hamp-Lyons, L. (Ed.) (1991). *Assessing second language writing in academic contexts.* Norwood, NJ: Ablex.

Hamp-Lyons, L. (2003). Writing teachers as assessors of writing. In B. Kroll (Ed.), *Exploring the dynamics of second language writing* (pp. 162–189). Cambridge: Cambridge University Press.

Hartshorn, J. K., Evans, N. W., Merrill, P. F., Sudweeks, R. R., Strong-Krause, D., & Anderson, N. J. (2010). The effects of dynamic corrective feedback on ESL writing accuracy. *TESOL Quarterly, 44*, 84–109.

Hendrickson, J. M. (1980). The treatment of error in written work. *Modern Language Journal, 64*, 216–221.

Hinkel, E. (2002). *Second language writers' text: Linguistic and rhetorical features.* Mahwah, NJ: Erlbaum.

Horner, B., Lu, M-Z., & Matsuda, P. K. (Eds.) (2010). *Cross-language relations in composition.* Carbondale: Southern Illinois University Press.

Hyland, K. (2002). *Teaching and researching writing.* Harlow, UK: Pearson Education.

Janopolous, M. (1992). University faculty tolerance of NS and NNS writing errors. *Journal of Second Language Writing, 1*, 109–122.

Krashen, S. D. (1984). *Writing: Research, theory, and application.* Oxford: Pergamon Press.

Long, M. H., & Robinson, P. (1998). Focus on form: Theory, research, and practice. In C. Doughty & J. Williams (Eds.), *Focus on form in second language acquisition* (pp. 15–41). Cambridge: Cambridge University Press.

Lunsford, A. A., & Lunsford, K. J. (2008). "Mistakes are a fact of life": A national comparative study. *College Composition and Communication, 59,* 781–806.

Reilly, R. (2012). *The sins of the father.* Available online at http://espn.go.com/espn/story/_/id/8162972/joe-paterno-true-legacy

Russell, J., & Spada, N. (2006). The effectiveness of corrective feedback for the acquisition of L2 grammar: A meta-analysis of the research. In J. Norris & L. Ortega (Eds.), *Synthesizing research on language learning and teaching* (pp. 133–164). Amsterdam: John Benjamins.

Santos, T. (1988). Professors' reactions to the academic writing of nonnative-speaking students. *TESOL Quarterly, 22,* 66–90.

Schachter, J. L. (1974). An error in error analysis. *Language Learning, 24,* 205–214.

Schmidt, R. (1995). *Attention and awareness in foreign language learning.* Honolulu: University of Hawai'i Press.

Shaughnessy, M. P. (1977). *Errors and expectations.* New York: Oxford University Press.

Silva, T. (1993). Toward an understanding of the distinct nature of L2 writing: The ESL research and its implications. *TESOL Quarterly, 27,* 657–677.

Sommers, N. (1982). Responding to student writing. *College Composition and Communication, 33,* 148–156.

Vann, R., Meyer, D., & Lorenz, F. (1984). Error gravity: A study of faculty opinion of ESL errors. *TESOL Quarterly, 18,* 427–440.

Zamel, V. (1982). Writing: The process of discovering meaning. *TESOL Quarterly, 19,* 79–102.

APPENDIX A[1]

Sample Mini Lesson on Verb Tense Shifts

Discovery Activity

Examine the following student text excerpt. In this paragraph, the student writer shifts from past tense to present tense. Examine the paragraph and describe (a) when the shift happens, (b) why it happens, and (c) whether you think the writer handled the shift accurately.

> As a first generation Asian-American, my main focus growing up was not reading or writing but in the art of mathematics. To my parents' understanding, as long as I was proficient at speaking the English language, the words on the pages will begin to read and write by themselves. I began to refute this notion vigorously once I stepped into my first public school classroom where I found that the words Barney once spoke so adamantly could not be written down with such ease. As time slowly drifted by and my understanding of the mechanics of reading and writing vastly improved, I found that my understanding of other subjects also began to improve. I agree with the many professors and students who find that reading and writing abilities are very important for success in college and future careers. I also believe that improving my reading and writing skills will be very critical to my success as a college student.

Explanation

Writers often will shift back and forth between past and present tense, especially in writing that includes *narrative*—a story from personal experience, a retelling of a plot in a literary analysis paper, a description of a historical event, or even a report on a science experiment or statistical procedures. As we saw in the Discovery Activity, such shifts can be perfectly appropriate and correct:

> I **found** that my understanding of other subjects also **began** to improve. I **agree** with the many professors and students who **find** that reading and writing abilities **are** very important for success in college and future careers.

In this example, the writer moved from describing an experience in the past to a statement of opinion that he holds in the present. In other words, the shift from past tense to present tense, even from one sentence to the next in the middle of the same paragraph, can be natural and accurate. However, writers do sometimes make errors by incorrectly shifting their tenses in the middle of a narrative, for example starting a story in the past tense but shifting to present in the middle (while still telling the story from the past):

> A couple of years ago, my mom **took** my friend Sydney and me to Southern California on vacation. As we **drove** down the Pacific Coast Highway on the way to our hotel, our friend Heidi **texts** us, saying that she and her boyfriend Zack **broke** up again. Sydney **calls** her right away to see if Heidi **is** doing OK, but really it **was** because Sydney **used** to date Zack and **wants** him back herself.

In this narrative, the past tense verbs are in bold, and the present tense verbs are in bold italics. The entire story happened in the past, and the time frame should have stayed in past tense throughout the whole paragraph. However, the writer shifted to present tense in the middle of the second sentence, starting with the verb **texts**, and then went back and forth between present and past for the rest of the story.

Practice and Application Activities

Practice Exercise: Identifying Inappropriate Verb Tense Shifts. The following text excerpt was from a literary analysis paper written for a high school English class. Find and mark any erroneous verb tense shifts in the paragraph, and suggest ways to correct them in the context of the passage.

> There are also monsters that are more fantasy-like. In "A Sound of Thunder," the characters time-traveled into the time of dinosaurs, and the monster was the T-Rex. There is one final kind of monster in a couple of the stories. When stress and bad things go on between people, it can lead to horrible things, and the bad things are the "monster" in these situations. In "The Sniper," there was a civil war going on, and it led one brother to kill another. Even though the man who killed his brother didn't know it was him when he shot him, it's still a very depressing situation. Or like in "The Interlopers,"

two Native American tribes have been in rivalry for ages over a certain area of land that they both wanted and the chiefs of these tribes were in the forest fighting each other and ended up not being able to get out of the woods. They decided to make up while they were trapped together, but in the end it wasn't good enough to save them because a pack of wolves went after them.

Application Activity: Find a paper you wrote that includes narrative and/or that describes a text(s) written by another author. Look through that paper and examine:

a. If you shifted tenses while telling the story, and if so, if you did so correctly. Are there explicit text markers that show when/why you switched from present → past or past → present?
b. If you used the correct verb tense when talking about the text(s) by another author(s). Try to explain why you chose to use either past or present tense in that particular context.

Note

1 Ferris and Hedgcock (2014, figures 9.7–9.9: 323–325); adapted from Ferris (2014: 300–302).

APPENDIX B

Language Self-Study Project: Overview and Instructions

Background and Purpose: A successful piece of writing involves many things: compelling ideas, effective organization, and awareness of one's audience (readers). It also, of course, involves *language:*

- Texts that are virtually free of grammatical and mechanical errors.
- Texts with precise, interesting word choice.
- Texts with varied, effective sentences.
- Texts with attention to style/voice (which includes word/sentence choices as well as "extralinguistic" features such as punctuation and formatting).

The goal of this assignment is to help you become more aware of these language choices in your own writing. However, rather than your instructor selecting language points for you to study, this will be a *self-directed* assignment: *You* will choose the language features on which to focus.

Grading: This assignment is worth 100 points (10%) of your final course grade. You will receive full credit if you complete the assignments on schedule and according to instructions and do a thoughtful, thorough job on the project. I may give partial credit if it seems appropriate. You also will have the option of adding up to 50 points (5%) of *extra credit* by doing additional project choices (see below for more details).

Options: You will choose from one of three options to complete this project. We will spend time in class on Day 2 doing some diagnostic activities that might help you decide which option to select.

- **Option 1: Vocabulary Journal.** For each of your five entries, choose *three* words or phrases that you have encountered in your reading (for this class or other courses or in pleasure reading). These should be words that are *new or unfamiliar* to you (including words you know but that are used differently in the text you read). See the attached sample for the information you should include.

- **Option 2: Style Journal**. Copy sentences or longer excerpts from texts you read where the author's style really catches your attention—for either good or bad reasons. Note the sentence/excerpt and its source, and write a paragraph of analysis: what you notice about the style, what your reaction to it is, and how it might inform your own writing (as a strategy or tool to use or avoid). See attached "Sample Vocabulary Journal Entry."
- **Option 3: Grammar/Mechanics Self-study**. In the course website, there is a selection of self-study tutorials on a range of language topics (grammar, vocabulary, punctuation, and style). You should pick five topics that you think would be the most useful/valuable for your needs. For each one, you should work through the tutorial (do the activities and read the material). For grading, choose, complete, and submit one "Practice" exercise and one "Apply" exercise (including, as applicable, any texts you analyze to complete those exercises).

Introduction and Reflection Entries. In addition to your five vocabulary, style, or grammar entries, you will begin your project with an introduction of 200–250 words. In this introduction, you should explain which option you have chosen and why. For your final reflection, look back on your introduction entry and the five entries you completed. Write a 200–250 reflection on how this project went for you. Was it useful, difficult, confusing, interesting, or . . . what? Were you happy with your project choice, or do you now wish you'd selected one of the other options? Did you notice any heightened awareness of your language use while writing this quarter? Do you predict that the project will have future benefits for your writing? Why or why not?

Sample Vocabulary Journal Entry

Word	*Muster*
Source	"Write or Die" by Stephen King (p. 29)
Sentence	"Now that I was away from the administrative offices of Lisbon High, I felt able to muster a little honesty."
General meaning	Muster means to assemble things together, as in armies or courage.
Specific meaning	Muster was used to mean gathering the quality of honesty.
Grammatical info	Verb (transitive)
Sample sentence	Former presidents and world leaders have all tried to muster the sympathies of a global population in order to fight human rights violations.

Sample Style Journal Entry

"Shitty First Drafts" by Anne Lamott (pp. 321–322)

Passage

> First there's the vinegar-lipped Reader Lady, who says primly, "Well, *That's* not very interesting, is it?" And there's the emaciated German male who writes these Orwellian memos detailing your thought crimes. And there are your parents, agonizing over your lack of loyalty and discretion; and there's William Burroughs, dozing off or shooting up because he finds you as bold and articulate as a houseplant; and so on.

Analysis

The word choice and tone of this passage all intrigued me.

For instance, Lamott carefully chose her words to make her feelings easier to understand. She used *vinegar-lipped, emaciated German male,* and *Orwellian memos,* all of which carry unique images, but it's not like these are cliché kinds of phrases. So that made her writing memorable without using worn-out phrases. I was surprised, though, by her pronoun usage. Lamott starts off by describing what she herself feels, but in the third sentence, she changes the pronoun to *your* in order to suggest that we all feel the same kinds of voices. I think her assumption is correct, but the switch in pronoun was a little jarring. Switching pronouns is something I try not to do, so I was surprised that Lamott did it.

12

WRITING WITH ATTITUDE

Conveying a Stance in Academic Texts

Ken Hyland

Life on Mars: Encounters with University Writing

Students often see academic writing as an alien form of literacy designed to disguise the author and deal directly with facts. Style guides and textbooks commonly advise them to remove themselves from their texts and provide the grammatical means to do so. This advice, however, ignores the fact that effective academic writing always carries the individual's point of view. In this paper I briefly explore the most visible expressions of a writer's presence in a text, the use of hedges and first person pronouns, to show there is actually considerable scope for the negotiation of identity in academic writing.

Many students arriving at university think they have landed on Mars. From the beginning, they encounter what looks like a completely different communication system as the texts they are asked to read and the essays they are expected to write seem alien and unreal. The textbooks that sought to stimulate their interest and the assignments that asked for their opinions have largely disappeared, to be replaced by written texts that are as dry as dust and apparently produced without the hand of human intervention. This is academic discourse: a form of literacy designed to hide the author and deal directly with facts.

In this context, students are often advised to leave their personalities at the door and use an impersonal, faceless style of writing to disguise their own opinions behind linguistic objectivity. The *I* pronoun is probably the most obvious expression of a writer's presence in a text, and style guides and textbooks are particularly hard on the use of this, generally exhorting students to avoid it at all costs. This advice is typical:

The total paper is considered to be the work of the writer. You don't have to say 'I think' or 'My opinion is' in the paper. (. . .) Traditional formal writing does not use I or we in the paper.

(Spencer and Arbon 1996: 26)

To the scientist it is unimportant who observed the chemical reaction: only the observation itself is vital. In this situation, passive voice and the omission of the agent of action are justified.

(Gong and Dragga 1995)

Write your paper with a third person voice that avoids 'I believe' or 'It is my opinion'.

(Lester 1993: 144)

But is this really good advice? It is certainly true that the first person pronoun is sometimes misused by students, who often stake personal claims to what may be common knowledge (*I believe that the sun rises in the East*) or to other people's ideas (*I think that dreams are a window to the unconscious*). But the presence or absence of a pronoun does not determine whether a piece of writing is 'academic' or not.

Clearly some disciplines observe conventions of impersonality and anonymity more than others, and students in some fields will find the texts they need to read and write look more like those they have encountered outside university. But while disciplines have very different ways of talking about their subjects, writing at university means crafting texts in a way that insiders can see as 'doing biology' or 'doing history'. Following the conventions of a particular field of study restricts how something can be said, but despite its apparently frozen surface, academic writing is full of attitudes and opinions. Writers still need to convey their ideas, but they have to do this using a language their readers are likely to find familiar and appropriate, and this is very different to everyday talk. So instead of representing things as we see them, as we normally do, academic writing encourages us to foreground events rather than actors, disguise the source of our ideas and downplay our personal reactions to things. This involves using different grammatical resources and, most importantly, different resources to convey our attitudes to what we are talking about and to our readers. This is an *interpersonal* grammar, and I will refer to these resources as contributing to a *stance*.

What Is Stance?

This chapter is about stance, but what does that mean? *Stance* concerns the ways writers step into their texts to stamp their personal authority or beliefs onto their arguments. It refers to the language features writers use to comment on their statements in order to convey their attitudes, opinions and degrees of commitment to what they say, boosting or toning down their claims and criticisms, expressing surprise or importance, intruding though self-mention and commenting on their topics. There are three main parts to expressing a stance as writers ask themselves the following questions about any statement:

1. How certain do I want to be about this?
2. What is my attitude towards it?
3. Do I want to make myself prominent here?

To do these things, writers use *hedges, boosters, attitude markers* and *self-mention.*

Hedges are words like *might, likely, perhaps* and phrases such as *it may be due to, it is possible that,* which change an assertion into something less certain. They allow writers to withhold complete commitment to a statement and imply that it is based on plausible reasoning rather than on certain knowledge. They indicate that the writer thinks it may not be a good idea to be too confident about the truth of a claim and, at the same time, allow the reader a space to dispute it. In Example 1, which follows, we can see how a definite assertion is toned down by the use of hedges (italicized). This allows the reader to feel that he or she is being considered by the reader and that the writer recognizes that there may be alternative views on the matter:

Example 1

Our results suggest that rapid freeze and thaw rates during artificial experiments in the laboratory *may* cause embolism. However, such experiments *may* not represent the true amount of embolism in nature as low temperatures *usually* result in gradual freezing and thawing.

Boosters have the opposite pragmatic effect to hedges. They are personal assessments of certainty that something is true or correct, and they close down opportunities for readers to express alternative viewpoints. Affectively, they also mark involvement and solidarity with an audience, stressing shared information, group membership and direct engagement with readers. They are conveyed lexically through words like *definitely, prove, must,* etc. and by fixed phrases such as *it seems obvious that, as we know, I strongly believe,* etc. In Example 2, from a philosophy research article, the writer employs a series of boosters to underline the conviction he wishes to attach to his argument:

Example 2

This brings us into conflict with Currie's account, for static images *surely* cannot trigger our capacity to recognize movement. If that were so, we would see the image as itself moving. With a few interesting exceptions we *obviously* do not see a static image as moving. Suppose, then, that we say that static images only depict instants, but this also seems *highly* dubious. (Philosophy article)

In addition to conveying either a tentative or definite stance, writers have the option of indicating an affective attitude to propositions using *attitude markers*. These convey whether the writer feels positively or negatively towards something and typically draw on another set of items of interpersonal grammar such as attitude verbs (*agree, prefer*), adverbials (*unfortunately, surprising*) and complement clauses (*we hope that*). The conventions of academic writing certainly restrict the range of attitudes that can be appropriately expressed, so we find very little emotion in academic texts, but we do see expressions of surprise, agreement, importance, frustration and so on, rather than just commitment. Students, however, typically draw on a larger number of markers and express stronger emotions than professional academic writers, as these examples from a Hong Kong student's essays show:

Example 3

The percentage of people being positive had increased *unbelievably* from 30% to 46% between 1989 to 1998. It was *stunning* that the percentage had decreased from 40% to 18% during the earlier period.

Example 4

With *tremendous* increase in the usage of Internet, the world was truly wired with *wonderful* electronic information.

These strong attitudes establish a very different stance to that taken in research articles or textbooks, where persuasion is typically managed by softer expressions.

The final and perhaps the most obvious marker of the writer's stance is the use of *self-mention*. This concerns how far writers want to intrude into their texts though the use of *I* or *we* or of impersonal forms. To some extent, which form a writer uses is a matter of personal preference, determined by seniority, experience, confidence, personality etc., but research shows that the discipline the student is writing in plays a big part, and the social sciences and humanities are particularly 'author-saturated' in this way (Hyland 2001), as in Example 5 from a sociology research article:

Example 5

Our investigation of writing at the local government office comprised an analysis of the attitudes of each individual. *We* asked the different employees about their norms concerning a good text and a good writer. *We* also asked them about their attitudes toward writing at work. What *we* found interesting about this context, however, is the degree of uniformity in their answers.

The presence or absence of explicit author reference is therefore a conscious choice by writers to adopt a particular stance and authorial identity.

Why Is Stance Important?

Presenting a self is central to the writing process (Ivanic 1998), and we cannot avoid projecting an impression of ourselves and how we stand in relation to our arguments, discipline and readers. It is impossible *not* to take a stance. Whether this is a confident and assertive author, a tentative interpreter or a modest scientist, carefully hiding behind what findings may show or what tables may demonstrate are important rhetorical decisions that affect how the message is received and the ways readers react to the text.

The different conventions of personality and author presence in different academic disciplines are key features of academic writing (e.g. Hyland 2004; Swales 2004). Table 12.1, for example, shows the average number of author pronouns (mainly *I* and *we*) in 240 published journal articles from eight disciplines (Hyland 2002). Broadly, we can see that a stronger identity and more explicit writer stance are claimed in the humanities and social sciences papers.

It is clear that writers in different disciplines represent themselves, their work and their readers in very different ways, with those in the humanities and social sciences taking far more personal positions than those in the sciences and engineering. The positivist understandings of the sciences mean that the authority of the individual is subordinated to the authority of the text and that facts are meant to 'speak for themselves' with little author visibility. Writers disguise their personal interpretations behind linguistic objectivity, downplaying their personal role to suggest that results would be the same whoever conducted the research.

In the hard sciences, writers assume that the methods, procedures and equipment they use will invariably produce the same result. In the 'soft' fields, on the other hand, there is less control of variables, more diversity of research outcomes and fewer clear bases for accepting claims than in the sciences. Writers can't report research with the same confidence in the methods and objectivity of the sciences, and so spinning a convincing argument involves creating a credible stance. Standing

TABLE 12.1 Self-mention per Research Paper (per 1,000 words) (Hyland 2002)

Philosophy	5.5	Physics	4.1
Sociology	4.3	Biology	3.4
Applied linguistics	4.5	Mechanical engineering	1.0
Marketing	5.5	Electrical engineering	3.3
Average	**5.0**		**2.9**

behind your arguments, with hedges, boosters, attitude markers and self-mentions can therefore help promote an impression of self-assurance and authority (Hyland 2012).

What is crucial in all this is that students are aware of what readers expect to find in the texts they write in their disciplines. What kind of stance do they have to adopt in their writing to present an effective argument and a competent self? Unfortunately, writing textbooks often fail to give students advice on these issues, and style guides simply repeat the intuitions of their authors without evidence. Lindsay, for example, advises that:

> [i]f you have no conclusive evidence don't dither around with expressions such as 'it may be possible that . . .' or (worse) 'the possibility exists that . . .', which immediately suggests that you do not believe your own data.
>
> *(Lindsay 1984: 21)*

More metaphorically, the classic *Elements of Style* refers to hedges as "the leeches that infest the pond of prose, sucking the blood of words" (Strunk and White 1999). Overall then, textbooks tend to ignore or under-represent the significance of hedging and other indicators of stance as they seem to add little to the propositional information or writer's argument. The importance of the writer's representation of self and how he or she constructs a relationship with the reader, however, is crucial to whether the argument is seen as persuasive and effective.

Student Difficulties and Practices

Students not only get bad advice about these features, but second language students often find it difficult to adapt to the different patterns of interaction involved when writing in English. Unlike many languages, English is said to be *writer responsible* (Hinds 1987), which means that, rather than forcing the reader to dig the meaning out of a dense and difficult text, it is the writer's job to make ideas accessible and connections as explicit as possible. Writers always have to consider their readers and try to anticipate the style of writing that they expect and that will best suit the writer's purposes. Features of stance seem particularly vulnerable to language differences, however, so that while academic writing in Finnish (Ventola 1997), Spanish (Oliver del Olmo 2004) and Bulgarian (Vassileva 1997) show a higher degree of commitment and less reader deference than their English counterpart, articles written in German (Kreutz and Harres 1997), Polish (Duszak 1994) and Czech (Cmerjrková and Danes 1997) show a higher degree of tentativeness than those written by English-speaking writers.

Consequently, stance features are often difficult for students to use appropriately. The ability to express doubt and certainty in English, for example, is a complex task for language learners so that Hinkel (1997) found that essays written in English by Japanese, Korean and Chinese students tended to be overhedged and to exhibit a great deal of hesitancy. While she attributes this to the influence of the 'Confucian tradition', Hyland and Milton's (1997) study of Hong Kong writers showed that they massively underused hedges and tended to boost their statements compared with native English writers, conveying an inappropriate force to their arguments. It was apparent that in essays written by more proficient learners, hedging and boosting frequencies were similar to those in essays by native English writers, suggesting that proficiency and prior teaching play an important role. In fact, Hong Kong students are often taught to present their work in a direct and confident style, as this extract from a Hong Kong undergraduate essay suggests:

Example 6

There is *strong* evidence to *demonstrate* the relationship between EQ and the academic performance. High EQ is *definitely* an advantage in any domain of life and *we all know* that a person with high EQ can *certainly* manage their own feelings well and deal effectively with others. *The fact that* the trend from overseas is *always* affecting Hong Kong people means that schools *must* now teach boys to be equal to female.

To many readers, used to a more cautious style, this seems too strong and perhaps leads us to make judgements about the writer as being overassertive and disrespectful to the reader's opinions.

Similarly, self-mention tends to be problematic for non-native English writers. Hinkel (2002), for instance, found that first person singular pronouns were significantly more frequent in essays written in English by speakers of Japanese, Korean, Chinese, Vietnamese and Indonesian than in those of American native English speakers, while the passive voice was significantly greater and occasionally twice as common in the native speakers' texts. My own corpus study comparing Hong Kong undergraduate dissertations with published research articles found the expert writers were *three times* more likely to use author pronouns in their texts, and this ratio held across both hard and soft disciplines. (See Table 12.2.)

These results are all the more interesting because it is actually *easier* to construct active sentences with the agent in subject position (*I believe that* . . .), which means these second language writers went to some trouble to avoid author pronouns.

TABLE 12.2 Self-mention in Research Articles and Essays (per 10,000 words)

Field	*Totals*	
	Articles	*L2 Essays*
Science and engineering	30.7	11.7
Business and professional	46.9	16.1
Overall	41.2	14.4

When interviewed, students gave two main reasons for this: First, they had been taught not to bring their own opinions into their texts, and, second, they felt uncomfortable with the personal authority that the use of *I* implied. First person pronouns are a powerful way of projecting a strong writer identity, and this individualistic kind of stance clashed with their cultural beliefs about being too assertive, particularly when it meant getting behind views for a teacher who was also judging their work for a grade:

> I don't think the use of "I" is appropriate as it gives personal opinions and my tutor may disagree with it. It is too strong.
>
> *(Computer science student interview)*

> I am just a student not a big academic with important ideas. How can I use I in the report?
>
> *(Sociology student interview)*

This sensitivity led them not only to avoid *I* but also to restrict its use to safe, low-stakes functions that carried only a very weak expression of identity, such as explaining methods (*I interviewed three teachers*) or setting out purposes (*My purpose is to*), rather than getting behind their arguments.

So, despite their exposure to academic texts in their courses, students, and particularly second language speaking students, therefore find it difficult to control the features that help manage writer–reader interactions. In the following sections, I suggest some examples of classroom activities to encourage students to think about, by making these interpersonal features salient to learners, and then use them in their writing.

Awareness of Stance: Interpersonal Analysis of Texts

There are various approaches to helping students to notice these conventions, and I will group them here under *consciousness-raising, genre* and *corpus methods*.

Consciousness Raising

Socio-rhetorical consciousness raising assists students to notice, comprehend and reflect on the ways texts work as discourse rather than on their role as bearers of content. Instead of building up a text from grammatical forms in a slot-and-filler kind of way, this is a top-down approach to understanding language that encourages writers to see grammatical features as "the on-line processing component of discourse and not the set of syntactic building blocks with which discourse is constructed" (Rutherford 1987: 104). It therefore focuses on the ways meaning is constructed as part of the overall intentions of writers. While this kind of inquiry can take a variety of forms, it most simply involves training students to read rhetorically and to reflect on the practices they observe and use themselves. It means providing classroom activities to expose students to discourses from different contexts and encourage them to inquire into their own writing behaviors and those of others (Johns 1997).

One approach to consciousness raising is to involve students in contrastive reflection, asking them to compare how features are used in different texts or contexts. This can suggest something of the relativistic nature of writing and, when used with EAL (English as an additional language) students, can highlight how English might differ from the practices they may be familiar with from their native language. Task 1, adapted from Swales and Feak (2000), asks advanced academic writers to reflect on the features we are considering in this chapter.

Task 1

Academic English, in comparison to other research languages, is often said to:

1. Be more impersonal and use fewer personal pronouns.
2. Be more cautious in making claims.
3. Use a limited range of adverbs expressing attitudes towards what is discussed.
4. Have stricter conventions for avoiding personal opinions.
5. Offer readers an opportunity to hold alternative interpretations.
6. Place the responsibility for clarity and understanding on the writer rather than the reader.

From your reading of academic articles, do you agree with these statements?

Reflect upon your own first academic language. Place ticks beside those points where academic writing in your L1 and academic English differ. Do you think other differences ought to be mentioned?

Do you think you need to fully adopt these conventions, or can you preserve your own academic culture in your academic writing?

Alternatively, students might be encouraged to see how hedges are used in their first language and in academic texts written in English or compare the advice they find about, say, the use of the first person in style guides and textbooks with the actual practices of academic writers. Commercial materials play an important part in literacy education at university, and students should learn to view their advice critically. Often textbooks rely heavily on intuition and conventional wisdom rather than on analysis of texts, and by analysing texts, considering advice and discussing uses, students can work towards a more informed understanding of language use.

Similarly, students can be asked to compare the treatments of the same topic in a research article and a popularization, the latter being an altogether more definite and certain presentation of information for a nonspecialist audience (e.g. Hyland 2010). Hedges allow writers to comment on the factual status of propositions and are therefore abundant in research genres, where authors need to carefully handle their claims to avoid overstating their case and risk inviting the rejection of their arguments. This example from a research paper is typical of this recognition of alternative voices:

Example 7

An early flowering response to high temperature is maintained in pif4 mutants, *suggesting* that architectural and flowering responses *may* operate via separate signaling pathways. The role of PIF4 in temperature signaling does not, however, *appear to* operate through interaction with either phytochrome or DELLA proteins, *suggesting* the existence of a novel regulatory mechanism. We conclude that PIF4 is a *potentially* important component of plant high temperature signaling and integrates multiple environmental cues during plant development.

[Current Biology 2009: 19 (5)]

The frequent use of hedges therefore marks out a modest and careful researcher trying to keep interpretations close to the data and unwilling to make overblown claims.

Journalists, on the other hand, take a very different view towards facts. The process of transforming research into popular accounts involves removing doubts and upgrading the significance of claims to emphasize their uniqueness, rarity or originality. This can be seen in the way that the same research is reported in a popular science journal, with the tentativeness removed in favour of unmodified or boosted assertions that amplify the certainty of the claims and, in so doing, the impact of the story:

Example 8

Researchers at the universities of Leicester and Oxford have made a *discovery* about plant growth which *could have an enormous impact* on crop production as global warming increases. Dr Franklin said: "This study provides *the first major advance* in understanding how plants regulate growth responses to elevated temperature at the molecular level. This *discovery will prove fundamental in understanding* the effects of global climate change on crop productivity."

(Science Today April 2009)

For the science journalist, hedges simply reduce the importance and newsworthiness of a story by drawing attention to its uncertain truth value, but in glamorizing material for a wider audience, popular science texts do not help readers to see how scientific facts can be questioned. These kinds of considerations can be useful in showing students how stance is adjusted for different contexts.

Finally, students should be encouraged to reflect on their own use of stance features through questions that ask them to discuss their thoughts and practices and their impressions of seeing them in the work of others. (See Task 2.)

Task 2

Consider the following statements, and discuss them with a partner.

- Do you use *I* or *my* in your academic writing?
- Do you feel comfortable using these words?
- Do you try and avoid them? How would you express the same idea instead?
- Do you think academics use this in your field? What do you think about this?
- Why do you think some writers use *I* and others don't?
- Why do you think some writers use *I* in one part of their paper and not in others?
- Do writers typically use or avoid *I* in your first language?
- Look at an essay or academic paper written by your partner, and discuss why he/she has used or avoided *I*. What alternative ways did he/she use to present ideas?

While the points appear to refer to surface features of academic writing, they raise wider issues of argument structure, reader awareness, the role of knowledge, appropriate interactions and cultural identity, all of which are important features of academic writing.

Genre-Based Tasks

Consciousness raising is often achieved by asking students to conduct mini analyses of the genres they have to write. *Genre* refers to abstract, socially recognized ways of using language. It is based on the idea that members of a community usually have little difficulty in recognizing similarities in the texts they use frequently and are able to draw on their repeated experiences with such texts to read, understand and perhaps write them relatively easily. Essentially, a genre approach to writing instruction means attending to grammar, but this is not the traditional idea of a grammar as a system of rules that operate independently of contexts and users. In genre-based writing instruction, this is a top-down procedure, starting with texts. Knapp and Watkins observe that this is an approach that:

> first considers how a text is structured and organised at the level of the whole text in relation to its purpose, audience and message. It then considers how all parts of the text, such as paragraphs and sentences, are structured, organised and coded so as to make the text effective as written communication.
>
> *(Knapp and Watkins 2005: 8)*

Here grammar is a resource for producing texts: a repertoire of available choices for achieving particular purposes in particular contexts.

Genre-based instruction involves deconstructing texts to enable students to construct their own, firstly with teacher and peer support and then independently with attention to setting genres in their social context and building up an understanding of their knowledge structures (e.g. Martin and Rose 2007). The basic idea is that students are not asked to write anything without first knowing what is expected of them, through teaching methods that make use of exemplars and that explicitly share knowledge about genres. Genre methodologies therefore describe target texts and strategies for reaching these targets rather than setting our 'rules' to follow, encouraging students to bring their often considerable research skills to the classroom to develop an exploratory attitude towards texts. For example, in academic writing classes, teachers can ask students to identify where authors have chosen to use or avoid *I* and determine possible reasons for this. A simple example is illustrated in Task 3.

Task 3

Select a research article, student report or other relevant genre, and read it carefully.

1. Mark all occurrences of *I* in a research article from the target discipline with a highlight pen; then count them and tabulate the findings.
2. Compare the results with a classmate's analysis (preferably in a different discipline).
3. Can you explain any differences?
4. Notice how impersonal and personal forms change in the text. Why might this be?
5. Select *five* places where *I* can be replaced with a passive. What effect does this have on the meaning of each sentence?

6.   What main verbs occur most often with *I* in this text? Can you group them in any way? Do they correspond to the following rhetorical functions?
     a.   Explaining what was done (*We interviewed 10 teachers from six schools.*)
     b.   Structuring the discourse (*First, I will discuss the method, then present my results.*)
     c.   Showing a result (*My findings show that the animation distracted the pupils.*)
     d.   Making a claim (*I think two factors are particularly significant in this regard.*)
7.   Now write a report to present your findings.

An awareness of hedges can also be approached in the same way. (See Task 4.)

Task 4

1.   Examine a text and distinguish statements that report facts and those that are unproven.
2.   Identify all hedges in a text, circling the forms used.
3.   Explain why you think the writer used them at this point.
4.   Locate and remove all hedges, and discuss the effect on the meaning of the text.
5.   Identify hedged propositions in a text, and substitute them with statements of certainty.
6.   Identify the hedges, and compile a scale ranking the amount of certainty they express,
7.   Consider a series of reformulations that vary the levels of certainty of a text, and decide how far they accurately report the original statements.

This kind of analysis provides students with a simple grammatical technique for distinguishing facts from opinions and identifying what assumptions the writer is making about a topic.

Corpus Material

While looking at single texts is a productive way of familiarizing students with stance features, a fundamental tool in developing students' awareness of these features is a concordancer. A concordance programme is a tool for searching large amounts of computer-readable text for particular words and combinations, but while it can isolate, sort and count data, the actual analysis is performed by humans. Thus such programmes can turn students into researchers and help them search for patterns that are not readily apparent. Many years ago, Wu summarized the advantages of a concordance approach in this way:

> Only when words are in their habitual environments, presented in their most frequent forms and their relational patterns and structures, can they be learnt effectively, interpreted properly and used appropriately.
>
> *(Wu 1992: 32)*

This approach to raising awareness therefore both stimulates inquiry and encourages independent engagement with the language.

Corpora provide two kinds of important information to students about grammatical and lexical patterning in texts: frequency and association. High-frequency items and collocations (or how words regularly occur together with other words) present repeated, taken-for-granted choices, as of all the different ways of saying roughly the same thing, writers in particular disciplines select the same items again and again. Thus students can see how disciplines differ in their use of first person or boosters by searching for high-frequency items.

For example, corpora reveal how the positivist epistemologies of the natural sciences are reflected and constructed through repeated rhetorical preferences that hide interpretative activities behind linguistic objectivity. Thus one way of minimizing the researcher's role is through less frequent use of hedges and, when hedging is used, using modal verbs over cognitive verbs. This is because modal verbs can more easily combine with inanimate subjects to downplay the person making the evaluation. So we are more likely to find instances of Example 9 in the sciences and those with cognitive verbs in the soft discipline fields (Example 10):

Example 9

For *V. trifidum*, ANOVA showed a significant increase from L to L and FI, which *could be interpreted* as reflecting the dynamics of fungal colonization. The deviations at high frequencies *may* have been caused by the noise measurements.

Example 10

I think this would be a mistake.
We suspect that the product used in this study may have contributed to the result.

Students can also be taught to search for patterns that replace personal pronouns, such as *abstract rhetors*, where tables, graphs and results replace authors as the agents of interpretations in patterns (e.g. *The table shows* . . . , *the results indicate* . . . , *the assays suggest* . . .). Similarly, science students can identify strategies to replace the use of first person by searching for frequent reporting verbs such as *suggest, demonstrate* and *prove*.

Concordance software is also useful when searching for word combinations, revealing frequencies and meanings of key phrases that vary by intervening words. Thus entering the expression *it* ＊ *that* will search for the word *it* followed by *that* in the near vicinity, producing examples such as these in a corpus of academic research papers:

it is likely that	*it shows that*	*it is worth noting that*
it seems that	*it is claimed that*	*it is shown that*
it is clear that	*it is true that*	*it is more likely that*

Academic writers use this phrasing extremely frequently to convey a stance, expressing their evaluation of whether the following statement is likely to be true or not.

Computer data also allow students to classify hedges according to their surface forms (parts of speech and therefore how they can be used grammatically) or their functions (according to the strength they have or their impact on the reader). By providing large numbers of examples, corpora can also help students to deduce 'rules' for the appropriate use of confusable pairs such as *infer* and *imply* or *suggest* and *propose*.

Finally, corpus materials can stimulate small projects among advanced learners that focus on the use of stance features in their own disciplines. Thus each student might select one of the eight disciplines from the COCA (Corpus of Contemporary American English, http://corpus.byu.edu/coca/) and analyse it in terms of the frequencies of common hedges, boosters or attitude words. The interface for the programme also allows the user to compare features in one discipline with another, and students can work together to discuss similarities and differences, compiling the results to draft an essay, research paper or class presentation on the subject. Relating tasks to students in this way means they can activate their acquired linguistic competence and discipline knowledge in a context of immediate relevance.

Productive Tasks: Using Stance Features in Writing

In addition to identifying stance items and gaining an appreciation of their appropriate use, students require guidance to use them effectively in their own writing. This necessarily begins with grammar-focused tasks that help learners to gain familiarity with the typical functions, forms and syntactic patterning of key features. Rather than treating the practice of these features as developing isolated, autonomous rules to be learnt, however, writing must include assisting students towards both a sense of audience and a sense of purpose in using these features correctly to produce, eventually, a complete piece of work. This requires that teachers specify a clear communicative context and create writing tasks that are as authentic as possible in terms of relevant objectives, genre and audience.

Despite the variety of means to convey stance, particularly hedges and attitude markers, there is some justification for concentrating initially on high-frequency items as these offer the greatest benefit for the least learning effort. Such a strategy will provide learners with a means of expressing themselves with subtlety in situations where they might lack the confidence to use a wider range of less familiar patterns. This knowledge will also foster familiarity with the concepts and the circumstances when it can most appropriately be employed, allowing more complex means of expression to be developed later.

Instead of expecting students to master the semantic complexities of the modal verb system to convey hedges and boosters, for example, attention could focus on the use of the highest-frequency modals *would, may* and *could*. Moreover, attention should be given to lexical verbs and adverbials as these have an extremely high frequency in the writing of many fields and present students with far less semantic confusion (Hyland 1998). Verb phrases with *indicate, suggest, appear* and *propose*, for example, represent 56% of all mitigating lexical items in academic writing (Hyland 1998) and are also sufficiently common in casual conversation to permit their transfer to other contexts (Biber, Johansson, Leech, Conrad, and Finegan 1999). Instruction can then proceed to related adjectival and nominal forms, gradually helping students acquire an understanding of the importance of hedging, the resources to express it and the assurance to employ forms appropriately.

Tasks that require an explicit focus on the productive use of stance features, for example, include the following:

- Provide students with statements that they then have to link by adding or omitting hedges to convey an accurate assessment of the truth relations between them.
- Ask learners to complete sentence frames, in an appropriate context, which employ common hedges such as *in spite of ..*, *if. . . . then, under these conditions . . . , the model implies . . .* , etc.
- Ask students to paraphrase a description of an experiment using hedges to refer to uncertain claims.
- Ask students to rewrite one of their academic papers to either replace self-mention with impersonal forms or vice versa and then to consider the effect of this.
- Ask students to highlight all attitude markers in different genres (say, a textbook, research article and popularization), categorize them according to the type of attitude expressed (surprise, importance, novelty, etc.) and see how they differ across genre.

- Ask students to select the most appropriate supports for a particular claim from a list and then link them to the controlling idea with appropriate hedges or certainty markers.

Many of these activities can provide the basis of 'reformulation' activities (e.g. Allwright et al. 1988) whereby a proficient user, perhaps a subject specialist, rewrites a non-native speaker's draft for class discussion. The discussion could focus on the level of claims made and the form and function of the hedges or boosters employed. This would serve to both encourage reflection on the effectiveness of the suggested alterations and assist learners in drafting their own claims by offering an expert reader's perspective.

Reader response is critical to effective writing, and in addition to making appropriate stance choices, students also need to consider the likely background knowledge and expectations of their readers. Learners generally have little experience in writing for real audiences and therefore need to be sensitive to genre-specific and community-specific practices. Tasks must therefore incorporate the students' particular socio-rhetorical situation, encouraging awareness of the kind of knowledge claims it is appropriate to make, the kinds of attitudes that are acceptable, the degree of author involvement that is expected and the level of conviction to invest in statements.

To develop a consideration of audience and purpose in writing, teachers can consider the following tasks:

- Provide students with a few paragraphs from a research article, and ask them to rewrite it for a popular audience, replacing uncertain claims with greater certainty or vice versa.
- Reformulate a textbook passage from the perspective of a scientist presenting the ideas for the first time in a research report, making the claims more tentative.
- Write a speculative paper explaining the possible cause-and-effect relationships in arguments about, say, the reasons for inflation, drug abuse, PhD dropout rates, juvenile crime, etc.
- Write a Discussion section of a research article that hypothesises about future possibilities from photographs, graphs, statistical trends, experimental results, etc.
- Contribute a short essay for a class journal about the state of knowledge on a topic or the implications of a new development in the student's discipline.
- Describe an experiment in the form of a Results or Discussion section of a research article for a subject teacher using hedges to convey the appropriate level of claim.
- Conduct a group investigation of the use of hedging in students' various disciplines, and write a research paper or essay on their similarities and differences.

Conclusion

Conveying an appropriate stance towards one's reader and arguments is a key aspect of academic writing, although one that tends to receive little attention in textbooks or academic writing classes. Appreciation of the importance of the set of features that realize it and the competence to manage it effectively involves both a rhetorical consciousness, or perceived rationale for its communicative use, and an ability to appropriately employ it for maximum interpersonal and persuasive effect. By exposing students to the choices frequently made by expert writers and an ability to analyse their own writing, teachers can assist students towards an understanding of these devices. This competence can contribute to actively empowering students to become members of their disciplinary communities.

The pedagogic tasks sketched here suggest a few ways in which students might be led to appropriate means of rhetorical expression by drawing on their linguistic resources, authentic models of language use and an explicit focus on stance devices. By emphasizing textual products and an intended readership, this approach encourages students to consider the relationship among writers, claims and readers and to introspect on the reasons for why writers adopt a stance and the effect it can have. In this process, the teacher and learner can each draw on their respective specialist knowledge and contribute as equals.

Discussion Questions

1. Do you recognize the features discussed in this paper as important? Do you currently teach them, and if so how do you teach them?
2. Which features discussed in this chapter are likely to present the greatest difficulty to your students? Design some consciousness-raising and writing tasks that you could use to help them.
3. How could you, as a teacher, draw on stance in nonacademic genres as a way of helping students to understand the role of stance in academic writing?
4. Select a textbook or set of materials you are familiar with, and identify how it treats attitude, self-mention, hedges and boosters. Do you feel it provides adequate coverage? How would you improve it?
5. Are there other features, not mentioned in this chapter, that help convey a writer's/speaker's stance?

Essential Reading

Biber, D. (2006). Stance in spoken and written university registers. *Journal of English for Academic Purposes*, 5(2), 97–116.

Hyland, K. (2002). Options of identity in academic writing. *ELT Journal*, 56(4): 351–358.

Hyland, K. (2009) *Academic discourse*. London: Continuum.

Martin, J. R., & Rose, D. (2007) Working with discourse: Meaning beyond the clause (2nd ed.). London: Continuum.

References

Allwright, R., Woodley, M.-P., & Allwright, J. (1988). Investigating reformulations as a practical strategy for the teaching of academic writing. *Applied Linguistics*, *9*(3), 236–256.

Biber, D., Johansson, S., Leech, G., Conrad, S., & Finegan, E. (1999). *Longman grammar of spoken and written English.* London: Longman.

Cmerjrková, S., & Danes, F. (1997). Academic writing and cultural identity: The case of Czech academic writing, In A. Duszak (Ed.), *Culture and styles in academic discourse* (pp. 41–62). Berlin: Mouton de Gruyter.

Duszak, A. (1994). Academic discourse and intellectual styles. *Journal of Pragmatics*, *21*, 291–313.

Gong, G., & Dragga, S. (1995). *A writer's repertoire.* New York: Longman.

Hinds, J. (1987). Reader vs. writer responsibility: A new typology. In U. Connor & R. B. Kaplan (Eds.), *Writing across languages: Analysis of L2 texts* (pp. 141–152). Reading, MA: Addison-Wesley.

Hinkel, E. (1997). Objectivity and credibility in L1 and L2 academic writing. In E. Hinkel (Ed.), *Culture and second language teaching and learning* (pp. 90–108). Cambridge: Cambridge University Press.

Hinkel, E. (2002). *Second language writers' texts.* Mahwah, NJ: Erlbaum.

Hyland, K. (1998). *Hedging in scientific research articles.* Amsterdam: John Benjamins.

Hyland, K. (2001). Humble servants of the discipline? Self-mention in research articles. *English for Specific Purposes*, *20*, 207–226.

Hyland, K. (2002). Options of identity in academic writing. *ELT Journal*, *56*(4), 351–358.

Hyland, K. (2004). *Disciplinary discourses: Social interactions in academic writing.* Ann Arbor: University of Michigan Press.

Hyland, K. (2010). Constructing proximity: Relating to readers in popular and professional science. *Journal of English for Academic Purposes*, *9*(2), 116–127.

Hyland, K. (2012). *Disciplinary identities.* Cambridge: Cambridge University Press.

Hyland, K., & Milton, J. (1997). Hedging in L1 and L2 student writing. *Journal of Second Language Writing*, *6*(2), 183–206.

Ivanic, R. (1998). *Writing and identity: The discoursal construction of identity in academic writing.* Amsterdam: John Benjamins.

Johns, A. M. (1997). *Text, role and context: Developing academic literacies.* Cambridge: Cambridge University Press.

Knapp, P., and Watkins, M. (2005). *Genre, text, grammar.* Sydney: University of NSW Press.

Kreutz, H., & Harres, A. (1997). Hedging in German and English academic writing. In A. Duszak (Ed.), *Culture and styles of academic discourse* (pp. 181–201). Berlin and New York: Mouton de Gruyter.

Lester, J. D. 1993. *Writing research papers* (7th ed.). New York: Harper Collins.

Lindsay, D. (1984). *A guide to scientific writing.* Melbourne: Longman.

Martin, J. R., & Rose, D. (2007). *Working with discourse: Meaning beyond the clause* (2nd ed.). London: Continuum.

Oliver del Olmo, S. (2004). *Análisis contrastivo español/inglés de la atenuación retórica en el discurso médico. El artículo de investigación y el caso clínico.* Doctoral thesis. Universitat Pompeu Fabra, Barcelona.

Rutherford, W. (1987). *Second language grammar: Learning & teaching.* London: Longman.

Spencer, C., and Arbon, B. (1996). *Foundations of writing: Developing research and academic writing skills.* Lincolnwood, IL: National Textbook.

Strunk, W., & White, E. B. (1999). *The elements of style* (4th ed.). Needham Heights, MA: Allyn & Bacon.

Swales, J. (2004). *Research genres.* Cambridge: Cambridge University Press.

Swales, J., & Feak, C. (2000). *English in today's research world: A writing guide.* Ann Arbor: University of Michigan Press.

Vassileva, I. (1997). Hedging in English and Bulgarian academic writing. In A. Duszak (Ed.), *Culture and styles of academic discourse* (pp. 203–223). Berlin: Mouton de Gruyter.

Ventola, E. (1997). Modalization: Probability—an exploration into its role in academic writing. In A. Duszak (Ed.), *Culture and styles in academic writing* (pp. 157–179). Berlin and New York: Mouton de Gruyter.

Wu, M. H. (1992). Towards a contextual lexico-grammar: An application of concordance analysis in EST teaching. *RELC Journal, 23*(2), 18–34.

LIST OF CONTRIBUTORS

Anne Burns, University of New South Wales, Australia

Marianne Celce-Murcia, University of California, Los Angeles, USA

Susan Conrad, Portland State University, USA

Rod Ellis, University of Auckland, New Zealand

Dana R. Ferris, University of California, Davis, USA

Keith S. Folse, University of Central Florida, USA

Eli Hinkel, Seattle Pacific University, USA

Ken Hyland, University of Hong Kong, Hong Kong

Michael J. McCarthy, University of Nottingham, UK

Sandra Lee McKay, San Francisco State University, USA (Emeritus), and University of Hawai'i (Affiliate Member), USA

Randi Reppen, Northern Arizona University, USA

Jack C. Richards, University of Sydney, Australia (Honorary Professor), University of Auckland, New Zealand (Honorary Professor), and Regional English Language Center, Singapore

Penny Ur, Oranim Academic College of Education, Israel

INDEX